Reading Corinthians and Philippians within Judaism

Other volumes in this series:

Reading Paul within Judaism: Collected Essays of Mark D. Nanos, Vol. 1
Reading Romans within Judaism: Collected Essays of Mark D. Nanos, Vol. 2
Reading Galatians within Judaism: Collected Essays of Mark D. Nanos, Vol. 3

Reading Corinthians and Philippians within Judaism

Collected Essays of Mark D. Nanos, Vol. 4

MARK D. NANOS

CASCADE Books • Eugene, Oregon

READING CORINTHIANS AND PHILIPPIANS WITHIN JUDAISM
Collected Essays of Mark D. Nanos, Vol. 4

Copyright © 2017 Mark D. Nanos. All rights reserved. Except for brief quotations in critical publications or reviews, no part of this book may be reproduced in any manner without prior written permission from the publisher. Write: Permissions, Wipf and Stock Publishers, 199 W. 8th Ave., Suite 3, Eugene, OR 97401.

Cascade Books
An Imprint of Wipf and Stock Publishers
199 W. 8th Ave., Suite 3
Eugene, OR 97401

www.wipfandstock.com

PAPERBACK ISBN: 978-1-5326-1758-4
HARDCOVER ISBN: 978-1-4982-4237-0
EBOOK ISBN: 978-1-4982-4236-3

Cataloguing-in-Publication data:

Names: Nanos, Mark D., 1954–

Title: Reading Corinthians and Philippians within Judaism : collected essays of Mark D. Nanos, vol. 4 / Mark D. Nanos.

Description: Eugene, OR: Cascade Books, 2017 | Includes bibliographical references and index.

Identifiers: ISBN 978-1-5326-1758-4 (paperback) | ISBN 978-1-4982-4237-0 (hardcover) | ISBN 978-1-4982-4236-3 (ebook)

Subjects: LCSH: Paul, the Apostle, Saint | Bible. Corinthians, 1st—Criticism, interpretation, etc. | Bible. Philippians—Criticism, interpretation, etc. | Jews in the New Testament |

Classification: BS2506.3 N36 2017 (print) | BS2506.3 (ebook)

Manufactured in the U.S.A.   07/27/17

For Vicky

Contents

Permissions | ix
Preface | xi

Part I: Corinthians

1. The *Polytheist* Identity of the "Weak," and Paul's Strategy to "Gain" Them: A New Reading of 1 Corinthians 8:1—11:1 | 3
2. Why the "Weak" in 1 Corinthians 8–10 Were Not Christ-believers | 36
3. Paul's Relationship to Torah in Light of His Strategy "to Become Everything to Everyone" (1 Corinthians 9:19–23) | 52
4. Was Paul a "Liar" for the Gospel? The Case for a New Interpretation of Paul's "Becoming Everything to Everyone" in 1 Corinthians 9:19–23 | 93

Part II: Philippians

5. Paul's Reversal of Jews Calling Gentiles "Dogs" (Philippians 3:2): 1600 Years of an Ideological Tale Wagging an Exegetical Dog? | 111
6. Paul's Polemic in Philippians 3 as Jewish-Subgroup Vilification of Local Non-Jewish Cultic and Philosophical Alternatives | 142

Index of Ancient Sources | 193

Permissions

The articles are reproduced here with permission.

"The Polytheist Identity of the 'Weak,' And Paul's Strategy to 'Gain' Them: A New Reading of 1 Corinthians 8:1—11:1." In *Paul: Jew, Greek, and Roman*, edited by Stanley E. Porter, 179–210. Pauline Studies 5. Leiden: Brill, 2008.

"Why the 'Weak' in 1 Corinthians 8–10 Were Not Christ-believers." In *Saint Paul and Corinth: 1950 Years Since the Writing of the Epistles to the Corinthians: International Scholarly Conference Proceedings (Corinth, 23–25 September 2007)*, edited by Constantine J. Belezos, Sotirios Despotis, and Christos Karakolis, 385–404. Athens, Greece: Psichogios, 2009.

"Paul's Relationship to Torah in Light of His Strategy 'to Become Everything to Everyone' (1 Corinthians 9:19–22)." In *Paul and Judaism: Crosscurrents in Pauline Exegesis and the Study of Jewish-Christian Relations*, edited by Reimund Bieringer and Didier Pollefeyt, 106–40. Library of New Testament Studies 463. London: T. & T. Clark, 2012.

"Was Paul a 'Liar' for the Gospel?: The Case for a New Interpretation of Paul's 'Becoming Everything to Everyone' in 1 Corinthians 9:19–23." *Review & Expositor* 110.4 (2013) 591–608.

"Paul's Reversal of Jews Calling Gentiles 'Dogs' (Philippians 3:2): 1600 Years of an Ideological Tale Wagging an Exegetical Dog?" *Biblical Interpretation* 17.4 (2009) 448–82.

"Paul's Polemic in Philippians 3 as Jewish-Subgroup Vilification of Local Non-Jewish Cultic and Philosophical Alternatives." *Journal for the Study of Paul and His Letters* 3.1 (2013) 47–91.

Preface

THE COMMENTARY TRADITION's "PAUL, the convert," who characteristically denounced the value of being a Jew or practicing Judaism, has come under suspicion on both historical and moral grounds. Nevertheless, readers of the commentaries on Corinthians and Philippians might not realize the traditional perspective is no longer self-evident. They will more than likely encounter the familiar, traditional interpretations as well as the theological and moral reasoning upon which they depend. But the challenges are mounting, and change is on the horizon. This volume collects my published contributions to this changing environment for reading Paul in his context.

The research undertaken for these studies examines and often finds wanting many of the commentary tradition's presuppositions, methodologies, translation decisions, and interpretive conclusions, as well as the basic sensibilities often expressed in descriptions and valuations of Jews and Judaism, including those about the Christ-following Jews who continued to value and practice a Torah-oriented way of life. These studies are informed by new methodologies, such as Social Identity Theory, epistolary-oriented rhetorical studies, and People's History approaches, and focus on Greco-Roman as well as Jewish dynamics that might better account for the texture of Paul's arguments; after all, Paul's Judaism, like the Judaism (used throughout to mean "ways of living developed by and for Jewish communities") of his contemporaries, was by definition Greco-Roman.

The text portions for these essays were chosen because they are among those central to the "Paul, not Judaism" paradigm that dominates Pauline studies. As you might expect from the title of the volume, these essays instead address several of these "flashpoints" from a "Paul within Judaism" perspective. For more details on the development of this perspective, see the first volume of this series (*Reading Paul within Judaism*), and the recent collection of essays by several scholars at the forefront of this research paradigm (Mark D. Nanos and Magnus Zetterholm, eds.,

Paul within Judaism: Restoring the First-Century Context to the Apostle. Minneapolis: Fortress, 2015).

In addition to the historical matters of interest to the exegete, elements explored in these essays are relevant for those involved in Christian-Jewish relations. Paul's voice is often of concern, but unlike that of Jesus, ironically enough, Paul's has represented more of an obstacle than an opportunity for advancing a more promising future.

The essays are divided into two sections, according to the letter of Paul they investigate, and subsequently arranged according to their publication dates. The first section presents studies of the texts from 1 Corinthians; the second, those from Philippians.

The commentaries on 1 Corinthians unanimously identify the "weak" as Christ-followers whose faith was supposedly not yet sufficient enough to indulge in the eating of idol food with indifference, as if ideally Paul wanted them to become "strong" enough to do so. Commentators have not had to argue at any length for this perspective. Unchallenged since the church fathers, this interpretive trajectory still proceeds as if its readers necessarily share the traditional view that Paul neither practiced nor promoted Torah. Paul's "Christianity" was not only supposedly Torah-free, but just as importantly, it embraced decidedly non-Jewish polytheistic ways of life as the ideal. Many significant implications for defining normative thought and behavior for followers of Jesus have naturally followed from these interpretive choices.

It is no surprise that the proponents of such readings of Paul's arguments in 1 Corinthians 8–10 about idol food do not hesitate to explain that in the midst of his argument in 9:19–23, Paul informed the Corinthians that in order to win non-Jews to Christ he *behaved* like non-Jews (i.e., ate idol food). They claim that Paul insisted that he and his communities were free from any obligation to observe Jewish covenantal behavior—except when he expediently chose *to mimic* Jewish behavior among Jews in order to win them to Christ too. The many logical and ethical problems these decisions raise, such as the fact that it could not have been performed in mixed communities of Jews and non-Jews without being recognized immediately by everyone as duplicitous, are seldom if ever discussed. Paul's ostensible misrepresentation of his convictions to sustain such a bait and switch strategy has been justified as putting the gospel first. Independent of such significant matters of conscience, there are numerous exegetically oriented problems that pose obstacles to this consensus view. For example, Paul does not state that to win different constituent groups to the gospel he "behaved like" them, but enigmatically that he "became as/like [ἐγενόμην ... ὡς]" them. As will be discussed, there is good reason to understand that

Paul meant he variously "argued as/like" each, that is, from the premises of each to conclusions that each would not be expected to otherwise draw. How could Paul have expected his audiences to deduce this? He needed only to know that they knew what later interpreters could not know and have not considered when seeking to interpret his arguments; namely, that when he had preached to and taught among non-Jews such as themselves he had always behaved like a Torah-observant Jew. Raising and testing this kind of simple yet radically different alternative way of reading Paul is at the heart of the investigations these studies undertake.

Turning to Philippians, commentators on this letter continue to inform their readers—usually without caveat—that Paul called Jews "dogs" for upholding the value of undertaking circumcision, and that he renounced such identification as "mutilation." This polemic is justified—and often repeated as if empirically true and appropriate to perpetuate—based upon reasoning articulated since at least Chrysostom's fourth-century ce commentary on Philippians. He proclaimed that Paul simply turned upon Jews an epithet that Jews commonly used to deride non-Jews. Chrysostom worked from the assumption that Paul not only switched his allegiance from Judaism to Christianity, but also essentialized the value of his own identification as a "Christian" by way of a binary contrast with (his former) identification as a "Jew." In approaching Paul this way, Chrysostom was, and is, not alone. Be that as it may, the evidence does not confirm that Jews called non-Jews dogs, which undermines the basis for declaring this to be a reversal of invective. Moreover, as other recent studies have noted, nowhere else in the letter are Jews or a Jewish context for the addressees' concerns indicated. Of whom then would the recipients of the warning that suddenly arises in 3:2 regarding the "dogs," "evil workers," and "mutilation," have supposed they were "to beware"?

These essays will argue that the interpretations repeated in the commentaries on these texts do not likely represent what Paul meant originally, or what his audiences would have supposed that he meant. Each essay explains why, and provides new alternatives for re-reading Paul's language *within Judaism*. I trust that the results will be of interest to Christians as well as to Jews and anyone else seeking to understand these enigmatic texts in their probable contexts, or in our own. I welcome your feedback. You can reach me through the (email) "contact" tab on my web page, www.marknanos.com.

A SHORT HISTORY OF THESE ESSAYS

At the most elementary level, I have been convinced of the need to investigate a relatively simple but paradigmatically radical question: what if Paul observed Torah, and did so as a matter of covenant fidelity? To explore that hypothesis, one must at the same time consider the perception of those who received his letters: What if the communities to whom he wrote these letters knew Paul faithfully observed Torah, instead of what has been traditionally assumed? What if they knew that he not only practiced but also promoted Judaism, and that he maintained that this Jewish communal way of life applied to Christ-followers who remained non-Jews as well? How then would his recipients have most likely interpreted his arguments?

I am convinced that to understand Paul in his most probable context, hypotheses should be developed around these and similar questions, and the data tested. I have focused on the texts that have been most influential for the traditional constructions of Paul, beginning with Romans, followed by Galatians. I am by no means done working through them, but having produced initial monographs and a number of essays on those texts, these studies attend to a few of the other "flashpoint" texts from his corpus that I have been able to investigate.

1 Corinthians

My research on 1 Corinthians began with probes made in the early and mid-90s. The identity of the "weak" in 1 Corinthians 8–10 as well as the topic of Paul's view on the eating of idol food by Christ-followers often arise in discussions of the identity of the "weak" in Romans 14–15, which was a central topic in my monograph on Romans. Those who maintain the traditional view that Paul no longer practiced or believed that other Christ-followers should observe Torah-based norms on matters like diet, certainly not as a matter of covenant fidelity, also point to Paul's language in 1 Corinthians 9:19–23 for support. These texts remain major factors for the prevailing constructions of Paul, especially regarding his relationship to Jews and Jewish ways of living, and I naturally consulted them over the years when concentrating on other texts for which they appeared relevant.

A welcome invitation from the Prefecture and the Municipality of Corinth to offer a paper in September 2007, at their celebration of 1,950 years since the writing of Paul's letters to their city, presented the venue to tackle these texts in detail. This was a fascinating conference, with many colleagues from around the world presenting papers in their native languages, many in Greek. My wife and I not only enjoyed Corinth for several days, we traveled throughout Greece afterwards, including to Philippi (more on that below). The paper title I presented in Corinth was, "'But this knowledge is not in everyone' (1 Cor 8:7): Who Were the 'Weak' in Corinth, and What Was the Harm Paul Feared They Would Suffer?" The timing for researching that paper coordinated well with plans to develop an essay for a Brill series volume on Paul as a Jew, Greek, and Roman. In addition, I had the opportunity to share this research as it progressed at a seminar at Lund University, Sweden, in May of 2008, thanks to the invitation of Magnus Zetterholm. The version published in the Brill volume is chapter 1 herein, and the version for the Corinth volume is chapter 2. The two chapters cover much of the same material, but the Corinth volume is not as widely available, and the non-specialist reader may appreciate the essay's less detailed style.

While working on the essays for the Brill and Corinthian conference volumes in early 2008, an invitation from Reimund Bieringer and Didier Pollefeyt to participate in a seminar entitled, "New Perspectives on Paul and the Jews: Interdisciplinary Academic Seminar," which was held at Katholieke Universiteit, Leuven, Belgium, September 14–15, 2009, led to another stage in the development of this research. I want to thank Emmanuel Nathan along with them for their graciousness; it was a very enjoyable and productive seminar, and the timing could not have been better. For this venue I focused on the research I was undertaking for how 9:19–23 worked within Paul's overall argument in chapters 8–10. This allowed me to develop two areas of emphasis simultaneously in the kind of detail that each warranted, while still attending to how they worked together. I presented a summary version as a paper to my peers in the Pauline Epistles section of the SBL Annual Meeting in New Orleans, November 22, 2009, entitled: "Did Paul Observe Torah in Light of His Strategy 'to Become Everything to Everyone' (1 Corinthians 9:19–23)?" I am grateful for the feedback in both venues, which, I am pleased to report, was generally positive; at the same time, I benefited also from the immediate resistance expressed by others. The final version for the conference volume represents the third chapter herein.

Finally, following the publication of the Leuven conference volume, David May graciously invited me to bring my work on Paul's relationship with Jews and Judaism to the readership of *Review and Expositor* in a volume focused on the Corinthians letters. This afforded the opportunity to revisit the research on 9:19–23 in a more summary style with a slightly different emphasis, as well as to cover some insights that had been omitted for the other venues. That version is republished here as the fourth essay.

Philippians

The research on Paul's polemics in Philippians 3, especially verses 2 and 18–19, began a couple of years before beginning to work in earnest on 1 Corinthians 8–10, and overlapped thereafter. These passages in Philippians similarly constitute a focal point for the traditional construction of a Paul understood to be against the continued value of Judaism. In fact, these passages are often used to suggest that Paul was against continued identification of himself as a Jew, at least certainly indifferent to it. These interpretive traditions tend to weave together Paul's ostensible distance from his own (former) Jewish identity out of the language in Philippians 3 in combination with that in 1 Corinthians 9:19–23.

I began working on the passages from Philippians as I do generally for a new project, trying to get a sense of the likely context of the audience and of Paul's concerns and messages, working on translation, and consulting the secondary literature. This process naturally involves checking the sources that have historically been brought to bear on the exegesis of the text. I was quite surprised to find that the original sources simply did not support the seemingly unquestioned decisions about whose influence Paul was supposedly creating this enigmatic polemic to oppose, or why he would have done so. So my focus became, first, to figure out if the commentaries were as mistaken as seemed probable from my initial review of the sources, and second, to imagine and construct what the alternatives to investigate might be. The research results are presented in the final two essays in this volume. The first of those two, the fifth chapter herein, examines each of the polemical yet cryptic references to the figures mentioned in these verses, with special attention to "the dogs" as well as to the overall thrust of the polemical triad; the second, the sixth chapter herein, investigates certain new options arising from, and suggested within the first essay.

While engaged in this research, I was involved in the Paul and Politics working group on Philippians, which, beginning in 2005, met on the Fridays before the Annual Meeting of the Society of Biblical Literature. This offered me an opportunity to learn much more about recent research on the letter, and to subject my own new research to examination and discussion. I am deeply grateful for the feedback and encouragement from the group, especially Dick Horsley and Joe Marchal. The seminar group's focus on a People's History approach was productive for evaluating what his audiences might have been experiencing that could make sense of Paul's polemics. The first paper I presented was largely focused on deconstructing the received views, with some suggested alternatives to explore. It was discussed before the meeting in Washington D.C. on November 17, 2006: "You say

'Judaizers,' I say, 'Why so?': The Context Implied by Paul's Name-Calling in Philippians 3."

My wife and I were able to visit Philippi in September, 2007, following the Corinth conference, mentioned earlier. There we met Alex Lambrianidis, a interesting person as well as helpful guide who knew where to find the inscriptions of various gods and goddesses on the cliffs from which the stones were quarried to build the city, which he led us to see. Since seeing them in person I cannot help but wonder all the more: could Paul's threefold warning to "beware" have played off of a locally recognizable, perhaps uniquely Philippian (or Pauline) way of referring to the "inscribed ones" (rather than the "mutilated ones")? This word choice in Greek generally denotes carving into stone (rather than into flesh). These reliefs, *inscribed* in the cliffs overlooking the city, simplistically depicted (what, from Paul's vantage point were almost certainly to be considered) "evil workers" like the god Silvanus and goddess Diana (Artemis) in hunting poses, each accompanied by "dogs" at their feet. (See the photos in chapter 6.)

Over the course of 2007 I had several opportunities to present this research project and receive helpful feedback, for which I am very grateful. These included presenting a paper at the Central States SBL in St. Louis, March 25; at a seminar at the University of Helsinki, Finland, May 14, by the invitation of Matti Myllykoski, and at a seminar at Gothenburg University, Sweden, May 22, by the invitation of Samuel Byrskog. During this trip, Dieter Mitternacht helped me examine German works relevant to this project, and we traveled together from Sweden to the wonderful and directly relevant museums in Berlin. We snapped many photos of images and statues of dogs and related inscriptions, as well as of "evil workers" and cult figures associated with "mutilation." Finally, I presented an updated version of this paper to the Early Jewish Christian Relations session of the Annual Meeting of the Society of Biblical Literature in Boston, Mass., November 21, 2008. I am pleased to say that immediately after it was published in *Biblical Interpretation* in 2009, peers began to cite it favorably, rather than to simply repeat the received view.

Studies of Paul naturally tend to focus on what Paul probably thought and meant to communicate. The question less often pursued is: What did the recipients of his letters think? This question, as mentioned, was the focus of the Paul and Politics Philippians seminar from a People's History perspective. In November 2010, I presented the updated research. Having already covered the many reasons to question the prevailing views, this paper focused on exploring the new options for identifying the polemical referents as well as the implications of each option, especially the Cynics (who, for different reasons, also play a role above when exploring 1 Cor

9:19–23), for re-conceptualizing the probable contexts and concerns of his audience in Philippi. The paper discussed was entitled, "The Greco-Roman Context of Paul's Struggling Jewish Subgroup Community in Philippi." The insights from that research paper were to some degree incorporated within the second Philippians essay reproduced herein, which was published in *The Journal for the Study of Paul and His Letters* in 2013.

It was not until fully rethinking the implications for a third essay—not included in this volume to avoid repetition of the many shared elements—that I was able to articulate in more detail the insights of most interest from a People's History perspective. That essay was developed specifically for the volume arising from the Philippians seminar: "Out-Howling the Cynics: Reconceptualizing the Concerns of Paul's Audience from His Polemics in Philippians 3" (in *The People Beside Paul: The Philippian Assembly and History from Below*, edited by Joseph A. Marchal, 183–221. Early Christianity and Its Literature. Atlanta: SBL Press, 2015). During this research, I presented a paper at the Central States SBL regional meeting in St. Louis, on March 17, 2013, entitled: "'Judaizers'? 'Pagan' Cults? Cynics?: Reconceptualizing the Concerns of Paul's Audience from the Polemics in Philippians 3:2, 18–19." That paper is available on my website.

A WORD ABOUT THE COVER IMAGE

Painting by Jean-Léon Gérôme, 1860; Walters Art Museum: Diogenes Laertius, 5th century BCE Cynic ("Doggish") philosopher, surrounded by dogs at the *Metroön* (temple for the Cybele cult in Athens), lighting his lamp to search for an honest man.

The artist's portrayal of Diogenes, the quintessential Cynic philosopher, drew together many elements of his mythological importance to this philosophical tradition. As surprising as it may seem in a volume investigating *Paul*, and all the more Paul *within Judaism*, several chapters consider the relevance of Cynic thought and behavior for interpreting Paul's language in 1 Corinthians 9 and Philippians 3, including specific elements developed in this painting (see especially chapter 6).

EDITORIAL NOTES

The reader will encounter numbers in brackets ("[00]") in the text of each article. These indicate the page numbers in the original publication of the essay.

Other essays included in this volume or other volumes of these collected essays are indicated in the bibliographic information listed for them at the end of each chapter; e.g., "(Available in this volume)"; "(Available in volume 1 of this essay collection)."

ACKNOWLEDGEMENTS

There are many to thank for their help along the way. In addition to those noted above or mentioned in the essays, I want to express my gratitude to all of you who have helped me with research and responded along the way to the papers and essays that grew out of it, which naturally includes peer reviewers, editors, fellow panelists and respondents at seminars and conferences, audience participants, students, colleagues, and friends. Thank you.

My editor at Cascade, Robin Parry, has been more generous with his help from the very beginning of the process than I can recount here, not least the technical elements of bringing these essays into consistent typeset form. Thank you.

I cannot thank my wife Vicky enough. She listened to these ideas as they developed, were researched and presented as papers and then in essays, and offered helpful feedback all along the way. She accompanied me on several of these research and conference trips, and helped me debrief after others. She good-naturedly proofed each paper and essay over the years, and now once again has done so: thank you! *I gratefully dedicate this volume to you, wonderful Gran to our three wonderful granddaughters.*

Mark D. Nanos, June 12, 2017

PART I
Corinthians

1

The *Polytheist* Identity of the "Weak," and Paul's Strategy to "Gain" Them
A New Reading of 1 Corinthians 8:1—11:1

[179] WHEN IT COMES to identifying those Paul describes as ἀσθενής in 1 Corinthians 8—usually translated "weak"—there are many interpretations on offer. But when it comes to the question of their identity as Christ-believers, there is only one.[1] That they are Christ-believers is apparently so obvious that interpreters often proceed without discussion. However, I propose that the consensus is likely mistaken, that the ἀσθενής are "polytheists" who do not believe in the message of good in Jesus Christ that Paul proclaims, and in which his recipients believe. From Paul's perspective, the Corinthians need to recognize that the ἀσθενής are also ἀδελφοί (brothers/sisters) on behalf of whom Christ died. They should thus be sincerely con-

---

1. The terms "Christian" and "Christianity" are anachronistic for discussion of Paul, who did not employ them, and also not helpful, because they suggest a developed institutional identity independent of Judaism. The term "polytheist" is adopted to denote those who are neither Jews nor Christ-believers, even though some Greco-Roman philosophers might not be helpfully described as polytheists either, but continued reference to them as "non-Christ-believing-non-Jews," or something similar, is cumbersome. "Greeks" is misleading, since most Jews and Christ-believers are likely also Greeks in Corinth, and a similar problem applies to using Romans; "idolaters" could be confusing, because many interpreters understand the Corinthians to be Christ-believers who are still in some sense idolaters; "pagan" is anachronistic, although it could have also been adopted, with similar caveats.

I am grateful for the suggestions made to earlier versions of this essay by Andy Johnson, William E. Mendus, Dieter Mitternacht, Loren Rosson, and Magnus Zetterholm.

cerned with the harmful impact that their proposed eating of idol food as if merely ordinary food would have upon these "unbelievers."

I will employ the translation "impaired" to refer to the ἀσθενής.[2] Impaired highlights that they are being objectified by Paul (if not already [180] by his audience as well) to be *unable* to function in the way that he expects of those with properly working sensibilities, lacking the proper sense of what is true about the divine. For Paul writes that the συνείδησις, that is, the "consciousness," "awareness," "sensibilities," or "sense of what is right" of these ones is impaired.[3] This aspect of their state of being makes less sense for the modifier "weak." If the impaired eat idol food, it is their "sensibilities," rather than themselves, that will become "soiled" (8:7) and "wounded" (v. 12).[4] The impaired ones are described as those without "the knowledge" Paul's addressees share, namely, that there is no such thing as an idol in the world, and that God is one (vv. 1, 4, 7), or the different roles of God the Father and Jesus Christ (v. 6). It is the impaired ones' sense of what is right that is ironically "strengthened" to continue to perceive things incorrectly (v. 10), to continue without the knowledge that could keep them from destroying themselves (vv. 7, 11).

In contrast to the impaired ones, Paul addresses those in Corinth with γνῶσις ("knowledge") that idols are meaningless, and that there is no God but the One (8:4), as well as the roles of God the Father and Jesus Christ (v. 6), whom I will refer to as "the knowledgeable."

Paul's terms for these people or groups do not precisely express oppositional categories. The ones with "knowledge" or "wisdom" (specifically, about idols and gods being meaningless) are contrasted with [181] those

2. Cf. Stowers, "Paul on the Use and Abuse of Reason," for discussion of the sense of "sick," including in philosophical discourse.

3. These examples reflect translation equivalents regularly offered for συνείδησις; see Maurer, *TDNT* 7.897–918; Jewett, *Paul's Anthropological Terms*, 402–46; Horsley, "Consciousness and Freedom among the Corinthians"; Gooch, "'Conscience' in 1 Corinthians 8 and 10"; Tomson, *Paul and the Jewish Law*, 208–15; Thiselton, *The First Epistle to the Corinthians*, 640–44, offers a recent overview of research history. The translation of συνείδησις is generally now distinguished from modern notions of "conscience" as in a moral compass, and it is noted that the knowledgeable are not urged to act according to their conscience. The point here is that the impaired have a sense of what is right that Paul calls the knowledgeable ones, with their own different sense of what is right, to consider.

4. Note the subtle change of language between v. 7 and v. 10. In v. 10 it is not the συνείδησις but the person who is described to be ἀσθενοῦς, based on agreement with the masculine participle, while in v. 7, where the issue of defiling/soiling (μολύνεται) arises, and v. 12, where the issue is wounding (τύπτοντες), it is the συνείδησις that is described as ἀσθενής. Grammatically observed, but to different conclusions, see Jewett, *Anthropological Terms*, 422–24; Cheung, *Idol Food in Corinth*, 132–33.

without this knowledge or wisdom (ἀλλ' οὐκ ἐν πᾶσιν ἡ γνῶσις), the ignorant, one might say, although Paul does not use precisely that term for them. Instead, once he has explained in v. 7 that for those who lack knowledge it is their "sense of what is right" (συνείδησις) that is ἀσθενής, he continues to refer to them as the impaired ones. The opposite of the identifications "weak" or "impaired ones" would logically be to "the strong" or "healthy ones," and indeed many interpreters refer to the ones with knowledge as the strong. But apart from referring to them having "power (ἐξουσία)" (actually to "that power of yours [ἡ ἐξουσία ὑμῶν αὕτη]," which carries a sarcastically dismissive tone),[5] Paul does not use "strong" or "powerful" to refer to their state. Thus, to refer to the weak versus the strong implies a different contrast than the one Paul articulates. The contrast he draws has the *knowledgeable* on one side, the *impaired* on the other. That uneven comparison is useful to keep in view. And while he addresses his instructions to the knowledgeable, it is less clear that he addresses the impaired, that they are even part of the encoded or the actual audience Paul envisages will hear the letter read; rather, he writes *about* the impaired, and the impact of the behavior of the knowledgeable upon them.[6] In addition, Paul seems to employ "knowledgeable ones" with an ironic edge, even to be sarcastic, since they do not exhibit appropriate knowledge of what Paul esteems to be the most important concepts and values, like love over rights, which he spells out to them. His parent-like ironic response to the questions they apparently raised to him about eating idol food implied, if not outright stated, disagreement. It reflects his perception, at least his posture, that they think they know more than Paul does [182] about the matters at hand. To call them knowledgeable in the midst of an instruction that signals what they fail to perceive, cuts with an ironic edge calculated to put them in their place.

Probable objections to the idea that Paul's message in these chapters primarily addresses issues across a Christ-believing/polytheist line instead of inter-Christian factionalism, and to the notion that Paul would write of polytheist idolaters as "brothers/sisters" of the Corinthians addressed, will

---

5. Smit, 'About the Idol Offerings', 88–89.

6. Jewett, *Anthropological Terms*, 426–27, among others, argues that 10:25 refers to the impaired. But Brunt, "Love, Freedom, and Moral Responsibility," 29 n. 12, observes that Paul can instead "be telling those with knowledge that they do not need to worry or ask questions in the meat market context." That is the case, all the more, if the knowledgeable do not eat idol food, but have enquired about whether they can. If the impaired are simply the polytheist idolaters of Corinth, then they will be impacted by the consequences of the behavior of the knowledgeable if the knowledgeable heed Paul's letter, as well as if they do not. But Paul's language does not require that the impaired are being addressed, or even among the knowledgeable when they meet to hear this letter read. The constant third person references to them suggest that they are not.

be discussed after the prevailing views, and a new proposal based upon the issues arising in the text itself, have been presented.

THE PREVAILING VIEWS FOR THE IDENTITY OF THE IMPAIRED

The "impaired" are generally perceived to be Christ-believers insecure about the implications of their newly found faith.[7] They are unable to eat food dedicated to idols as if religiously meaningless, having been "until now accustomed to eating idol food as if [sanctified] to idols (τῇ συνηθείᾳ ἕως ἄρτι τοῦ εἰδώλου ὡς εἰδωλόθυτον ἐσθίουσιν)" (8:7). If they were to see the knowledgeable ones "reclining at an idol's temple," they might "be strengthened to eat food sacrificed to idols" (8:10), against their own sense of what is right, which has not yet adjusted to Christ-believing ideals.[8]

Whether described as coming to Christ-faith as Greek or Roman polytheists, or as Jews, the impaired have supposedly retained some measure of their former sensibilities that inhibits them from experiencing [183] fully the ideal of freedom in Christ. In the case of former Greek or Roman idolaters, they retain the sense that participating in the rites and food associated with idols constitutes religious—i.e., idolatrous—behavior, and thus sense that it is right to avoid it now that they are Christ-believers.[9] In the case of Jews who have come to faith in Christ, the problem is supposed to be

---

7. Murphy-O'Connor, "Freedom or the Ghetto," 561–62, writes clearly what most uphold, variously stated: "The Strong assumed that the subjective world of all believers was the same simply because all subscribed to the same objective truth. Their abstract logic did not allow for the time-lag between intellectual acceptance of truth and its emotional assimilation. For some this interval was very short, but not for all. . . . Some had not shaken off the emotional attitude towards idols that had dominated their previous existence. In hidden corners of their hearts they still thought of them as possessing power and were afraid to come anywhere near their orbit"; 568: "Their instinctive revulsion against eating idol-meat was understandable insofar as they had not succeeded in fully interiorizing the fact that idols were nothing"; 569: "The instinctive reaction of the Weak could be overcome only as a by-product of their growth towards Christian maturity"; 573: "Through fear the Weak would have forced the community into a self-imposed ghetto."

8. The majority view is that the impaired have eaten idol food and suffered pangs of guilt thereafter. That is critical, e.g., to the reading of Murphy-O'Connor, "Freedom," 555–56.

9. This view can be traced back at least to Chrysostom, who nevertheless maintained that a Christian should not participate in these rites or eat this food, but not because of the infirmity that arises from fear of idols; see "Homily 20 on First Corinthians" (Philip Schaff [ed.], *NPNF. First Series.*, 111, 114–15).

that they mistakenly retain the Torah-based notion that they must avoid anything associated with idolatry,[10] including food.[11]

Some interpreters suggest that the label ἀσθενής is an indication of their low socio-economic standing.[12] They are unaccustomed to [184] eating sanctified meat independent of religious festivals, when free "meat" was made available to them, whereas the "strong," who had economic means, were used to eating sacrificial "meat" as a part of normal Greco-Roman social and business life. Being better educated, the knowledgeable were also able to reason more clearly, to understand the logical consequences of believing that there is no God but One, that food offered to idols was not actually sacred, and could be eaten as a matter of religious indifference. Yet it is not clear that all of the knowledgeable were elites. If even any of them were not, it would undermine defining the groups along that axis. There is also evidence that non-elites did eat meat, if often less desirable cuts and parts, and regularly enough, for example, at corner cook-shops (*popinae* and *ganeae*) and *tabernae*.[13] Moreover, the food at issue is not defined strictly to be

---

10. Paradoxically, in Scripture idols are trivialized as not gods and meaningless and yet proscribed as demonic and dangerous for those in covenant with the One God (e.g., compare Deut 32:21 with vv. 16–17; Isa 8:19 and 19:3 with chs. 40 and 44; cf. Wis 13–16; see also Ps 106:36–39; 1 En. 19; Jub. 11.4–6); other gods and lords are implicitly recognized to exist, albeit to be lower than Israel's God, and they are not to be honored by Israelites (Exod 15:11; 20:2–6; 22:28; Deut 4:19; 29:26; 32:8–9; Ps 82:1; Mic 4:5; Jas 2:19); images of other gods are to be destroyed in the Land (Exod 23:24; Deut 7:5).

11. There are many reasons to believe that Israelites were prohibited from food and other items involved in the rites of other nations, although most of the evidence is more general, referring to the prohibition of actual participation in the rites, as is the case to which Paul refers in ch. 10, from Exodus 32 and Numbers 25; see also 4 Macc 5:1–4, although probably later than Paul. In addition to these and other passages mentioned in the above note, see Exod 24:11; Deut 14:22–26; Ps 106:28; 1 Sam 9:13; 1 Kgs 1:25; Hos 8:13. The rabbis proscribed eating idol food, although making subtle distinctions, such as the difference between interaction with idolaters and their goods, and between goods that had been used in idolatrous rites and those intended for such use, which have some similarities to the kind of distinctions that arise in Paul's discussion of eating marketplace food not known to be idolatrous, or at someone's invitation, in 10:25–31: *m. Abod. Zar.* 1.4–5; 2.3; 3.4; 4.3–6; 5.1; see Tomson, *Paul*, 151–77, 208–20; Cheung, *Idol Food*, 39–81, 152–64, 300–301; Smit, 'About the Idol Offerings', 52–58, 65; Zetterholm, "Purity and Anger: Gentiles and Idolatry in Antioch," 15; Rudolph, "A Jew to the Jews," 97–104.

12. Theissen, *The Social Setting of Pauline Christianity*, 121–43; this suggestion has proven to be popular in subsequent commentaries: Witherington, *Conflict and Community in Corinth*, 186–202; Thiselton, *Corinthians*, 607–61. See also Hock, *The Social Context of Paul's Ministry*, 50–65; Marshall, *Enmity in Corinth*, 284–85, 290; Martin, *The Corinthian Body*, 70–76, for Cynic/Stoic implications.

13. Meggitt, "Meat Consumption and Social Conflict in Corinth," 137–41; de Vos, *Church and Community Conflicts*, 223.

meat, but idol food (εἰδωλόθυτον), which everyone in Greco-Roman society commonly ate (or drank, in the case of wine).[14]

[185] A few interpreters argue that there actually was no one or group in Corinth fitting the description of the impaired; rather, the sensibilities being expressed are those of Paul himself, for various reasons.[15] This is an interesting alternative; however, it does not sit well with several issues to be discussed, including that Paul, like most Jews, certainly anyone who had been a Pharisee, does not exemplify the profile: he was not one who was accustomed to eating idol food as sacred food. This also likely rules out that those whose sensibilities are at issue (the impaired) were Jews, or had been Jews, for the impaired were by habit idolaters.

According to the prevailing views, those who "know" that eating idol food is acceptable, being merely profane (ordinary) food, uphold this ideal to apply to *all* Christ-believers. Thus, the *"knowledgeable"* Christ-believers are understood to believe that the *"impaired"* Christ-believers should not object to the eating of idol food, and are generally believed to hold the impaired ones in contempt for doing so. In a slightly different direction, some interpreters maintain that the knowledgeable advocate that the impaired should be challenged and trained to overcome their mistaken notion that

14. That Paul mentions he would not even eat any "meats (κρέα)" if it would cause harm to his brother (v. 13) is not to be denied, but that point is made to emphasize how much further Paul would go than what he is asking of his audience, and does not mean the idol food in question is specifically meat (see Gooch, *Dangerous Food*, 53–55, 149–50). One should not overlook that he also mentions βρῶμα in v. 13: "if *food* would cause the brother to stumble...." It may well suggest that Paul would not eat anything that could be even mistaken to be idol food, which might apply to much of the meat in Corinth outside of that processed by a Jewish community (but not all, or Paul's statement of exception would be meaningless). But idol foodstuffs consist of many other materials than meat, and idolatry was practiced by every segment of society, not just those wealthy enough to afford meat. Nevertheless, the point stands that the poor may not often eat meat beyond civic or private association rituals which provided such expensive fare; what is at question is whether it would not also be the case that some of those with "knowledge" in Corinth are among the poor, and thus economic level would not serve as the logical basis for defining the difference between the impaired ones and the knowledgeable ones. Cf. Meggitt, *Paul, Poverty and Survival*; Friesen, "Poverty in Pauline Studies," 323–61. For interaction between Meggitt and Theissen as well as Dale Martin, see their essays in *JSNT* 84 (2001) 51–94. See also Friesen, "Prospects for a Demography of the Pauline Mission"; Pickett, "Conflicts at Corinth."

15. Hurd, Jr., *The Origins of 1 Corinthians*, 123–25, 147–48, argues that Paul is here creating a hypothetical case, that the knowledgeable were not eating in temples as v. 10 suggests, and that there are no weak ones, although the term can be imagined to apply to recent converts who had been idolaters, so that the case presented makes sense to them. Gooch, *Dangerous Food*, 65–72, 83–84, 97, 108, develops this idea also, but notes that it is problematic, since one would assume that upon entering this faith group they would learn that "there is no God but one."

there is some significance to the eating of idol food, and thereby persuaded to abandon their reluctance to eat it.[16]

The judgments of the knowledgeable are generally understood—apart from mitigating circumstances, such as he describes in the case at hand—to reflect Paul's own convictions about indifference to eating [186] idol food.[17] Because of the immediate concern with the sensibilities of the impaired in Corinth, Paul is portrayed to be momentarily willing to forgo upholding the ideal of indifference to idol food, so that their "awareness of what is right will not be soiled (μολύνεται)" (v. 7), and so that "the sense of what is right (συνείδησις)" of the impaired will not lead him or her to be "strengthened (οἰκοδομηθήσεται) to eat food sacrificed to idols" (v. 10), "causing him/her to cause self-ruin (ἀπόλλυται)" (v. 11).

THE IMPAIRED AS CHRIST-BELIEVERS

The consensus view that the impaired ones are specifically *Christ-believers* appears to be based on several factors. Although often not discussed, the primary reason is probably that Paul refers to the impaired ones as ἀδελφοί (brothers/sisters) of his "knowledgeable" audience, who have the ability to trip up and thus harm the impaired if they continue to eat idol food in their presence.[18] Also, Paul refers to Christ having died on behalf of the impaired brothers/sisters, so that sinning against them is sinning against Christ (8:11–12).[19] Moreover, many understand the impaired to be vulnerable to the influence of the knowledgeable in a way that implies that the impaired would thus be led to act against their own sense of what is right, to "destroy

---

16. Glad, *Paul and Philodemus*, 278–87, develops the latter viewpoint; see also Willis, *Idol Meat in Corinth*, 75, 98, 104, who notes variations on this theme among several earlier authors (Weiss, Lietzmann, Jewett); Yeo, "The Rhetorical Hermeneutic of 1 Corinthians 8 and Chinese Ancestor Worship," 298. A slightly different approach that draws on Theissen's socio-economic distinction for identifying the knowledgeable and impaired is offered by Fotopoulos, *Food Offered to Idols in Roman Corinth*, 216.

17. Cf. Weiss, *Der erste Korinthbrief*, 212; Murphy-O'Connor, "Freedom or the Ghetto," 556–58; Barrett, *Essays on Paul*, 50–56 ["Things Sacrificed to Idols"]; Theissen, *Pauline Christianity*, 138–40 ["Strong and Weak"]. This remains the case even among many who recognize that some of Paul's statements are likely recitations of Corinthian positions, or slogans, and may not express his own views.

18. Gooch, *Dangerous Food*, 64, at least raises the possibility that those still intimate with idols are not Christ-believers only to dismiss it, because "Paul identifies these others as Christians: the consciousness of these who eat idol-food as idol-food is weak and is polluted by the act of eating (8:7); this weak one is a brother for whom Christ died (8:11)" (full discussion: 65–72).

19. The second reason Gooch provides in the above note.

him or herself" (ἀπόλλυται) (8:11), because they have not yet completely broken free of their former way of thinking about idols (8:7–13).[20] That is presumed to be because [187] the impaired are not mature enough in their Christ-faith to think like the knowledgeable ones, who have perhaps been Christ-believers longer, or are of higher economic standing and education. They are thus better able to rationalize the issues, granting the knowledgeable some degree of moral authority.

Many interpretations of this section are also shaped by larger constructions of a tension between Pauline and Jewish Christianity, variously conceptualized, or between Jewish and gentile Christians.[21] These naturally limit the options to be explored to identify the possible players and situations addressed in Corinthians; at the same time, decisions fundamental to those portrayals depend upon interpretive elements gathered from previous interpretations of Corinthians.

Finally, the impact of the traditional and still prevailing constructions of Paul and his theology play an important role in suggesting the options to be explored. Interpreters generally uphold that the Corinthians understand Paul to proclaim a Torah-free gospel, and to be Torah-free as a matter of principle, although he may practice Torah when it is expedient for him to do so to reach Jews—notions at the heart of "Paulinism." It is also generally agreed that Paul believes Christ-believing Jews should not observe Torah either, certainly not as an expression of covenantal faith, and that Christ-believing non-Jews should not observe Jewish cultural norms, such as those set out in the Apostolic Decree of Acts 15, or in the Noahide Commandments of rabbinic Judaism.[22] Even if he may have appealed to these or something like them in his earlier letter, it did not and does not represent his own convictions.[23]

---

20. The first reason is provided by Gooch in the above note. It is conceptualized some-what differently by Gardner, *The Gifts of God and the Authentication of a Christian*, 40–64, who understands the impaired to want to be like the knowledgeable. Drawing on the confidence of the knowledgeable, they imitated them. But they were insecure about taking this course, and carried along into idolatry. It logically follows that the impaired are at that point idolaters.

21. Baur, *Paul the Apostle of Jesus Christ*, 137, 145–48, 268–320; Baur, "Die Christuspartei in der korinthischen," 70–94, 222–53, 291–329; differently, Goulder, *Paul and the Competing Mission in Corinth*, esp. 92–124, 152–64.

22. Murphy-O'Connor, "Freedom or the Ghetto," 558.

23. Cf. Hurd, *Origins*, 240–70, 271–96, discusses an ambiguous relationship between Paul and the Jerusalem apostles over the Decree, and even that Paul had behaved "as one outside the law" during his first stay in Corinth (280), to which he returned "at a far more mature level" and based on a more "independent theological bases for ethical action" following the negative reaction to his first letter, which was based on a veiled agreement with the Decree (289, 94).

[188] It is also commonly believed that Paul's argument here implies that he regards eating idol food independent of idolatrous rituals to be a matter of indifference, even that he ate it himself.[24] Hence, it is natural for Paul to be understood to be sympathetic to the propositional "knowledge" of the Christ-believers addressed, if not their lack of concern for how this might impact others, but also to be sensitive to the qualms of those ostensibly new to the idea of freedom to eat idol food as a matter of indifference. He too is understood to have experienced this transformation of attitude when moving from a Jewish- to a Christ-believing-based value system, and thus away from a Torah-defined life.

Paul's approach to the topic of idol food, based on the prevailing view that both the knowledgeable and the impaired are Christ-believers, and thus should ideally practice freedom in Christ to eat anything,[25] is generally combined with his supposed strategy to adopt the behavior of those to whom he seeks to relate, which allegedly involves compromising [189] Torah as a matter of policy (9:19–23).[26] Hence, it is those who know that

---

24. The majority view; e.g., Barrett, *Essays on Paul*, 50–56, upholds that Paul would not participate in idolatrous rituals (52), but he speaks for most interpreters of 1 Corinthians and of Paul in general when he observes: "in the matter of εἰδωλόθυτα (not to mention others) Paul was not a practicing Jew" (50). In contrast, several interpreters uphold that Paul did not and would not eat idol food, although most do not mean by this that Paul observes kashrut, or Torah per se: see Tomson, *Paul*, 185, 195–96, 201–3, 206–8, 219–20, 275–76, 280; Gooch, *Dangerous Food*, 94–95 (although he does not uphold Paul to observe kashrut conventions; 96 n. 60, 127, 129, 131–32, 135, 296–97); Dunn, *The Theology of Paul the Apostle*, 701–6 (but he does not observe kashrut or observe Torah as a matter of faith: *passim*, e.g., when discussing the Antioch Incident); Cheung, *Idol Food*, 76–81, 108–9, 136–41, 296–305 (he also distinguishes kashrut, which Paul did not practice, 78–79); Smit, 'About the Idol Offerings,' 3, 56–57, 154–65; Still III, "Paul's Aims Regarding ΕΙΔΩΛΟΘΥΤΑ," although not dealing with the topic of whether Paul would eat idol food, argues that he does not permit it at all for the Corinthians; Fotopoulos, *Food Offered to Idols*, 222–23 (but on 226: "he [Paul] does not observe the Law"); Garland, "The Dispute over Food Sacrificed to Idols (1 Cor 8:1—11:1)," also emphasizes the complete proscription of idol food, but Paul "rejected Jewish food laws that erected barriers between Jews and Gentiles. . . . Idol food is a different matter entirely" (182, 184). Rudolph, "A Jew to the Jews," like myself, upholds that Paul did not eat idol food, or permit it to be eaten knowingly, and consistently observed kashrut too.

25. Widely attested; see e.g., Weiss, *Der erste Korinthbrief*, 211–18 (esp. 212–13), 227–31; Barrett, *Essays on Paul*, 50, 54–56; Meeks, *The First Urban Christians*, 97–100. Willis, *Idol Meat*, 116, challenges the idea that Paul is affirming the Corinthian slogans of 8:1, 4–6, as if giving priority to freedom, but tempered with love as required.

26. This is especially evident with interpretations that describe the impaired to be Jewish Christ-believers who are not yet secure enough in their faith to eat idol food, or who are engaged in a Jewish Christian mission in opposition to Paul, but it can also be detected when the impaired are described as non-Jews: Weiss, *Der erste Korinthbrief*, 264; Barrett, *The First Epistle to the Corinthians*, 194–95, describes the "weak" in 8:7 to

eating idol food is a matter of indifference who are labeled by interpreters to be "strong," in concert with Paul's own projected ideals. The other ones, those Christ-believers whose supposed lack of maturity leaves them uncomfortable with this Pauline propositional truth, are labeled "weak."[27] This view, interestingly, implies that the church fathers were "weak," because they upheld that no Christians were to eat idol food, based in part on their understanding that this passage prohibited it.[28]

A NEW PROPOSAL: THE IMPAIRED AS NON-CHRIST-BELIEVING POLYTHEISTS

In spite of several reasons to identify the impaired ones to be Christ-believers, which have been discussed, the consensus view is nevertheless [190] far from certain, and I do not think that it is probable. I am convinced neither that from Paul's perspective the impaired ones are insecure in their faith, specifically, that they are troubled by eating idol food,[29] nor that he fears

---

be non-Jewish Christ-believers who are "foolish," being "scrupulous where scrupulosity rests on pure error" about not eating idol food, and on 215, the "weak" in 9:22 are "Christians not yet fully emancipated from legalism."

27. Barrett, *First Epistle to the Corinthians*, 240, represents a good example of the basic point I seek to challenge, commenting on 10:25: "So far as the essential point of principle is concerned he [Paul] is at one with the strong Christians, . . . neither food nor abstention from it will commend us to God. He makes a clean break with Judaism, where conscience demanded of the devout Jew the most searching inquiry before he might eat. Paul had in fact ceased to be a practicing Jew." Similar comments are made with reference to ch. 8 and on 9:19–23. Barrett draws a monolithic portrait of Jewish observance that is mistaken (see above note discussing the nuanced views of the rabbis on idol food).

Willis, *Idol Meat*, 119–20, for a list of other arguments along similar lines, which he challenges, since Paul does not offer instruction to the impaired, and does not side with the knowledgeable; rather, Paul disagrees with the knowledgeable about there being no such thing as idols in the world, and does not favor eating idol food, although Willis believes that Paul regards food to be neutral. I would argue slightly differently, that food is theoretically neutral, since purity is not inherent, but imputed, and since Paul respects Torah as the word of God, idol food is imputed to be that which those belonging to the One God cannot eat. That is also in keeping with rabbinic teaching discussed in an earlier note.

28. In addition to the proscriptions in Acts 15:20, 29; 21:25; Rev 2:14, 19–20; Did. 6.1–2; Ign. *Magn.* 8–10; Justin, *Dial.* 35; Tertullian, *Apol.* 9.13–14; see the discussions in Tomson, *Paul*, 177–86; Gooch, *Dangerous Food*, 122–27, 131–33; Cheung, *Idol Food*, 165–295.

29. Willis, "1 Corinthians 8–10: A Retrospective after Twenty-five Years," 11, observes: "Almost everyone sees the 'weak' as simply those who are troubled by the eating of sacrificial meat."

they will revert to idolatry if the knowledgeable behave against their sensibilities.[30] Rather, I propose that the impaired are *polytheist idolaters* with whom the Christ-believers in Corinth interact, even those to whom they are proclaiming the gospel message. The impaired are not *resistant* to eating idol food; rather, *the impaired have always eaten idol food as an act of religious significance*.[31] After all, is it not more logical to suppose that Christ-believers "know" the truth about idols now, by definition, being Christ-*believers*? In what sense have they become Christ-believers if not by confessing the truth of the One, thus turning from the truth they had supposed before about idols and other gods and lords?[32]

I thus suggest that the impaired are not insecure in their faith, they do not share faith in Christ with the knowledgeable. They are not troubled by eating idol food, that is what they do and have always done as a matter of course, "until now." Thus, Paul's concern is not that the impaired will *revert* to idolatry, but that they will never turn away from it. If they witness that even Christ-believers, who otherwise deny the impaired ones' convictions, nevertheless still eat idol food, they will *continue* to sense that idolatry is right, leading to their self-destruction, when it should be the role of the knowledgeable to live in such a way as to prevent that outcome. Their "impaired" sense of what is right will ironically be "built up (οἰκοδομηθήσεται)," that is, they will be "edified" or [191] "strengthened"[33] to continue the course on which they have spent their whole lives, instead of challenged by the fact that Christ-believers are willing to abandon even the pretense of worshipping their many gods and lords (v. 10). They are brothers and sisters for whom Christ died, but they would not be reached

---

30. Cheung, *Idol Food*, 128–29.

31. Rauer, *Die 'Schwachen' in Korinth und Rom nach den Paulusbriefen*, 27–29, identifies the impaired to be Christ-believers, yet when arguing why they were not Christ-believing Jews, he recognizes that the impaired eat idol food as sacred to the idols and not common food because of their previous way of regarding it to be sacred to idols.

32. Cf. 1 Thess 1:9–10. This does bring up the interesting issue of whether the impaired might include some who have sought to add Christ-faith to their pantheon; see my discussion below of option four, about how Paul might fear the self-destruction of the impaired could follow from failure to conform to his teaching about idol food. See discussion of his instructions in ch. 5 about Christ-believers who engage in idolatry, for why I do not believe they are included among the impaired.

33. Interpreters regularly note that Paul uses the word meaning "to build up" ironically, to signify tearing down by arrogantly behaving in a way that encourages the other to do something harmful to themselves. However, Paul's comment here need not mean that the impaired were not already doing the harmful thing at issue, which most interpreters understand to be implied. Building up need not signify the same thing as starting from scratch. The point is that they are strengthened in resolve to do it.

with that message if the Christ-believers live according to the rights they suppose themselves to have, regardless of the consequences for those who do not share their knowledge.

It is not necessary here to define which specific idolatrous rites are at issue in Corinth, such as those carried out at the many religious temples, in mysteries, associations, homes, and festivals, most of these in some way integrated into the expression of imperial cult.[34] What is significant is that the "impaired ones" are so labeled because they do not share in the "knowledge" of Christ-believers that there is no god but the One; hence, their *"sense of what is right"* is *"impaired."*[35]

In other words, Paul fears that if these "impaired" idolaters were to see the Christ-believers eating idol food—which is notably introduced as a *hypothetical possibility* in 1 Cor 8:10[36]—their own sensibilities would be *confirmed* instead of challenged to be *misguided*. That outcome would be the opposite of what the knowledgeable Christ-believers, as former idolaters themselves, have apparently supposed to be the case. That case may be theoretical, that is, the knowledgeable may not be eating idol food, but they have enquired about the possibility of doing so.[37] Paul explains why they cannot begin that course.

[192] Although Paul begins to explain why they cannot eat it on the basis of consideration of the negative impact on the impaired in ch. 8, in 1 Cor 10:1–22 Paul betrays the ultimate Jewish convictions that are at work in his thinking, and to which he will seek to move his audience as the argument unfolds: there are such things as daemons involved in idol worship, and thus food that has been associated with idolatry cannot be eaten by those who eat at the table of the Lord.[38] Although secondary to strategically agreeing with the knowledgeable that "we know that there are no idols in the *kosmos*" (8:4), and concluding that "for us there is One God" (8:6), as well as diminishing their importance when stating "even if there are those

---

34. For full discussions of the options, see, e.g., Willis, *Idol Meat*; Chow, *Patronage and Power*; Gooch, *Dangerous Food*; Newton, *Deity and Diet*; Fotopoulos, *Food Offered to Idols*; and the essays in Schowalter and Friesen (eds.), *Urban Religion in Roman Corinth*.

35. Willis, *Idol Meat*, 92, although upholding that the impaired are Christ-believers, makes an observation that fits my proposal that they were not: "Those who were 'weak' in συνείδησις were simply those who were 'not knowing' (8:7) the truth about idols and idol meat." See also Martin, *Corinthian Body*, 179–89.

36. Similarly noted by Garland, "Dispute over Food," 180.

37. Sandelin, "Drawing the Line: Paul on Idol Food and Idolatry in 1 Cor 8:1—11:1," esp. 119. Whether the questions were posed to Paul in a challenging tone or not does not alter the point.

38. For sources, consult notes 10 and 11 above.

being called gods" (8:5a), Paul nevertheless includes from the start of his argument the admission that "there are many gods and lords" (8:5b).[39] While the knowledgeable know these gods represented by statues made by humans do not measure up to the God to whom they have now turned, and apparently are asking about eating idol food for any number of other reasons, not least probably to demonstrate that conviction or to avoid negative social consequences for failing to do so, they *cannot* eat it. Paul will finally make clear: What is sacrificed to daemons and not to God *must not be eaten*! God is *jealous* and does not accept for his people to associate in any way with such things. Thus, like the Israelites, the Corinthians, as members of the family of the One God must *flee from idolatry*; food that has been involved in idolatrous rites cannot be on their table (10:1–22).

What is the "ruin" Paul fears will result for the impaired if they witness Christ-believers eating idol food? Although the "ruin" or "destruction" (ἀπόλυται) is self-inflicted by the impaired one in 8:11 ("he will cause himself to be ruined"), it is the knowledgeable who "strengthen" them to choose that course for themselves, who thus cause them to "stumble" in the direction of self-destruction, who "sin" against them, who "wound" their "sense of what is right" (vv. 9–13). At least several possibilities can be imagined to describe what Paul envisages:

(1) Idolaters may fail to *understand* that Christ-faith makes exclusivistic claims for the One God and Christ over against the claims of any other gods, since it appears to incorporate eating of food offered to other [193] gods.[40] Hence, the message of good in Christ is not being proclaimed as it should be, and cannot effect the changes Paul believes should result from proclamation of this news (cf. 14:22–25). The knowledge of the One that can save the impaired is being obstructed by the very ones who have themselves already benefited from understanding that message.

(2) Idolaters may not take the message of Christ-faith *seriously*, that is, on the exclusivistic and superiority terms that it claims against other gods and lords, such as the worship of the One God alone, and the message of salvation in Christ.[41] Idolaters may conclude that even those who

---

39. See also 2:8; 15:24–27, all of which admit the role of other gods and lords to articulate God's superiority (also Rom 8:38–39; 16:20; 2 Cor 4:4; Phil 2:10).

40. Deut 4:6–7, speaks of the nations who witness the Israelites observing Torah, which will therefore lead them to call Israel wise and understanding, and will recognize that there is no other God like theirs. Alternatively, often the prophets warn of the mocking of them and their God that failure to observe Torah will bring.

41. Somewhat similarly, Tomson, *Paul*, 216, states that to eat idol food after it is

profess faith in Christ and the One God do not want to risk the wrath of the gods, or any of the other socio-economic, physical, and psychological consequences that polytheists might expect to result from neglect or abstention of various rites, or from opting out of the social networks within society that participation in these rites entails. That would likely lead to the *a priori* dismissal of the claims of the message of good in Christ. The message of good is thus being compromised, corrupted by its messengers.

(3) If idolaters did understand and take their exclusivistic claims seriously, and recognized that they claimed to have something superior to that which idolaters uphold to be true, then idolaters may regard those who profess it to *lack integrity*: they are hypocrites, arrogant troublemakers, or simply foolish.[42] There is little force to their confession of faith in God and Christ to be exclusive of and superior to other gods. For these Christ-believers fail to live up to the truths proclaimed when they still participate in idolatrous rites, and eat idol-related food they have otherwise renounced to be inferior. This is different than being regarded to be foolish because of believing in the message of a crucified lord, and behaving consistent with that confession in the face of resistance, which Paul expects and experiences for his faithfulness to [194] the message. If idolaters conclude that Christ-believers are hypocrites, they will likely dismiss the message of good in Christ out of hand as lacking integrity.

(4) The Christ-believers' faith might be perceived *to incorporate the worship of other gods alongside* faith in Christ. If any polytheists are interested in Christ-faith for themselves, they may conclude that they can add the One God and Christ to their pantheon, in keeping with the common practice in Greco-Roman culture of incorporating new gods. This would appear to be fully compatible with their polytheistic sensibilities, based on observing the behavior of those who proclaim this news.[43] Ironically, the "superstitions" of their idolatrous family

announced, would "*de facto* renounce the belief that 'For us there is One God the Father'"; Cheung, *Idol Food*, 159, suggests: "If the Corinthians eat the food regardless, they will compromise their confession of the One God and abandon the basic Christian (and Jewish) critique of pagan gods."

42. Similarly, Garland, "Dispute over Food," 196.

43. Somewhat similarly, Conzelmann, *1 Corinthians*, 178, observes: "the Christian would objectify the power of the gods, and thereby 'preach' faith in them"; and Willis, *Idol Meat*, 241, notes: "the pagan who observes a Christian eating ἱερόθυτον might either think Christianity was syncretistic, or the Christian really is uncommitted in faith." Garland, "Dispute over Food," 196, who interprets the impaired in chs. 8 and 10 to

members, friends, neighbors, fellow association members, and social and political contacts, will all be confirmed, not denied. They will be caused to stumble, taking the form of merely adding God and Christ to their idolatrous way of life. The already impaired are thus rendered unable to know that which the knowledgeable know, and are being destroyed by continuing to live in idolatry. From Paul's implied point of view, if the knowledgeable eat food that idolaters (i.e., the impaired ones) regard to be sacred, it will confirm that it is indeed sacred, and the idolaters will be ruined as a result.[44]

This option can be amplified by altering the language of Peter Borgen's argument for the consensus view: "Paul here seems to assume that the recent convert will interpret this [the knowledgeable eating idol food] positively and see it as permission to participate in polytheistic sacrificial meals. This may lead him to attempt a syncretistic fusion of [195] Christianity and polytheistic worship. According to Paul the convert is in this way destroyed."[45] *Mutatis mutandis*, this could describe someone "impaired" who never desisted from polytheism, but sought to add Christ-faith, and indeed, it is possible that someone was regarded to be a member of the community by some other gospel than Paul's, which did not include turning from idols to Christ. But that seems unlikely, since Paul does not here confront the Corinthians about what the proclamation of the gospel entails, but draws upon a shared understanding of that knowledge. Moreover, as will be discussed, this fails to take into account the implications of Paul's instructions in ch. 5 about those *named* brothers and sisters who persist in idolatry: they are not to be accommodated, but challenged or dislodged. Rather, the alternative I wish to suggest to Borgen's description is this: If the impaired one is not a "recent convert" but a polytheistic idolater who is not a Christ-believer, would not this lead him or her to see Christ-believers eating idol food sanctioning continued participation in idolatry, without knowing that

---

be Christ-believers, nevertheless observes the consequences concerning the unbeliever who identifies the food to be idol food in 10:27–29 in a way that is sympathetic to my argument throughout: if a Christ-believer knowingly eats idol food, "It would confirm, rather than challenge, the unbeliever's idolatrous convictions and would not lead the unbeliever away from the worship of false gods. If a Christian were to eat what a pagan acquaintance regards as an offering to a deity, it signals the Christian's tacit endorsement of idolatry"; Rudolph, "A Jew to the Jews," 91; see also Cheung, *Idol Food*, 159.

44. t. 'Abod. Zar. 6.4–6, discusses the rabbinic concern to avoid any behavior that could be seen by a polytheist and create the impression of idolatry; cf. Tomson, *Paul*, 162–63.

45. Borgen, "'Yes,' 'No,' 'How Far?': The Participation of Jews and Christians in Pagan Cults," 51.

it should be otherwise? Might he or she not conclude that Christ-faith can be added to his or her current mix of beliefs—"lead[ing] him to attempt a syncretistic fusion of Christianity and polytheistic worship"? Would that not lead the non-Christ-believer to self-ruin in a way not unlike the supposed Christ-believer Borgen posits—all the more so?

In each of these scenarios, the impaired can be understood to be *strengthened* in their misguided sense of what is right, failing to perceive "the truth" about idolatry, and thus Paul may conclude that the *perpetuation* of their *impaired* state as a result of the wrong behavior by the knowledgeable will lead the impaired *to their ruin*. All of these outcomes, including various combinations of them, would represent alienation from the message of good in Christ that Paul believes can be avoided if the Christ-believers refrain from eating idol food on behalf of the sensibilities of idolaters. He does not want idolaters to be "scandalized" by behavior not befitting those confessing the faith. He wants them to know the One God through Christ-faith. He wants his audience to follow his own example, for he would not even eat "meat" if the eating of any kind of "food" would cause the stumbling of some over the message of Christ (8:13); moreover, he adapts his presentation of the [196] message to "everyone" in order that he might "gain" even "some" to be "saved" (9:19–23).

I thus conclude, in direct contrast to the consensus views, that the impaired ate idol food without any qualms; that is what idolaters do. Moreover, the knowledgeable most likely did not eat idol food,[46] or dine at polytheist's temples,[47] just as Christ-believers would not be expected to do.[48] This point is accentuated all the more to the degree that we accept that these Christ-believers likely met as subgroups within the Jewish communities of Corinth.[49] Although these former polytheists wondered if it would be acceptable to eat it, most likely for a host of the socio-economic and psychological reasons associated with remaining "in the world," in addition to the notion

---

46. Similarly, Sandelin, "Drawing the Line," 118–19.

47. Thus giving weight to Paul's example as an hypothetical construction to respond to their questions about whether they could do so. Note the conditional clause and subjunctive verb when Paul sets out the example: "for if (ἐάν) someone was to see (ἴδῃ) you . . ." (8:10).

48. But see Zetterholm, "Purity and Anger," 11–16. Although I agree that it is not the intrinsic nature of idol food that is at issue for Paul, or for that matter the rabbis, when discussing this topic (Nanos, *Mystery of Romans*, 199–200), the basic premises of Paul's argument here (and in Romans) suggests that he instructed from the start that any food known to have been involved in idolatrous rites was not to be eaten by those committing to Christ-faith. The implications of this policy have likely intensified after Paul left Corinth, leading to the questions that this discourse aims to answer.

49. Cf. Horsley, "Paul's Assembly in Corinth."

that it would demonstrate their faith proposition of indifference to idols, Paul herein sought to make it plain that they must not. It would perpetuate the impaired state of their idolatrous neighbors, rather than helping to bring them to faith in Christ, and it involved a relationship with evil forces that should be avoided at all costs (10:16-22). Paul reminds them what happened to Israelites who indulged in similarly mistaken logic (10:5-22, drawing on Numbers 25).

Paul's original audience knew what we cannot know; namely, whether there were any Christ-believers behaving in the way in which the impaired are described, or whether his descriptions and concerns naturally matched those of their polytheist families, friends, and neighbors. Are there any other clues either within or outside of chs. 8-10 that might support the notion proposed herein, that it was polytheistic [197] brothers and sisters' sensibilities and outcomes in Corinth with whom Paul was concerned?

PAUL'S CONCERN ABOUT POLYTHEISTS IN 8:1—11:1, AND THROUGHOUT THE LETTER

That there were divisions among the Christ-believers in Corinth is not to be denied (cf. 1:11-12; 3:3-4; 6:6-8; 11:18-19).[50] Paul is apparently responding to issues reported to him (1:11; 5:1), or, more likely, that the recipients raised in correspondence to him (7:1; 8:1), which probably arose in response to his earlier letter, lost to us (cf. 5:9-11).[51] But it is not clear whether Paul was specifically responding to a division between or among the addressees over idol food in 8:1—11:1,[52] or instead addressing questions raised, or implications arising from the attitudes they expressed, perhaps in the way certain questions were posed, about how Christ-believers should behave "in the world." A concern with factionalism in this letter does not exclude a concern with how Christ-believers should think and live in view of their role among their polytheist families, friends, neighbors, and larger

---

50. Baird, "'One against the Other': Intra-Church Conflict in 1 Corinthians"; Mitchell, *Paul and the Rhetoric of Reconciliation*.

51. Hurd, *Origins*, 47-94, *passim*.

52. I accept that this section was written as a composite: ibid., 43-94, 114-49, who also raises questions about the prevailing assumption that there are two parties quarreling in the Corinthian church about this matter, albeit to a different conclusion, that the quarrel is between Paul and Corinthians, which I also find to be convincing. But I maintain that the impaired are real people, although not members of the community of God (*ekklēsia*). They are the topic around which the issues (conflicts?) turn concerning how Christ-believers should live in the world among idolaters, and bear witness to their faith; cf. Smit, 'About the Idol Offerings,' 29-46.

world. Learning to eliminate factionalism amongst themselves is an important aspect of how they are to stand out from the world, as in, but not of it. They are those who celebrate the dawning of the age to come in the midst of the present age in a spirit of oneness, who must uphold that ethos on behalf of the service of their brothers/sisters of the world.

Paul draws a contrast between those who believe in many gods and lords and "us," who believe in the One God, and in Christ Jesus (8:6). [198] While in 8:1 Paul apparently agrees that "we realize that everyone has knowledge" about things sacrificed to idols, that is, "we realize that there is no such thing as an idol in the world" (v. 4), at the same time Paul undermines this ostensible agreement: "however, there is not in everyone this knowledge" (8:7). Are not the "we" and "us" Christ-believers, versus the "them" who believe in idols, who do not realize that God is One, or believe in Jesus Christ?[53] It cannot be proven that the impaired "for whom Christ died" in 8:11 is intended to describe polytheist idolaters, or that to sin against polytheists is "to sin against Christ" (v. 12), but how can it be dismissed as if not within the conceptual range of such a statement? Did Christ not die for the unbeliever? Would not living in such a way as to prevent polytheists turning to Christ be considered by Paul to be sinning against Christ? Are not polytheists also "brothers/sisters" of God's creation for whom Paul's addressees should be unselfishly concerned?

It is hard to imagine that the addressees did not perceive that Christ died for those who do not yet believe in him, or that they could read his comments in 15:3 to mean that it was only the sins of Christ-believers for which he died, or upon receipt of the comments later in 2 Cor 5:14–15, that the "all" for whom he died was only all Christ-believers. And although I do not wish to claim that the Corinthians anticipated Romans, certainly Paul made the case in that letter that Christ died for those who did not yet believe in him. Not only that, but he describes the unbelievers of the world to be ἀσθενής, before Christ died for them. Paul writes:

> For while we were *still weak* (ἀσθενῶν), at the right time Christ died for the ungodly. Indeed, rarely will anyone die for a righteous person—though perhaps for a good person someone might actually dare to die. But God proves his love for us in that *while we still were sinners Christ died for us*. Much more surely then, now that we have been justified by his blood, will we be saved through him from the wrath of God. For if *while we were enemies*, we were reconciled to God through the death of his

---

53. Fee, *The First Epistle to the Corinthians*, 379, maintains that the impaired are Christ-believing former idolaters, nevertheless he observes that, "yet for *them* (i.e., the pagans) there are many 'gods' and many 'lords.'"

Son, much more surely, having been reconciled, will we be saved by his life. (Rom 5:6–10 NRSV; emphasis added)

[199] Throughout 1 Corinthians Paul addresses matters arising from the polytheist communal context of the recipients (especially in chs. 7–11, 14).[54] Note, for example, that 5:9–13 sets out the difference between being in the world and behaving like the world, and his references to gentiles (ἔθνεσιν) and the outsider (τοὺς ἔξω) function more like later usage of "polytheist" or "pagan." In 6:1–11, Paul contrasts their identity as well as treatment of each other to that of the "unrighteous" (ἄδικοι) and "unbelievers" (ἀπίστων). 7:12–16 involves a discussion of marriage to an "unbeliever," including how their partner is thereby "sanctified," and the hope that he or she will be thereby "saved." In 9:19–23, in the midst of this discussion of idol food in chs. 8 to 10, Paul states explicitly that he does everything he does for the sake of the gospel in order "to gain" and "to save some."[55] He concludes ch. 10 with a seamlessly constructed concern to seek to avoid offending not only the Christ-believing ἐκκλησία (community), but also the Jews and Greeks (v. 32). The topic of women's hair in 11:2–16 arguably involves how they will be perceived by outsiders.[56] Paul wraps up his instruction about proper conduct at the Lord's Supper with the powerful warning that those who undertake this rite improperly will be disciplined by the Lord: they are instructed to "judge" themselves in order that they "may not be condemned along with the cosmos" (11:27–32). Chapter 12 begins a discussion that extends through ch. 14 about how to conduct gifts and other behavior thus: "You know that when you were 'members of the nations (ἔθνη),' you let yourself be led away to dumb idols, however you were led" (v. 2). Paul expresses specific concern with the effect of the Christ-believer's "spiritual" behavior upon "unbelievers" in 14:16–17, 22–25. He argues: "Tongues, then, are a sign not for [200] believers (πιστεύουσιν) but for unbelievers (ἀπίστοις), while prophecy is [a sign] not for unbelievers (ἀπίστοις) but for believers (πιστεύουσιν). If, therefore, the whole church comes together and all speak in tongues, and outsiders (ἰδιῶται) or unbelievers (ἄπιστοι) enter, will they not say that you are out of your mind (μαίνεσθε)? But if all prophesy, an

---

54. Furnish, *The Theology of the First Letter to the Corinthians*, 16: "In one way or another, the issues taken up in the second section, 5.1—11.1, all derive from the church's struggle to *be* the church in a world to which it does not finally belong."

55. Although some argue that the impaired in this text are Christ-believers, they do not argue that Paul cannot be referring to winning polytheists to faith in Christ here; instead, they seek to extend the reach to include winning Christ-believers to Paul's way of thinking: cf. Willis, "An Apostolic Apologia?" 37; Carson, "Pauline Inconsistency," 14–15; Gardner, *Gifts of God*, 96–99, 104–5; Hays, *First Corinthians*, 155.

56. Fiorenza, *In Memory of Her*, 227–30.

unbeliever (ἄπιστος) or outsider (ἰδιώτης) who enters is reproved by all and called to account by all. After the secrets of the unbeliever's heart are disclosed (τὰ κρυπτὰ τῆς καρδίας αὐτοῦ φανερὰ γίνεται),[57] that person will bow down before God and worship him, declaring, 'God is really among you'" (14:22-25 NRSV). It is not difficult to see that Paul is not focused solely on intra-"Christian" matters in this letter: he wants his audience to learn how to live in order to "win" their polytheist families, friends, and neighbors to the confession of Jesus Christ.

Within the framework of 8:1—11:1, and allowing for the observation that there are dissimilarities between the cases described in chs. 8 and 10—the former about activity in a temple, and the latter seemingly about a home or other place that is not dedicated to cultic activity per se[58]—a pertinent example arises in 10:27. Paul discusses the possible case of accepting an invitation to dinner from "one of the unbelievers (ἀπίστων)." In v. 28, Paul notes the possibility of a certain one—it is unclear whether the host or another guest—pointing out that the food served is "sacred food (ἱερόθυτόν)."[59] This terminology appraises [201] the food from a non-Jewish and non-Christ-believing cultural point of view; in contrast, Paul uses "idol food (εἰδωλόθυτον)" everywhere else in this passage.[60] This strongly suggests that Paul is portraying this "someone" to have the perspective of a polytheist

---

57. NRSV adds the referent "unbeliever's" here, but literally this is a pronoun, "causing to be made known the secrets of *their* heart."

58. Smit, 'About the Idol Offerings,' 61-65, clearly sets out the similarities and dissimilarities between 8:1-3, 7-13 and 10:23-30. Fotopoulos, *Food Offered to Idols*, 241-43, for discussion of the options for the food at issue in 10:27—11:1, and *passim*, for investigation of the probable locations and dynamics of idol food eating in Corinth.

Contra proposals that require the references to idol food only be to food eaten in cultic contexts, or that limit Paul throughout this section to only be addressing the issue of eating food in cultic contexts, or that insist idol food in markets was no longer considered to be idolatrous and thus not objectionable to Paul: Fee, "Εἰδωλόθυτα Once Again"; Witherington, "Not So Idle Thoughts about *Eidolothuton*"; Gardner, *Gifts of God*, 183-85. See the challenges to Fee mounted by Fisk, "Eating Meat Offered to Idols"; Cheung, *Idol Food*, 101-12, 319-22; Still III, "The Meaning and Uses of ΕΙΔΩΛΟΘΥΤΟΝ"; see also Griffith, "ΕΙΔΩΛΟΝ as 'Idol' in Non-Jewish and Non-Christian Greek."

59. It should be considered whether only some of the food was identified to be idol food, as a host or another guest today might indicate certain food or preparation issues of concern to a known vegan guest, or one with allergies, to steer them away from certain choices, but also toward others.

60. Although non-Jews and non-Christ-believers did sometimes refer to these representations as εἴδωλον (idols or images), it was a common Jewish characterization that played negatively off a term connoting merely an appearance or copy rather than the real item it represented, and later it continued to be used in similar ways by Christ-believing groups (Griffith, "ΕΙΔΩΛΟΝ as 'Idol,'" 95-101; cf. F. Buchsel, *TDNT* 2.375-78).

idolater. Nevertheless, many interpreters maintain that this "someone" is an impaired Christ-believer.

Commentators have been baffled by the idea that Paul would express concern here for the "sensibilities" of polytheists, in language like that used in ch. 8 when discussing the impaired. But that is just the point! These interpretations travel in a circle that excludes consideration of the possibility that Paul might have been concerned with impaired unbelievers as "brothers/sisters" in ch. 8. Among other results, this leads to drawing sharp distinctions between the referent in 10:27 and the person described in vv. 28–29, and to other strained arguments.[61] But there does not seem to be any grammatical or contextual grounds for a change of the referent from a polytheist to a "Christ-believer" between these verses.[62]

The reasons that a non-Christ-believing host might inform a Christ-believer that the food had been sanctified could be many, including from helpful to malicious. For example, having offered the invitation, it could have been out of concern for the sensibilities of the [202] Christ-believing guest, or *someone* rumored to be such, or merely to cover the possibility of such guests among the invitees. That might be based on what the polytheist host has learned to be the *possible* "superstitions" of Christ-believers, which are understood to be like those of which they might be aware among Jews, even if only aware in stereotypical or secondhand terms about their supposed beliefs.[63] Or, it could have been a way of testing a

---

61. E.g., Barrett, *First Epistle to the Corinthians*, 242; Gardner, *Gifts of God*, 96–105, 176–79; Fotopoulos, *Food Offered to Idols*, 245. Willis, *Idol Meat*, 235–45, offers a particularly useful discussion.

62. It is of interest to note that although many interpreters insist Paul always refers to Christ-believers when using ἀδελφοί (brothers/sisters), since he does not signal a change, the same standards are not always applied to his use of ἀσθενής (weak) in chs. 8 to 10, and all the more remarkably, between vv. 27 and 28–29 in ch. 10. Also, the case of 11:29–30 should not be overlooked, where being weak and sick and even asleep/dead are linked to eating and drinking without proper discernment of the body in a way that would seem to point to the knowledgeable rather than to the impaired, since it represents the more liberal who need to be more circumspect; is Paul still using ἀσθενής for the same referents? It is most likely that these terms do not represent only one possible meaning for Paul. Meaning is derived from within the changing contexts of usage. Later interpreters are disadvantaged, not knowing the context in Corinth in the ways that the addressees do.

63. Interpreters do not generally seem to consider the potential for a benign or even concerned effort on behalf of a polytheist idolater toward the sensibilities of the Christ-believer; e.g., Gooch, *Dangerous Food*, 69, dismisses the option of non-Christ-believers in view because "there is no evidence whatever that non-Christians were objecting to Christians eating idol-food." Indeed, but that does not mean that this possible identification "may be rejected immediately," for "objecting" need not be at issue based on what Paul describes. Moreover, this may be a case representing just that evidence

Christ-believer, for example, to find out if he or she would eat idol food and thus be exposed as a hypocrite.

In 10:23–31, Paul explains to the knowledgeable, after making it clear up until this point that they cannot eat any food known to be set apart to idols, that this does not mean that they are responsible to investigate whether food that is not known to be idol food (i.e., available outside of cultic situations) to be idol food, a concession to the practicalities of their lives in this Greco-Roman city. This exception does not pertain if someone informs them that it is idol food they are about to eat (v. 28). Similar rabbinic sensibilities are expressed in the sources listed in the discussion above. Paul's instruction also implies that the market has available for purchase non-idol-related-food; otherwise, everything there would be known to be idol food, and thus by definition proscribed, rendering Paul's point mute.

The concerns Paul expresses on both sides of chs. 8–10, which urge the audience to evaluate their behavior in terms of its impact upon polytheists, correspond to Paul's message in this section, as argued herein, for why Christ-believers cannot eat idol food on behalf of the impaired. But one more ostensible obstacle remains to discuss.

POLYTHEISTS AS "BROTHERS/SISTERS ON BEHALF OF WHOM CHRIST DIED"?

[203] Standing in the way of my proposed identification of the "impaired," as well as my interpretation of other language in 1 Cor 8:1—11:1, is the fact that Paul refers to the impaired as ἀδελφός/οί.[64] The translators of the NRSV are certain enough that Paul means by ἀδελφός fellow-believers in

---

which Gooch considers missing, because it is being dismissed out of hand via circular reasoning. Also arguing for the likelihood of positive motives, see de Vos, *Community Conflicts*, 213. Fee, *Corinthians*, 483–85, suggests that a pagan is in view, and takes a somewhat similar line to the argument offered here, however he accounts for accommodating a pagan's consciousness very differently: because "it [idol food] is *not* a matter of Christian moral consciousness" (485).

64. Elsewhere, I have argued in other letters for instances where Paul uses this kinship language to refer to non-Christ-believers: in Rom 9:3, for non-Christ-believing Jews as "my brethren (ἀδελφῶν μου)"; throughout Romans 14 with reference to the ἀσθένεια, whom I understand to be non-Christ-believing Jews; and in Gal 2:4, for the "pseudo-brothers (ψευδαδέλφους)" in Jerusalem, whom I understand to be fellow Judeans, but not Christ-believers; see Nanos, *Mystery of Romans*, 110–13; Nanos, "Intruding 'Spies' and 'Pseudo-brethren': The Jewish Intra-Group Politics of Paul's Jerusalem Meeting (Gal 2:1–10)," 65–68. Objections to my argument in the case of Romans have been made by Gagnon, "Why the 'Weak' at Rome Cannot Be Non-Christian Jews," which I have answered in Nanos, "A Rejoinder to Robert A. J. Gagnon."

Christ that the fact that Paul refers to them as ἀδελφός is masked in the text that English-only readers meet in 8:11: "So by your knowledge those weak *believers* for whom Christ died are destroyed," although literally Paul writes: "for by what you know you are causing the impaired one to destroy him/herself, the brother/sister (ἀδελφὸς) on behalf of whom Christ died."[65]

Throughout 1 Corinthians Paul regularly refers to Christ-believers in the kinship terminology of brotherhood (ἀδελφός/οί), referring to people who are not related to each other by other familial ties, such as by birth or legal adoption. Before ch. 8 he refers to "our brother" Sosthenes (1:1), addresses and exhorts them as "brothers/sisters" (1:10, 11, 26; 2:1; 3:1; 4:6; 7:24, 29), and uses this language to differentiate between Christ-believers and others (5:11; 6:5–8; 7:12–15). This kinship [204] language continues to be used in similar ways after ch. 8 as well: for specific Christ-believing fellow-workers: 16:11–12 (general: 16:20); in general address to the recipients of the letter: 10:1; 11:33; 12:1; 14:6, 20, 26, 39; 15:1, 31, 50, 58; 16:15; and to differentiate Christ-believers from others: 9:5 (note lit.: "*sister*-wife [ἀδελφὴν γυναῖκα]," as well as "*brothers* of the Lord and Cephas"); 15:6.

Such usage of fictive kinship language is common in other Pauline as well as other New Testament texts,[66] just as it is common in the Tanakh[67] and

---

65. Emphasis added; note that the KJV and NASV as well as RSV do not similarly substitute "believer" for "brother." Aasgaard, *My Beloved Brothers and Sisters!*, in an extensive and useful study, does not even express awareness that this question could arise for this passage. He begins a discussion of sibling language in Paul's letters with the subheading, "Christian Siblingship in Paul," and early in the introduction has already concluded that Paul uses ἀδελφοί only for fellow-Christians, except in Rom 9:3, where it is specifically "used in a traditional way, of compatriots"; "it occurs here in a metaphorical-ethnic sense, not in a metaphorical-Christian" (4 n. 5).

66. To note just Paul, for example, it is applied to fellow non-Christ-believing Jews by Christ-believing Jews: by Paul in Rom 9:3; and in speeches attributed to Jews in Acts 2:29; 3:17; 7:2; 13:15, 26, 38; 22:1; 23:1; 28:17.

67. Exod 2:11; 32:27; Lev 19:17; Deut 3:18; 15:2–3, 11–12; 23:19; 24:7; Judg 20:13; 21:6; 2 Chr 19:10; Neh 5:1; Job 30:29; Ps 22:22; Prov 18:24; Isa 66:20; Jer 22:18; Zech 11:14. von Soden, *TDNT* 1.144–46, observes categorically: "There can be no doubt, however, that ἀδελφός is one of the religious titles of the people of Israel taken over by the Christian community" (145).

other Second Temple literature,[68] and Greek and Roman literature too.[69] At the same time, many of these sources use familial language to reach across group boundaries in ways not unlike it is being proposed that Paul should be read in this case.[70]

The concept of a household or family was broader than generally conceptualized today, more extended and fluid. It could include a broad array of family members, slaves, former slaves who are now freepersons as well as their families, and other employees.[71] There were [205] also household-based associations,[72] and one should not discount the dynamics associated with patron-client relationships. The Hippocratic oath bound the medical student not only to his teacher as a son, but to the teacher's sons.[73] Fictive kinship labels were common not only in synagogue groups, but also among polytheist friends, political allies, fellow soldiers, members of religious groups, trade guilds, and voluntary associations, which are attested in surviving epigraphs and letters.[74] Members of the Great Mother cult regarded themselves to be family, and called each other mother and father as well as sister and brother, as did also participants in the Mithras cult, including reference to "holy brother" and "holy father," and fictive sibling language is attested for other cults.[75]

68. Tob 1:3, 10, 16; 5:10–14; 7:1–12; 10:6; 14:4; Jdt 7:30; 8:14; 1 Macc 5:16; 2 Macc 1:1; 1 Esd 1:5–9; 4:61; 8:77. For the Qumran group, see 1 QS 1.9; 2.24–25; 5.25; 6.10, 22; CD 6.20; 7.1; 1 QSa 1.18. Philo, *That the Worse* 140, universalizes the lesson to be learned from Cain's denial of responsibility to his brother; *On the Virtues* 82: "Therefore Moses forbids a man to lend on usury to his brother, meaning by the term brother not only him who is born of the same parents as one's self, but everyone who is a fellow citizen or a fellow countryman"; *Q and A on Gen.* 1.65–77, universalizes from Cain's murder of Abel, his brother; Josephus, *War* 2.122, to describe the brotherhood among the Essenes. See also m. Soṭah 7.8.

69. Plato, *Menex.* 238e–239a, for compatriots; Xenophon, *Anab.* VII.2.25, for friends; Plotinus, *Enn.* II.9.18, for all things in the world; in many papyri and inscriptions for members of religious societies; von Soden, *TDNT* 1.146; Aasgaard, *My Beloved Brothers and Sisters!*, 107–12.

70. E.g., 1 Macc 11:30; 12:10, 17, to refer to the bond between the Judeans and the Spartans; Philo, *Q and A on Gen.* 2.60, which universalizes brotherhood around "all we men are akin to one another, and are brothers, being connected with one another according to the relation of the highest kind of kindred; for we have received a lot, as being the children of one and the same mother, rational nature."

71. See Harland, *Associations, Synagogues, and Congregations*, 30–33; Aasgaard, *My Beloved Brothers and Sisters!*, 34–60.

72. Harland, *Associations*, 30–33.

73. *The Oath*, lines 5 to 15; cf. Johnson Hodge, *If Sons, Then Heirs*, 40.

74. Harland, *Associations*, 30–33, for examples; Aasgaard, *My Beloved Brothers and Sisters!*, 107–12.

75. Aasgaard, *My Beloved Brothers and Sisters!*, 109–11.

Fictive kinship is expressed in a more general sense within virtually any group, and in many overlapping, even disparate ways, including across different group boundaries. It is a constructed and thus dynamic concept based on the perception of shared history and characteristics that can either be understood to be inherent to a group of people, such as blood or seed or land (i.e., essentialist), or defined by a group around values which they perceive themselves to share in common and in contrast to other groups and their values (i.e., processual).[76] These two seemingly different concepts are actually both at work at the same time, for the claim to an inherent bond is itself the construction of identity, and both what is claimed and how it is emphasized can change. Kinship can also be used to signify non-human relationships.[77] Late in the first or early in the second century, Ignatius calls upon his addressees to pray for outsiders to the church, and to conduct themselves as "brothers/sisters (ἀδελφοί)" to them, which is expressed not by behaving like them, but by imitating how Christ lived humbly toward his neighbor, [206] including choosing to be wronged rather than to wrong them (*Eph.* 10).[78] Although Chrysostom understood the impaired in 1 Corinthians 8–10 to be Christ-believers, he made an argument relevant to the point I am trying to make, that on socio-economic grounds the Christian in his own audience ought to regard as *brother* the fellow-laborer more than the elite or wealthy.[79]

The concept of a brotherhood of humankind is not a Christian innovation, or only attested earlier among Israelites. It was at work in Alexander the Great's concept of uniting the world under his rule,[80] and it was an important concept among philosophical groups, especially articulated

---

76. Baumann, *The Multicultural Riddle*, 81–95; Johnson Hodge, *If Sons, Then Heirs*, 20–22, 118–20, and *passim*, for many implications for the study of Paul.

77. Cf. Philo, *Allegorical Int.* 1.8, "And appetite is the brother of imagination"; *That the Worse* 40; 66; *On the Posterity of Cain* 100; *On Drunkenness* 70–71; *On Flight* 90–91; *On Dreams* 109; *On the Contemplative Life* 7; *Q and A on Gen.* 2.12; 2.60; 3.43, 56.

78. Ignatius also writes of looking not only to one's own concerns, but to those of "one's neighbors (τοὺς πέλας)," which is juxtaposed with discussing how true love is not marked only by the desire "that oneself be saved (σώζεσθαι), but all the brothers (τοὺς ἀδελφούς) as well" (*Mart. Pol.* 1.2; M. Holmes trans.).

79. Schaff (ed.), *Nicene and Post-Nicene Fathers. First Series. Vol. XII. Chrysostom: Corinthians*, 117 [Homily 20].

80. In an effort to explain the universalistic aspirations and policies of Alexander, the first-century CE Roman historian Quintus Curtius, *History of Alexander* 10.3.11–14, portrays Alexander addressing his new Persian troops to understand themselves in his eyes to be "soldiers of our blood, not brought in from outside." Plutarch portrays Alexander envisioning a philosophical commonwealth united around the virtuous as kin, and the wicked as foreigners (*On the Fortune of Alexander* 329B–D).

by the Stoics and Cynics.[81] Although slightly later than Paul, Epictetus appealed to the brotherhood of humankind through the shared nature of all humans, including slaves, because all were offspring of Zeus, thus citizens of the universe and sons of god (*Diatr.* 1.9.4-6; 1.13.4). Elsewhere he describes the Cynics to revile all whom they meet because they regard them to be parents, children, brothers, and themselves to be servants of Zeus, father to all humans (*Diatr.* 3.22.81-82). Marcus Aurelius upheld that all humans were kin, including the sinner, who should cooperate with one another like various parts of one body, since all had within themselves an element of the divine (2.1; 7.22; 9.22-23).

But did Paul herein employ fictive kinship language for polytheist idolaters, or can he even be imagined to conceptualize them in such affectionate terms? Is that not just how he urges his audience to think and behave, and how he lives his whole life, on behalf of "the some" he can "gain" and "save"?[82] Are not the concerns he expresses in 10:24 made in the most general terms: "Let no one seek his own [interest], [207] but that of the other (τοῦ ἑτέρου)"? Does Paul not wrap up his overall case against eating idol food in just these terms: in 11:1, to imitate his example of imitating Christ, and in 10:32-33, with the call to "become inoffensive to Jews and to Greeks and to the ekklēsia of God," just as he does himself, in order to "save" "the many"?[83]

Paul's language in 5:9-12, especially v. 11, opens a window into his perspective on believers in Christ versus non-believers that is important to this discussion. Paul explains that when he instructed them in an earlier letter not "to be associated with immoral people (συναναμίγνυσθαι πόρνοις)" (v. 9), he did not mean all of the immoral people "of this world," such as "the greedy," "thieves," and "*idolaters* (εἰδωλολάτραις)," because that would necessitate departing from the world to be accomplished (v. 10). He meant that they should not associate with someone "calling themselves brother or sister (ἀδελφὸς ὀνομαζόμενος),"[84] "if" he or she "is an immoral person, a greedy person, *an idolater*, a swindler, a drunkard, or a thief"; indeed, they

---

81. Aasgaard, *My Beloved Brothers and Sisters!*, 108-9.

82. 1 Cor 9:19-23; Chrysostom observes that Paul claims "all things whatsoever I do, I do for the salvation of my neighbor" (Schaff [ed.], *NPNF. First Series. Vol. XII. Chrysostom: Corinthians*, 132 [Homily 23]).

83. Chrysostom observes the logical connection here: "Not only, however, should the brethren receive no hurt from us, but to the utmost of our power not even those that are without.... Since even Gentiles are hurt, when they see us reverting to such things: for they know not our mind nor that our soul hath come to be above all pollution of sense. And the Jews too, and the weaker brethren, will suffer the same" (Schaff [ed.], *NPNF. First Series. Vol. XII. Chrysostom: Corinthians*, 146 [Homily 25]).

84. Middle voice, accentuating the action of the one who chooses this kinship label.

are not to even eat with anyone [causing themselves to be called brother or sister] of that sort (v. 11). He continues in vv. 12–13, by way of ironic questions, to make the point that it is not his place to judge those "outside," which it is God's place to do, but it is however the audience's place to judge those "inside." He concludes with the imperative to remove from their midst the immoral man (v. 13), who was the topic of the preceding verses (5:1–8).

This usage of fictive kinship language distinguishes Christ-believers from others. But notice that there is a formality introduced in Paul's language to identify specifically those who choose "*to call themselves*" brother or sister, and he also uses inside/outside terminology to accentuate the point. It is relevant to observe that Paul's instruction does not suggest the kind of respect and tolerance toward a fellow-Christ-believer that the usual interpretations for the impaired in ch. 8 require. For the impaired ones continue to be idolaters if they eat food offered to idols, *since they continue* to believe that idols represent real gods, that food offered to them is sacred, which Paul refers to as their habit "*until* [208] *now*." On the prevailing interpretations, they would be Christ-believers, but nevertheless *idolaters*.[85] That anomaly could arise, as discussed in point four above, for one seeking to add Christ-faith to their pantheon, based upon witnessing Christ-believers eating idol food, coupled with a proclamation of a gospel quite different than the one Paul proclaims, which involves turning away from idols as fundamental. It is to ensure that just such a case does not arise that he undertakes several arguments in this letter. While in theory it could have already occurred—the implications of his instructions in ch. 5 seem to preclude it to be the case addressed in chs. 8–10.

In view of Paul's instruction in ch. 5, if they have eaten with a bothered sensibility about doing so, or even refrained because they sensed that food offered to idols remained sacred to the god it represented, as usually described, then this should suggest that, *instead of being accommodated* (the knowledgeable might say, "pandered too"), Paul would call for them to be properly instructed *to change* their ways, *or else be removed* from the assembly. Yet Paul does not call for the "impaired ones" to be instructed to change or be thrown out of the assembly in chs. 8–10. He makes it clear that those who are "called brothers and sisters" *cannot* practice idolatry, whereas those who are idolaters but do not believe in Christ are to be treated under a different, more tolerant standard, such as that articulated in the text under consideration: they are to adjust to the sensibilities of the impaired. Paradoxically, that is the kind of accommodation one might expect to be promoted toward a natural-born brother or sister, or a spouse (cf. 7:10–16!),

---

85. Lietzmann, *An die Korinther I/II*, 43, tellingly writes of an "Halbchristen."

but it is quite different from the judgment Paul commands toward those identified to be Christ-believing brothers and sisters.

The accommodation Paul expresses in ch. 8 toward the impaired corresponds to the position he champions in ch. 5 toward polytheists, not toward fellow Christ-believers. Why does Paul not also instruct the impaired, if Christ-believers, to undertake the ideas and behavior that he otherwise instructs the Corinthians to express, in this case, to give up idolatry? Because they are not Christ-believers, they are not "named" ἀδελφοί in terms of shared faith in Christ. They are not members of "the community of God." At the same time, why does he not address the knowledgeable as if they are Christ-believing [209] ἀδελφοί who would be guilty of idolatry if they ate idol food knowingly? Because the knowledgeable do not eat idol food. Although they have apparently enquired about the possibility, which likely arose for them on theoretical, logical grounds, because idols are now regarded by them to be neutral, and because they live within in an idolatrous culture, this issue arises for them on practical grounds too. How else are they to succeed in the world?

CONCLUSION

Paul's perspective reveals a sense of fictive kinship with all humankind—"on behalf of whom Christ died." Idolaters who do not yet profess faith in Christ are to be regarded as brothers and sisters too, fellow-members of the family of humans God created and seeks to restore in Christ. That is a dimension of their identity about which the knowledgeable needed to be set straight, in view of their resistance to his earlier instruction proscribing idolatry for all Christ-believers.[86] They have apparently failed to properly calculate the destruction such "know-it-all" behavior will bring both upon themselves, and upon their polytheist neighbors, whom they are instead to learn (to know how) to love as they do themselves.

The impaired are to be treated differently than fellow Christ-believers, those "being named" brother and sister. Rather than being judged, polytheists are to be gained by behavior consistent with the confession of Christ-faith. That involves not eating any food know to be set apart to idols. It involves not insulting the "mistaken" beliefs of the impaired, but learning how to develop speech and behavior calculated to implicitly undermine

---

86. Furnish, *Corinthians*, 55, similarly observes: "what drives and shapes his mission to 'outsiders' is the conviction that no one stands beyond the circle of God's saving purpose, and that, in this sense, even unbelievers are 'insiders' to God's grace (see 9.19–23)."

them. The knowledgeable are to relate to the impaired on terms that will communicate the "knowledge" of Christ to them, which means they must not live in a way that can be mistaken to deny their confession of the One.

Paul outlines his own strategy for accomplishing this on behalf of those whom he seeks "to save," by way of example, in the midst of his instructions in these chapters, in 9:19–23. Paul sketches how he relates [210] to various kinds of people according to their own premises in order to proclaim the gospel to each in terms to which they can relate. He does not behave like them, for example, he does not eat like them, but remains Torah-observant when he eats. But he adjusts his rhetorical behavior and posture to deliver the gospel to different people in different ways. For example, to the Jew he argues like a Jew, from Torah, to the lawless he argues like a lawless person would, apart from appeal to law, and to the impaired he argues like the impaired would argue. That is just how Luke portrays him to proceed in the Areopagos speech of Acts 17:16–31, where Paul discloses the Unknown God to which they have built a statue (idol) to be the Creator God (v. 23), that is, he begins his argument from within their own premises. But in the course of his argument he eventually reveals his own very different conviction about the appropriateness of building this or any image to represent the divine (v. 29), and challenges them to turn away from idols to the God who has raised Jesus Christ from among the dead (vv. 30–31; cf. v. 18). Notably, Luke understands Paul to appeal to the brotherhood of all humankind based upon common origin in one man (vv. 26–31).[87]

In Romans, Paul, the Christ-believing Jew, will teach non-Jews how to live in order to gain their Jewish brothers and sisters, those for whom Christ came first of all;[88] in 1 Corinthians we witness Paul teaching non-Jews how to gain their Greek (and Roman) polytheist brothers and sisters. Albeit informed by Paul's own Christ-faith-based Jewish group perspective, both instructions appeal to the development of empathy across communal lines where sibling rivalry, or worse, so often prevails.

BIBLIOGRAPHY

Aasgaard, Reidar. *My Beloved Brothers and Sisters! Christian Siblingship in Paul.* Early Christianity in Context: JSNTSup 265. London: T. & T. Clark, 2004.

Baird, William. "'One Against the Other': Intra-Church Conflict in 1 Corinthians." In *The Conversation Continues: Studies in Paul & John in Honor of J. Louis Martyn*

---

87. Cf. Acts 2:5; 10:35; Rom 5:12–19; 1 Cor 15:45–49; Bruce, *The Acts of the Apostles*, 382–83.

88. Nanos, *Mystery of Romans*.

edited by Robert T. Fortna and Beverly R. Gaventa, 116–36. Nashville: Abingdon, 1990.

Barrett, C. K. *Essays on Paul*. Philadelphia: Westminster, 1982.

———. *The First Epistle to the Corinthians*. BNTC. Peabody, MA: Hendrickson, 1968.

Baumann, Gerd. *The Multicultural Riddle: Rethinking National, Ethnic, and Religious Identities*. London: Routledge, 1999.

Baur, Ferdinand Christian. "Die Christuspartei in der korinthischen Gemeinde, der Gegensatz der petrinischen und paulinischen Christentums in der ältesten Kirche, Petrus in Rom." *Tübinger Zeitschrift für Theologie* 4.3 (1831) 70–94, 222–53, 291–329.

———. *Paul the Apostle of Jesus Christ: His Life and Works, His Epistles and Teachings*. Translated by Allan Menzies. Edited by Eduard Zeller. 2nd ed. Two vols. in one vol. Peabody, MA: Hendrickson, 2003.

Borgen, Peder. "'Yes,' 'No,' 'How Far?': The Participation of Jews and Christians in Pagan Cults." In *Paul in His Hellenistic Context*, edited by Troels Engberg-Pedersen, 30–59. Minneapolis: Fortress, 1995.

Bruce, F. F. *The Acts of the Apostles: The Greek Text with Introduction and Commentary*. 3rd rev. and enlarged ed. Grand Rapids: Eerdmans, 1990.

Brunt, John C. "Love, Freedom, and Moral Responsibility: The Contribution of 1 Cor. 8–10 to an Understanding of Paul's Ethical Thinking." In *Society of Biblical Literature 1981 Seminar Papers*, edited by Kent Harold Richards, 19–33. Atlanta: Scholars, 1981.

Carson, David. "Pauline Inconsistency: Reflections on 1 Corinthians 9.19–23 and Galatians 2.11–14." *Churchman* 100 (1986) 6–45.

Cheung, Alex T. *Idol Food in Corinth: Jewish Background and Pauline Legacy*. JSNTSup 176. Sheffield, UK: Sheffield Academic Press, 1999.

Chow, John K. *Patronage and Power: A Study of Social Networks in Corinth*. JSNTSup 75. Sheffield, UK: Sheffield Academic Press, 1992.

Conzelmann, Hans. *1 Corinthians: A Commentary on the First Epistle to the Corinthians*. Translated by James W. Leitch. Hermeneia. Philadelphia: Fortress, 1975.

de Vos, Craig Steven. *Church and Community Conflicts: The Relationships of the Thessalonian, Corinthian, and Philippian Churches with Their Wider Civic Communities*. SBLDS 168. Atlanta: Scholars, 1999.

Dunn, James D. G. *The Theology of Paul the Apostle*. Grand Rapids: Eerdmans, 1997.

Fee, Gordon. "Εἰδωλόθυτα Once Again: An Interpretation of 1 Corinthians 8–10." *Biblica* 61 (1980) 181–87.

———. *The First Epistle to the Corinthians*. NICNT. Grand Rapids: Eerdmans, 1987.

Fiorenza, Elisabeth Schüssler. *In Memory of Her: A Feminist Theological Reconstruction of Christian Origins*. New York: Crossroad, 1984.

Fisk, Bruce N. "Eating Meat Offered to Idols: Corinthian Behavior and Pauline Response in 1 Corinthians 8–10 (A Response to Gordon Fee)." *Trinity Journal* 10 NS (1989) 49–70.

Fotopoulos, John. *Food Offered to Idols in Roman Corinth: A Social-rhetorical Reconsideration of 1 Corinthians 8:1—11:1*. WUNT 2.151. Tübingen: Mohr Siebeck, 2003.

Friesen, Steven J. "Poverty in Pauline Studies: Beyond the So-called New Consensus." *Journal for the Study of the New Testament* 26.3 (2004) 323–61.

———. "Prospects for a Demography of the Pauline Mission: Corinth among the Churches." In *Urban Religion in Roman Corinth: Interdisciplinary Approaches*, edited by Daniel N. Schowalter and Steven J. Friesen, 351–70. HTS 53. Cambridge: Harvard University Press, 2005.

Furnish, Victor Paul. *The Theology of the First Letter to the Corinthians*. New Testament Theology. Cambridge: Cambridge University Press, 1999.

Gagnon, Robert A. "Why the 'Weak' at Rome Cannot Be Non-Christian Jews." *Catholic Biblical Quarterly* 62 (2000) 64–82.

Gardner, Paul Douglas. *The Gifts of God and the Authentication of a Christian: An Exegetical Study of 1 Corinthians 8—11:1*. Lanham, MD: University Press of America, 1994.

Garland, David E. "The Dispute over Food Sacrificed to Idols (1 Cor 8:1—11:1)." *Perspectives in Religious Studies* 30.2 (2003) 173–97.

Glad, Clarence E. *Paul and Philodemus: Adaptability in Epicurean and Early Christian Psychagogy*. NovTSup 81. Leiden: Brill, 1995.

Gooch, Paul W. "'Conscience' in 1 Corinthians 8 and 10," *New Testament Studies* 33 (1987) 244–54.

Gooch, Peter David. *Dangerous Food: 1 Corinthians 8–10 in Its Context*. SCJ 5. Waterloo, ON: Wilfrid Laurier University Press, 1993.

Goulder, Michael D. *Paul and the Competing Mission in Corinth*. Library of Pauline Studies. Peabody, MA: Hendrickson, 2001.

Griffith, Terry. "ΕΙΔΩΛΟΝ as 'Idol' in Non-Jewish and Non-Christian Greek." *Journal of Theological Studies* 53 (2002) 95–101.

Harland, Philip. *Associations, Synagogues, and Congregations: Claiming a Place in Ancient Mediterranean Society*. Minneapolis: Fortress, 2003.

Hays, Richard B. *First Corinthians*. Interpretation. Louisville, KY: John Knox, 1997.

Hock, Ronald F. *The Social Context of Paul's Ministry: Tentmaking and Apostleship*. Philadelphia: Fortress, 1980.

Horsley, Richard A. "Consciousness and Freedom among the Corinthians: 1 Corinthians 8–10." *Catholic Biblical Quarterly* 40 (1978) 581–89.

———. "Paul's Assembly in Corinth: An Alternative Society." In *Urban Religion in Roman Corinth: Interdisciplinary Approaches*, edited by Daniel N. Schowalter and Steven J. Friesen, 371–95. HTS 53. Cambridge: Harvard University Press, 2005.

Hurd, John Coolidge, Jr. *The Origins of 1 Corinthians*. New York: Seabury, 1965.

Jewett, Robert. *Paul's Anthropological Terms: A Study of Their Use in Conflict Settings*. AGJU 10. Leiden: Brill, 1971.

Johnson Hodge, Caroline. *If Sons, Then Heirs: A Study of Kinship and Ethnicity in the Letters of Paul*. New York: Oxford University Press, 2007.

Lietzmann, Hans. *An die Korinther I/II*. HNT 9. 5th ed. Tübingen: Mohr, 1969.

Marshall, Peter. *Enmity in Corinth: Social Conventions in Paul's Relations with the Corinthians*. WUNT 2.23. Tübingen: Mohr Siebeck, 1987.

Martin, Dale B. *The Corinthian Body*. New Haven: Yale University Press, 1995.

Meeks, Wayne A. *The First Urban Christians: The Social World of the Apostle Paul*. New Haven: Yale University Press, 1983.

Meggitt, Justin J. "Meat Consumption and Social Conflict in Corinth." *Journal of Theological Studies* 45 (1994) 137–41.

———. *Paul, Poverty and Survival*. Studies of the New Testament and its World. Edinburgh: T. & T. Clark, 1998.

Mitchell, Margaret Mary. *Paul and the Rhetoric of Reconciliation: An Exegetical Investigation of the Language and Composition of 1 Corinthians.* Louisville: Westminster/John Knox, 1992.

Murphy-O'Connor, Jerome. "Freedom or the Ghetto: 1 Cor viii, 1–13; x, 23–xi, 1." *Revue biblique* 85 (1978) 561–62.

Nanos, Mark D. "Intruding 'Spies' and 'Pseudo-brethren': The Jewish Intra-group Politics of Paul's Jerusalem Meeting (Gal 2:1–10)." In *Paul and His Opponents*, edited by Stanley E. Porter, 59–97. Pauline Studies 2. Leiden: Brill, 2005. (Available in volume 3 of this essay collection.)

———. *The Mystery of Romans: The Jewish Context of Paul's Letter.* Minneapolis: Fortress, 1996.

———. "A Rejoinder to Robert A. J. Gagnon's 'Why the "Weak" at Rome Cannot Be Non-Christian Jews.'" Unpublished paper (2000; 37pp), available at http://www.marknanos.com/Gagnon-rejoinder-6-20-03.pdf. (Available in volume 2 of this essay collection.))

Newton, Derek. *Deity and Diet: The Dilemma of Sacrificial Food at Corinth.* JSNTSup 169. Sheffield, UK: Sheffield Academic Press, 1998.

Pickett, Ray. "Conflicts at Corinth." In *Christian Origins*, edited by Richard A. Horsley, 113–37. A People's History of Christianity, Vol. 1. Minneapolis: Fortress, 2005.

Rauer, Max. *Die 'Schwachen' in Korinth und Rom nach den Paulusbriefen.* Biblische Studien. Freiburg: Herder, 1923.

Rudolph, David J. "A Jew to the Jews: Jewish Contours of Pauline Flexibility in 1 Corinthians 9:19–23." Ph.D. thesis, University of Cambridge, 2006.

Sandelin, Karl-Gustav. "Drawing the Line: Paul on Idol Food and Idolatry in 1 Cor 8:1—11:1." In *Neotestamentica et Philonica: Studies in Honor of Peder Borgen*, edited by David E. Aune *et al.*, 108–25. Leiden: Brill, 2003.

Schaff, Philip, ed. *A Select Library of the Nicene and Post-Nicene Fathers of the Christian Church. First Series. Vol. XII. Saint Chrysostom: Homilies on the Epistles of Paul to the Corinthians.* Grand Rapids: Eerdmans, 1978.

Schowalter, Daniel N., and Steven J. Friesen, eds. *Urban Religion in Roman Corinth: Interdisciplinary Approaches.* HTS 53. Cambridge: Harvard University Press, 2005.

Smit, Joop. *'About the Idol Offerings': Rhetoric, Social Context, and Theology of Paul's Discourse in First Corinthians 8:1—11:1.* Contributions to Biblical Exegesis and Theology 27. Leuven: Peeters, 2000.

Still III, E. Coye. "The Meaning and Uses of ΕΙΔΩΛΟΘΥΤΟΝ in First-Century Non-Pauline Literature and 1 Cor 8:1—11:1: Toward Resolution of the Debate." *Trinity Journal* 23 NS (2002) 225–34.

———. "Paul's Aims Regarding ΕΙΔΩΛΟΘΥΤΑ: A New Proposal for Interpreting 1 Corinthians 8:1—11:1." *Novum Testamentum* 44.4 (2002) 333–43.

Stowers, Stanley K. "Paul on the Use and Abuse of Reason." In *Greeks, Romans, and Christians: Essays in Honor of Abraham J. Malherbe*, edited by David L. Balch *et al.*, 253–86. Minneapolis: Fortress, 1990.

Theissen, Gerd. *The Social Setting of Pauline Christianity: Essays on Corinth.* Translated by John H. Schütz. Philadelphia: Fortress, 1982.

Theological Dictionary of the New Testament. (TDNT). 10 vols. Edited by G. Kittel and G. Friedrich. Translated by Geoffrey Bromiley. Grand Rapids: Eerdmans, 1964–76.

Thiselton, Anthony C. *The First Epistle to the Corinthians: A Commentary on the Greek Text.* NIGTC. Grand Rapids: Eerdmans, 2000.

Tomson, Peter J. *Paul and the Jewish Law: Halakha in the Letters of the Apostle to the Gentiles*. CRINT. Minneapolis: Fortress, 1990.
Weiss, Johannes. *Der erste Korinthbrief.* MeyerK. Göttingen: Vandenhoeck & Ruprecht, 1910.
Willis, Wendell Lee. "1 Corinthians 8–10: A Retrospective after Twenty-five Years." *Restoration Quarterly* 49.2 (2007) 103–12.
———. "An Apostolic Apologia? The Form and Function of 1 Corinthians 9." *Journal for the Study of the New Testament* 24 (1985) 33–48.
———. *Idol Meat in Corinth: The Pauline Argument in 1 Corinthians 8 and 10*. SBLDS 68. Chico, CA: Scholars, 1985.
Witherington, Ben. *Conflict and Community in Corinth: A Socio-Rhetorical Commentary on 1 and 2 Corinthians*. Grand Rapids: Eerdmans, 1994.
———. "Not So Idle Thoughts about *Eidolothuton*." *Tyndale Bulletin* 44.2 (1993) 237–54.
Yeo, K. K. "The Rhetorical Hermeneutic of 1 Corinthians 8 and Chinese Ancestor Worship." *Biblical Interpretation* 2.3 (1994) 294–311.
Zetterholm, Magnus. "Purity and Anger: Gentiles and Idolatry in Antioch." *Interdisciplinary Journal of Research on Religion* 1 (2005) 1–24.

2

Why the "Weak" in 1 Corinthians 8–10 Were Not Christ-believers

[385] INTERPRETERS UNANIMOUSLY IDENTIFY the ἀσθενής ("weak") in 1 Corinthians 8 to be Christ-believers. I propose, however, that the ἀσθενής—which I will translate "impaired"—are, unlike the Corinthians to whom he writes, polytheists who do not believe in the message of good in Jesus Christ.[1]

From Paul's perspective, the recipients of this letter, who had written to him about the possibility of eating idol food now that they did not believe idols represented real gods or lords, need to be brought to a new realization about the impaired, those who still do regard idols to represent gods. Namely, these polytheists, which the recipients had been themselves before turning to Christ, are still their ἀδελφοί ("brothers/sisters"), for whom Christ also died, but they have not *yet* realized this propositional truth. Thus, the proposed eating of idol food as if a matter of indifference must not be undertaken. In the first place, it would have a destructive effect upon these polytheists if they witness [386] it. In the second place, they would damage themselves. That is, the thinking of the "knowledgeable" is based upon mistaken logic: any association with idolatry is anathema for those who worship the One God in Christ, as it has always been for Israel as well,

---

1. Since the term "weak" does not properly modify the referent συνείδησις ("consciousness"), I suggest the term "impaired," and will use this term throughout, while refraining from calling those on the other side "strong."

even when the significance of idolatry, and of the gods it represents, have been denied.[2] These are the things those claiming knowledge should know.[3]

Note that Paul writes that it is the συνείδησις—that is, the "consciousness," "awareness," "sensibilities," or "sense of what is right"—of these ones that is impaired.[4] If encouraged to eat idol food in that state, their [387] sensibilities will become defiled (8:7). In contrast to those in Corinth with γνῶσις ("knowledge") that idols are meaningless, and that there is no God but the One (8:4), whom I will refer to as "the knowledgeable," the impaired are generally perceived to be insecure in their new-found Christ-faith. They are understood to be unable to eat food dedicated to idols as if religiously meaningless, having been "until now accustomed to eating idol food as sanctified for idols [τῇ συνηθείᾳ ἕως ἄρτι τοῦ εἰδώλου ὡς εἰδωλόθυτον εσθίουσιν]" (8:7).

Whether described as coming to Christ-faith as idolaters or Jews, the prevailing views uphold that the impaired have retained some vestige of their former sensibilities that inhibits them from fully experiencing the ideal of freedom in Christ.[5] In the case of former idolaters, they ostensibly retain the

---

2. Paradoxically, in Scripture idols are trivialized as not gods and meaningless and yet proscribed as demonic and dangerous for those in covenant with the One God (e.g., compare Deut 32:21 with vv. 16–17; Isa 8:19 and 19:3 with chapters 40 and 44; cf. Wis 13–16; see also Ps 106:36–39; 1 En. 19; Jub. 11.4–6); other gods and lords are implicitly recognized to exist, albeit to be lower than Israel's God, and they are not to be honored by Israelites (Exod 15:11; 20:2–6; 22:28; Deut 4:19; 29:26; 32:8–9; Ps 82:1; Mic 4:5; cf. Jas 2:19); images of other gods are to be destroyed in the Land (Exod 23:24; Deut 7:5).

3. Paul seems to employ "knowledgeable ones" with an ironic edge, even to be sarcastic, since they do not exhibit appropriate knowledge of what Paul esteems to be the most important concepts and values, but they think that they know more than Paul about the matters at hand.

4. These examples reflect translation equivalents regularly offered for συνείδησις; see Maurer, *TDNT* 7.897–918; Jewett, *Paul's Anthropological Terms*, 402–46; Horsley, "Consciousness and Freedom among the Corinthians," 581–89; Paul Gooch, "'Conscience' in 1 Corinthians 8 and 10"; Tomson, *Paul and the Jewish Law*, 208–15; Thiselton, *The First Epistle to the Corinthians*, 640–44, offers a recent overview of research history. The translation of συνείδησις is generally now distinguished from modern notions of "conscience" as in a moral compass, and it is noted that the knowledgeable are not urged to act according to their conscience. The point here is that the impaired have a sense of what is right that Paul calls the knowledgeable ones, with their own different sense of what is right, to take into consideration.

5. Murphy-O'Connor, "Freedom or the Ghetto," 561–62, writes clearly what most uphold, variously stated: "The Strong assumed that the subjective world of all believers was the same simply because all subscribed to the same objective truth. Their abstract logic did not allow for the time-lag between intellectual acceptance of truth and its emotional assimilation. For some this interval was very short, but not for all. . . . Some had not shaken off the emotional attitude towards idols that had dominated their previous existence. In hidden corners of their hearts they still thought of them as possessing

sense that the rites associated with idols constitute sacred behavior, and thus sense that it is right to avoid such rites now that they are Christ-believers.[6] In the case of Jews who come to faith in Christ, the problem is supposed to be that they mistakenly retain the Torah-based notion that they must avoid anything associated with idolatry.

THE CONTEXT OF PAUL'S CONCERNS ABOUT EATING IDOL FOOD

[388] There were divisions among the Christ-believers in Corinth (cf. 1:11–12; 3:3–4; 6:6–8; 11:18–19), and thus there is good reason to suppose that Paul may be addressing the knowledgeable and impaired as two factions within the community, as the consensus view maintains. Nevertheless, it does not seem that Paul is addressing the impaired directly, or even that he has any authority over them, but rather, that in 8:1—11:1, he seeks to make the Christ-believers in Corinth aware of their responsibility to the "unbelieving" polytheists with whom they share life in this city.[7] Paul writes *to* some who have knowledge of the One God, even if they have, according to Paul, mistaken views about the implications of that knowledge; the others, *about* whom he writes, do not have this knowledge at all. Paul writes on behalf of the latter, on behalf of whom Christ died *too*.

Throughout the chapters around our text, and in the midst of it, Paul addresses many matters arising from the "polytheist" or "pagan" context of the recipients (explicitly, cf. 5:9–13; 6:1–11; 7:12–16; 9:19–23; 10:32; 11:27–32; 14:16–17, 22–25).[8] He concludes chapter 10 with a seamlessly constructed concern to seek to avoid offending not only the Christ-believing ἐκκλησία ("assembly"), but also the Jews and Greeks (v. 32). [389] Paul is not focused solely on intra-"Christian" concerns, but also on "gaining"

---

power and were afraid to come anywhere near their orbit"; 568: "Their instinctive revulsion against eating idol-meat was understandable insofar as they had not succeeded in fully interiorizing the fact that idols were nothing"; 569: "The instinctive reaction of the Weak could be overcome only as a by-product of their growth towards Christian maturity"; 573: "Through fear the Weak would have forced the community into a self-imposed ghetto."

6. This extends to the arguments for a more socio-economic basis for defining them, cf. Theissen, *The Social Setting of Pauline Christianity*, 121–43.

7. Smit, 'About the Idol Offerings', 61–65, clearly sets out the similarities and dissimilarities between 8:1–3, 7–13 and 10:23–30. Fotopoulos, *Food Offered to Idols in Roman Corinth*, 241–43, for discussion of the options for the food at issue in 10:27—11:1, and *passim*, for investigation of the probable locations and dynamics of idol food eating in Corinth.

8. For a full discussion, see Nanos, "The Polytheist Identity of the 'Weak.'"

the rest of the world to his faith. It may well be that Paul's concern that the Christ-believers desist from factionalism is related to the other conduct he also proscribes so strongly among themselves, because of the concern for how their divisive and compromising behavior will negatively impact their polytheist family members, friends, and neighbors. A pertinent example arises in 10:27.

Paul discusses a hypothetical case of accepting an invitation to dinner from "one of the unbelievers [ἀπίστων]." In v. 28, he brings up how to behave if someone at the meal points out that some of the food being served is "sacred food [ἱερόθυτόν]."[9] This change in Paul's terminology from "idol food [εἰδωλόθυτον]," which he used before this point, is notable, for here Paul appraises the food from a non-Jewish and non-Christ-believing cultural point of view.[10] The point Paul makes is that once the Christ-believer is made aware that what is being served is food that has been sanctified to idols, the Christ-believer is not to eat it.[11] The reason is not because of a Christ-believer's own sensibilities about eating idol food, but on behalf of the sensibilities of the other, the polytheist host or guest who has made this matter known (vv. 28–29).

[390] Commentators have been baffled by the idea that Paul would express concern here for the "sensibilities" of "polytheists," who are however not referred to as "impaired," in language like that used in chapter 8 when discussing the impaired. But that is just the point! These interpretations travel in a circle that excludes consideration of the possibility that Paul might have been concerned with the salvation of the impaired unbelievers in chapter 8![12] But if the impaired in chapter 8 were understood by his audi-

---

9. It should be considered whether only some of the food was identified to be idol food, as a host or another guest today might indicate certain food or preparation issues of concern to a known vegan guest, or one with allergies.

10. Although non-Jews and non-Christ-believers did sometimes refer to these representations as εἴδωλον (idols or images), it was a common Jewish characterization that played negatively off a term connoting merely an appearance or copy rather than the real item it represented, and later it continued to be used in similar ways by Christ-believing groups (Griffith, "ΕΙΔΩΛΟΝ as 'Idol' in Non-Jewish and Non-Christian Greek").

11. Note that in 10:25, when Paul instructs them about eating food sold in the marketplace, following his explanation not to eat idol food, that he means they can only eat marketplace food not known to them to be idol food, not marked as idol food by the seller. This logically implies that there is marketplace food available that was not involved in idolatrous rites, just as there could be in a polytheist host's home. But once announced to be idol food, they cannot eat it.

12. E.g., Barrett, *The First Epistle to the Corinthians*, 242; Gardner, *The Gifts of God and the Authentication of a Christian*, 96–105, 176–79; Fotopoulos, *Food Offered to Idols*, 245. Willis, *Idol Meat in Corinth*, 235–45, offers a particularly useful discussion.

ence to be polytheists, then Paul's concern with the sensibilities of polytheists continuing into chapter 10 would have made perfect sense. Note that in 10:33, as Paul concludes this argument, he states that the behavior he advises is, as is everything in his own life, to do good to everyone, to seek the advantage of the many, "in order that they would be saved [ἵνα σωθῶσιν]."

THE IMPAIRED AS NON-CHRIST-BELIEVING "POLYTHEISTS"

I propose that the impaired throughout chapters 8–10 are polytheistic *idolaters* with whom the Christ-believers in Corinth interact, perhaps even those to whom they are proclaiming the gospel message. They are [391] neither insecure in their faith, for example, troubled by eating idol food,[13] nor does Paul fear that they will revert to idolatry.[14] They are not *resistant* to eating idol food, but quite the contrary: "until now" the impaired *have always eaten idol food* as an act of *religious significance*. Paul's fear is not that they will *revert* to idolatry, but that they will never turn away from it. The "impaired ones" are so labeled because they do not share in the "knowledge" of Christ-believers that there is no God but One; hence, their "*sense of what is right*" is "*impaired*."[15] Is it not more logical to suppose that Christ-believers "know" the truth about idols now, by definition, being Christ-*believers*? In what sense have they become Christ-believers if not by confessing the truth of the One, thus turning from the truth they had supposed before about idols and other gods and lords?[16]

Paul fears that if these "impaired" polytheists were to see the Christ-believers eating idol food, their own sensibilities would be confirmed instead

---

It seems to me that in 10:23–31, Paul is now explaining to the knowledgeable, after making it clear up until this point that they cannot eat any food known to be set apart to idols, that this does not mean that they are responsible to investigate whether food that is not known to be idol food (i.e., available outside of cultic situations) is idol food, a concession to the practicalities of their lives in this Greco-Roman city. This exception, of course, does not pertain if someone informs them that it is idol food they are about to eat (v. 28). The rabbis express similar sensibilities (see note 20 below).

13. Willis, "1 Corinthians 8–10: A Retrospective after Twenty-five Years," 11, observes: "Almost everyone sees the 'weak' as simply those who are troubled by the eating of sacrificial meat."

14. Cheung, *Idol Food in Corinth*, 128–29.

15. Willis, *Idol Meat*, 92, although upholding that the impaired are Christ-believers, makes an observation that fits my proposal that they were not: "Those who were 'weak' in συνείδησις were simply those who were 'not knowing' (8:7) the truth about idols and idol meat."

16. Cf. 1 Thess 1:9–10.

of challenged as *misguided*. That outcome would be the opposite from what the knowledgeable Christ-believers, as former idolaters themselves, have apparently supposed to be the case. That case may be hypothetical, that is, the knowledgeable may be eating idol food, or, more likely, they have not, but have enquired about the possibility of doing so.[17]

[392] Paul is probably surprised that they would deduce from the proposition of the One God that therefore eating idol food is a matter of indifference. Jews concluded instead that anything to do with idols must be avoided completely. So Paul explains to these non-Jewish Christ-believers why they cannot begin that course. His argument develops several reasons. The "impaired" sense of polytheists' notions of what is right will ironically be "built up [οἰκοδομηθήσεται]," that is, they will be "edified" or "strengthened"[18] to continue the course on which they have spent their whole lives ("until now"), instead of challenged by the fact that Christ-believers are willing to abandon even the pretense of worshipping their many gods and lords (v. 10). They are brothers and sisters "on behalf of whom Christ died," but they would not be being reached with that message if the Christ-believers live according to the "rights" they suppose themselves to have, regardless of the consequences for those who do not share their knowledge.

Paul calculates instead that if the knowledgeable eat food that idolaters regard to be sacred, it will confirm that it is indeed sacred.[19] Paul may suppose one of several unacceptable consequences will result from polytheists witnessing Christ-believers eating idol food. 1) The message may be obstructed, in that polytheists will fail to understand the non-polytheistic nature of Christ-faith. 2) The message may be compromised, in the sense that even though Christ-believers claim not to [393] believe in other gods, their continued participation will signal that this claim has no substance, and need not be taken seriously as an alternative. 3) Along the same line, if they take it seriously, they may regard its adherents to be hypocrites, and thus not consider it further. For apparently even those who profess faith in

---

17. Cf. Sandelin, "Drawing the Line," esp. 119.

18. Interpreters regularly note that Paul uses the word meaning "to build up" ironically, to signify tearing down by arrogantly behaving in a way that encourages the other to do something harmful to themselves. However, Paul's comment here need not mean that the impaired were not already doing the harmful thing at issue, which most interpreters understand to be implied. "Building up" need not signify the same thing as starting from scratch. The point is that they are strengthened in resolve to do it. For a detailed investigation of Paul's use of irony in his letters, with a focus on Galatians, see Nanos, *The Irony of Galatians*.

19. T. 'Abod. Zar. 6.4-6, discusses the rabbinic concern to avoid any behavior that could be seen by a polytheist and create the impression of idolatry (cf. Tomson, *Paul*, 162-63).

Christ and the One God do not want to risk the wrath of these gods, or any of the other socio-economic, physical, and psychological consequences that idolaters might expect to result from neglect or abstention. Or 4) if they are persuaded by the message of Christ, they may (mis)understand that what is required of them is simply to add the God of Jesus Christ to their pantheon, rather than being challenged to desist from the worship of all other gods. Thus, the "superstitions" of their idolatrous family members, friends, neighbors, fellow association members, and social and political contacts, will all be confirmed, not denied. They will be caused to "stumble." The impaired will be "strengthened" in their misguided sense of what is right, failing to perceive *the truth* about idolatry; the *perpetuation* of their *impaired* state will lead them "to ruin."

Although Paul begins to explain why they cannot eat idol food on the basis of consideration of the negative impact on the impaired in chapter 8, in chapter 10:1–22 Paul betrays the ultimate Jewish convictions that are at work in his thinking, and to which he will seek to move his audience as the argument unfolds: there are such things as daemons involved in idol worship, and thus food that has been associated with idolatry cannot be eaten by those who eat at the table of the Lord.[20] [394] Albeit secondary to strategically agreeing with the knowledgeable that "we know that there are no idols in the *kosmos*" (8:4), and concluding that "for us there is One God" (8:6), as well as diminishing their importance when stating "even if there are those being called gods" (8:5a), Paul nevertheless includes from the start of his argument the admission that "there are many gods and lords" (8:5b).[21] While the knowledgeable know these gods represented by statues made by humans do not measure up to the God to whom they have now turned, and apparently are asking about eating idol food for any number of other

---

20. There are many reasons to believe that Israelites were prohibited from food and other items involved in the rites of other nations, although most of the evidence is more general, referring to the prohibition of actual participation in the rites, as is the case to which Paul refers in chapter 10, from Exodus 32 and Numbers 25; see also 4 Macc 5:1–4, although probably later than Paul. In addition to these and other passages mentioned above in note 2, see Exod 24:11; Deut 14:22–26; Ps 106:28; 1 Sam 9:13; 1 Kgs 1:25; Hos 8:13. The rabbis proscribed eating idol food, although making subtle distinctions, such as the difference between interaction with idolaters and their goods, and between goods that had been used in idolatrous rites and those intended for such use, which have some similarities to the kind of distinctions that arise in Paul's discussion of eating marketplace food not known to be idolatrous, or at someone's invitation, in 10:25–31: m. 'Abod. Zar. 1.4–5; 2.3; 3.4; 4.3–6; 5.1; see Tomson, *Paul*, 151–77, 208–20; Cheung, *Idol Food*, 39–81, 152–64, 300–301; Smit, 'About the Idol Offerings', 52–58, 65; Zetterholm, "Purity and Anger," esp. 15; Rudolph, "A Jew to the Jews," 97–104.

21. See also 2:8; 15:24–27, all of which admit the role of other gods and lords to articulate God's superiority (also Rom 8:38–39; 16:20; 2 Cor 4:4; Phil 2:10).

reasons, not least probably to demonstrate that conviction or to avoid negative social consequences for failing to do so, they *cannot* eat it.

By the time they read 10:1–22 it will be clear: What is sacrificed to idols and not to the One God *must not be eaten*! God is *jealous* and does not accept for his people to associate in any way with such things. Thus, like the Israelites, the Corinthians, as members of the family of the One God must *flee from idolatry*; food that has been involved in idolatrous rites cannot be on their table.

I thus conclude, in direct contrast to the consensus views, that the impaired ate idol food without any qualms; that is what idolaters do. Moreover, the knowledgeable most likely did not eat idol food, just as Christ-believers would not be expected to do. Although the knowledgeable wondered if it would be acceptable to eat it, given their knowledge [395] that it is not sacred, Paul herein sought to make it plain that they must not. It would perpetuate the impaired state of their idolatrous neighbors, rather than helping to bring them to faith in Christ, and it involved a relationship with evil forces that should be avoided at all costs (10:16–22). Paul reminds them what happened to Israelites who indulged in similarly mistaken logic (10:5–22).

THE PROBLEMATIC ISSUE OF ἈΔΕΛΦΟΣ/ΟΙ

If the impaired do not share the knowledge of the meaning of Christ with the knowledgeable whom Paul addresses, this would account for the discrepancy between 8:1 and verse 7, wherein Paul writes both that *everyone knows*, and *yet* that *not everyone knows* the very same thing.[22] Paul's conflicting language makes sense if those who "know" are Christ-believers. His inclusive use of language signifies "every" Christ-believer, and those who do not know are those who do not "yet" believe in Jesus Christ. They are polytheist idolaters. Yet the unanimous consensus view is built around the conviction that since Paul refers to the impaired as ἀδελφοί, they must be fellow Christ-believers. Would Paul refer to polytheist non-Christ-believing idolaters as brothers and sisters? The approach of the interpretive tradition has been based upon an unequivocal "No."[23]

---

22. Whether Paul is merely repeating a Corinthian slogan or stating what he understands them to uphold, and thus feigning agreement rather than expressing his own view, it does not alter the fact that these two statements stand in stark contrast to each other: who is the everybody who knows, if not everybody knows? How is the identification of the "everybody" further defined by the contours of Paul's argument?

23. Interestingly, many interpreters do not discuss this matter, apparently assuming if not concluding that it is self-evident, probably at this point based upon a unanimous tradition of interpretation. Peter Gooch, *Dangerous Food*, 64, discusses the

[396] I propose the answer to be "Yes." Is that not just how he urges his audience to think and behave, and how he lives his whole life, on behalf of "the some" he can "gain" and "save"?[24] Are not the concerns he expresses in 10:24 made in the most general terms: "Let no one seek his own [interest], but that of the other [τοῦ ἑτέρου]"? Does Paul not wrap up his overall case against eating idol food in just these terms: in 11:1, to imitate his example of imitating Christ, and in 10:32–33, with the call to "become inoffensive to Jews and to Greeks and to the *ekklēsia* of God," just as he does himself, in order to "save" "the many"?[25]

There are too many factors to discuss the topic in any comprehensive way here.[26] But Paul's language in 5:9–12, especially verse 11, opens [397] a window into his perspective on believers in Christ versus non-believers that is directly relevant to this section of 1 Corinthians. Here Paul explains that his instructions to them in an earlier letter not "to be associated with immoral people [συναναμίγνυσθαι πόρνοις]" (v. 9), did not mean all of the immoral people "of this world," such as "the greedy," "thieves," and "*idolaters* [εἰδωλολάτραις]," because that would necessitate departing from the world

---

possibility that those still intimate with idols are not Christ-believers only to dismiss it, because "Paul identifies these others as Christians: the consciousness of these who eat idol-food as idol-food is weak and is polluted by the act of eating (8:7); this weak one is a brother for whom Christ died (8:11)" (full discussion: 65–72).

24. 1 Cor 9:19–23; Chrysostom observes that Paul claims "all things whatsoever I do, I do for the salvation of my neighbor" (Schaff, ed., *NPNF* XII:132 [Homily XXIII]). See also Romans 5.6–10, where Paul writes: "For while we were *still weak* [ἀσθενῶν], at the right time Christ died for the ungodly. Indeed, rarely will anyone die for a righteous person—though perhaps for a good person someone might actually dare to die. But God proves his love for us in that *while we still were sinners Christ died for us*. Much more surely then, now that we have been justified by his blood, will we be saved through him from the wrath of God. For if *while we were enemies*, we were reconciled to God through the death of his Son, much more surely, having been reconciled, will we be saved by his life" (NRSV; emphasis added).

25. Chrysostom observes the logical connection here: "Not only, however, should the brethren receive no hurt from us, but to the utmost of our power not even those that are without.... Since even Gentiles are hurt, when they see us reverting to such things: for they know not our mind nor that our soul hath come to be above all pollution of sense. And the Jews too, and the weaker brethren, will suffer the same" (Ibid., 146 [Homily XXV]).

26. For a detailed discussion, see Nanos, "The Polytheist Identity of the 'Weak.'" I have argued for cases in other letters where Paul uses this kinship language to refer to non-Christ-believers: in Romans 9:3, for non-Christ-believing Jews as "my brethren [ἀδελφῶν μου]"; throughout Romans 14 with reference to the ἀσθένεια, whom I understand to be non-Christ-believing Jews; and in Galatians 2:4, for the "pseudo-brothers [ψευδαδέλφους]" in Jerusalem, whom I understand to be fellow Judeans, but not Christ-believers: see Nanos, *Mystery of Romans*, 110–13; Nanos, "Intruding 'Spies' and 'Pseudo-brethren,'" esp. 65–68.

to be accomplished (v. 10). He meant that they should not associate with someone "calling themselves brother or sister [ἀδελφὸς ὀνομαζόμενος]," "if" he or she "is an immoral person, a greedy person, *an idolater*, a swindler, a drunkard, or a thief"; indeed, they are not to even eat with anyone [causing themselves to be called brother or sister] of that sort (v. 11). He continues in vv. 12–13, by way of ironic questions, to make the point that it is not his place to judge those "outside," that is for God to do; it is, however, the audience's place to judge those "inside." He concludes with the imperative to remove from their midst the immoral man (v. 13), who was the topic of the preceding verses (5:1–8).

This usage of fictive kinship language sharply distinguishes Christ-believers from others. But notice that there is a formality introduced in Paul's language to identify specifically those who choose "*to call themselves*" brother or sister, and he also uses inside/outside terminology to accentuate the point. It is relevant to observe that Paul's instruction does *not* suggest the kind of respect and tolerance toward a fellow-Christ-believer that the usual interpretations for the impaired [398] in chapter 8 require. For the impaired ones, if they continue to eat food offered to idols, which Paul refers to as their habit "*until now*," therefore remain idolaters. They *continue to believe* that idols represent *real* gods, so that food offered to them is deemed to be sacred.

On the prevailing interpretations, the impaired would be Christ-believers and yet idolaters at the same time. That anomaly could arise for one seeking to add Christ-faith to their pantheon. As discussed in point 4 above, Paul apparently fears that might happen, if polytheists witness Christ-believers eating idol food, while at the same time proclaiming the gospel. Any such message would be quite different than the one Paul proclaims, which involves turning away from idols as part of what it means to turn to Christ. He undertakes several arguments in this letter to ensure that just such a case does not arise. While in theory it could have already occurred, the implications of his instructions in chapter 5 seem to preclude it to be the case addressed in chapters 8–10. For then we would expect him to be similarly critical, instead of accommodating.

In view of Paul's instruction in chapter 5, if they have eaten with a bothered sensibility about doing so, or even refrained because they still believed that food offered to idols remained sacred to the god it represented, as they are usually described, then this should suggest that *instead of being accommodated* (the knowledgeable might say, "pandered to"), Paul would call for them to be properly instructed *to change* their ways, *or else be removed* from the assembly. Yet Paul does *not* call for the "impaired ones" to be instructed to change or be thrown out of the assembly in chapters

8–10. He makes it clear that those who are "called brothers and sisters" *cannot* practice idolatry, whereas those who are idolaters but do not believe in Christ are to be treated under a different, more tolerant standard, such as that articulated in the text under consideration: they are to adjust to the sensibilities of the impaired. Paradoxically, that is the kind of accommodation one might expect to be promoted toward a natural-born brother or sister, or a spouse (cf. 7:10–16!), but it is quite different from the judgment Paul commands toward those identified to be Christ-believing brothers and sisters.

[399] The accommodation Paul expresses in chapter 8 toward the impaired corresponds to the position he champions in chapter 5 toward polytheists, but it is decidedly different than the disposition he advises toward fellow Christ-believers. Why does Paul not also instruct the impaired, if Christ-believers, to undertake the ideas and behavior that he otherwise instructs the Corinthians to express, in this case, to give up idolatry? I suggest that it is because they are not Christ-believers, they are not "named" ἀδελφοί in terms of shared faith in Christ. They are not members of "the community of God." At the same time, why does he not address the knowledgeable as if they are Christ-believing ἀδελφοί who would be guilty of idolatry if they ate idol food knowingly? Because the knowledgeable do not eat idol food, although they have apparently enquired about the possibility, which likely arose for them on theoretical, logical grounds, because they now regard idols to be profane. Because they live within an idolatrous culture, this issue probably arises for them on practical grounds too: they would like to avoid the marginality "in this world" that undertaking the recommended course will almost certainly entail.

CONCLUSION

On this reading, Paul's perspective reveals a sense of fictive kinship with all humankind—"for whom Christ died." Idolaters who do not yet profess faith in Christ are to be regarded as brothers and sisters too—a dimension of their identity on which the knowledgeable needed to be set straight, in view of their resistance to his earlier instruction proscribing idolatry for all Christ-believers. They have apparently failed to properly calculate the profound results such behavior threatens both for themselves, and for their "polytheist" neighbor, whom they are to love as they do themselves.

The impaired are to be treated differently than fellow Christ-believers, those "being named" brother and sister. Rather than being judged, [400] the idolaters are to be gained by behavior consistent with the Christ-believers' confession of faith, accompanied by rhetorical sensitivity. They are not to insult the mistaken beliefs of the "impaired," but to learn how to undermine them. Paul outlines his own strategy for accomplishing this on behalf of "some" of them, by way of example, in 9:19–23.[27]

In Romans, Paul, the Christ-believing Jew will teach non-Jews how to live in order to gain their Jewish brothers and sisters, those for whom Christ came first of all;[28] in 1 Corinthians we witness Paul teaching non-Jews how to gain their Greek (and Roman) polytheist brothers and [401] sisters. Albeit informed by Paul's own Christ-faith based Jewish group perspective, both instructions appeal to the development of empathy across communal lines where sibling rivalry, or worse, so often prevails.

SUMMARY

I propose the translation equivalent "impaired" rather than "weak" for the ἀσθενής; and that "knowledgeable" or something similar be used for the τὸν ἔχοντα γνῶσιν ("the ones having knowledge"). "Strong" is not helpful, since it is better to keep the focus on their identity as the ones who "know" that there is no such thing as idols, and thus that food offered to them by idolaters

---

27. In 9:19–23, Paul sketches how he relates to various kinds of people according to their own premises in order to proclaim the gospel to each in terms to which they can relate. I do not believe that by "becoming like" that Paul means he behaves like them in the sense of adopting their conduct. For example, Paul does not eat like them, but remains Torah-observant when he eats. The prevailing interpretations revolve around Paul changing his conduct. But he does not actually become like them on the prevailing views, although this point does not seem to be generally realized. Rather, these views understand his conduct to represent "becoming like" only in the sense of "mimicking" their behavior, because he is not understood to share their propositional beliefs. In my view, he becomes like them in the sense that he adjusts his rhetorical behavior and posture to be meaningful to them from their own premises or worldviews, and thus that he delivers the gospel to different people in different ways. For example, to the Jew he argues like a Jew, from Torah, to the lawless he argues like a lawless person would, apart from appeal to law, and to the impaired he argues like the impaired would argue, as if there are other gods and lords represented by the statues humans make. That is just how Luke portrays him to proceed in the Areopagos speech of Acts 17:16–31. There Paul discloses that the Unknown God to whom they have built a statue (idol) actually signifies the Creator God (v. 23). He begins his argument from within their own premises. But in the course of his argument he eventually reveals his own very different conviction about the appropriateness of building this or any image to represent the divine (v. 29), and challenges them to turn away from idols to the God who has raised Jesus Christ from among the dead (vv. 30–31; cf. v. 18). Although a Jew, he relates to these non-Jewish philosophers from their own premises: he becomes like them in order to gain them to the message of good in Christ. Notably, in terms of kinship, Luke understands Paul to appeal to the brotherhood of all humankind based upon common origin in one man (vv. 26–31).

28. Nanos, *Mystery of Romans*.

is not actually sacred, which is not a precisely oppositional category to those whose συνείδησις is described as "impaired." I agree with those who argue that "consciousness" or "awareness" or even better "sensibilities" or "sense of what is right" should be used to translate συνείδησις. That helps to keep salient that at issue is the person's *sense* of what is *proper*, an aspect that can be conceptualized to be "defiled." I propose that means that if the impaired were to see Christ-believers eating idol food they would either misunderstand or dismiss the propositional claims of Christ-faith proclaimed by the "knowledgeable," or alternatively, would believe that they can add Christ-faith to their pantheon. Such conclusions would contribute, from Paul's point of view, to their destruction.

The ἀσθεναία were most likely non-Christ-believing idolaters. They did not share the knowledge of Christ-believers (or of Jews in general) that there is no God but One, and thus that any food offered to man-made statues of them is theoretically not sacred. They ate idol food. At the same time, Paul instructs those with "knowledge" of this Jewish and Christ-faith based propositional view of what is sacred not to eat idol food. It is not likely that the knowledgeable have done so already, but they wonder if this would be acceptable behavior. The answer is an emphatic "No!" Doing so would contribute additional harm to their [402] "polytheist" neighbors' already impaired sensibilities, which could lead to their inability to turn to the One God. Moreover, there *is* such a thing as real powers (daemons) associated with these idols and worship of them; thus, idol food is not without religious value, albeit harmful. It is dangerous for those who have turned to the One God, even as it is for those who have not. They must flee from it.

My approach focuses on Paul's concern with how Christ-believers in Corinth interfaced with the idolatrous world of their family, friends, neighbors, patrons or clients, and so on. The letter was not calling for accommodation of idolatrous sensibilities among Christ-believers, which in chapter 5 Paul made plain were not to be tolerated. Paul's use of ἀδελφός/οί in chapter 8 is not likely best understood on contextual grounds to always signify Christ-believers, but functions in the case of the impaired ones to refer to those who are fictive kin, in that Christ has died on behalf of them too, although they have not (yet) realized that to be the case.

When Paul describes his strategy for gaining and saving some to faith in Christ in 9:19–23, I imagine that he has in mind a strategy consistent with what he told the knowledgeable to adopt toward the impaired in chapters 8 and 10. Eating food offered to idols is *not* a matter of indifference, e.g., a demonstration of their freedom from their former conviction that idols and rites offered to them are sacred. And they are *not* to disregard the sensibilities of the impaired about what is meaningful. They are rather to "flee" from any association with idolatry, both for their own sake, and for the sake of the impaired. That strategy is evident in the way he has approached them rhetorically throughout the argument of chapters 8:1—11:1, which is not by direct appeal to Torah overall, since they are not Jews.[29] But because they are non-Jewish [403] Christ-believers, he appeals to concern for the other for whom Christ died, and also to the propositional truth that applies to them as well as to Jews, which he supports by examples from Torah: one cannot eat of the table of daemons and of the Lord.

Paul instructs the letter's recipients that even Christ-believing gentiles cannot eat idol food as a matter of indifference. His approach, moreover, implies that while they have understood him to be a Torah-observant Jew, they have nevertheless applied what they calculated to be the logical outcome of his message of good for gentiles who remain gentiles after Christ-faith, which led them to question his earlier letter's instruction for themselves (being non-Jews) to refrain from eating any food that they knew to be sanctified to idols (implied in 5:9–13 with 7:1 and 8:1).[30] On their reckoning, since it was not regarded to be sacred, it was thus profane, and eating it would bear witness to that propositional truth at work in their recent change of heart. But Paul saw things differently. He sought to shape the minds and actions of his non-Jewish audience from a worldview circumscribed by Torah, without at the same time bringing them under Torah, since they were, and remained, representatives from the other nations turning to the One God, and did not become Israelites. According to his interpretation of the implications of the new age having dawned in Christ, each was to remain in the state in which they had been when they became part of the community of believers, however, all were to uphold "the commandments of God" (7:17–24). In the case of non-Jews, now that they were members of these Jewish groups, that meant conforming to prevailing rules of conduct for righteous non-Jews, such as those set out in the Apostolic Decree in Acts 15.[31]

[404] Paul was flexible in his rhetorical approach toward both Jews and non-Jews based upon his perception of their sensibilities, their conceptualizations of reality. That it was an important element in his strategy to

---

29. That is not to say Paul does not appeal to Torah within his argument, which serves as the source for the Christ-believing movement, which is still Judaism for Paul and his assemblies, in my view. But note that he appeals to Torah in the midst of this argument directed to non-Jews as an example, and thus somewhat indirectly, whereas if addressing this topic to Jews, he would simply cite Torah's command not to eat idol food.

30. Cf. Hurd, *Origins of 1 Corinthians*, 289, 294.

31. Thus, Paul's instructions to non-Jews throughout his letters about turning from living as slaves to sin to living as slaves to righteousness (cf. Nanos, *Mystery of Romans*, 50–57, 166–238).

gain some from every nation to faith in the One God through Jesus Christ, is explained and exemplified throughout 1 Corinthians 8:1—11:1.

BIBLIOGRAPHY

Barrett, C. K. *The First Epistle to the Corinthians*. BNTC. Peabody, MA: Hendrickson, 1968.

Cheung, Alex T. *Idol Food in Corinth: Jewish Background and Pauline Legacy*. JSNTSup 176. Sheffield, UK: Sheffield Academic Press, 1999.

Fotopoulos, John. *Food Offered to Idols in Roman Corinth: A Social-rhetorical Reconsideration of 1 Corinthians 8:1—11:1*. WUNT 2.151. Tübingen: Mohr Siebeck, 2003.

Gardner, Paul Douglas. *The Gifts of God and the Authentication of a Christian: An Exegetical Study of 1 Corinthians 8—11:1*. Lanham, MD: University Press of America, 1994.

Gooch, Paul W. "'Conscience' in 1 Corinthians 8 and 10," *New Testament Studies* 33 (1987) 244–54.

Gooch, Peter David. *Dangerous Food: 1 Corinthians 8-10 in Its Context*. SCJ 5. Waterloo, ON: Wilfrid Laurier University Press, 1993.

Griffith, Terry. "ΕΙΔΩΛΟΝ as 'Idol' in Non-Jewish and Non-Christian Greek." *Journal of Theological Studies* 53 (2002) 95–101.

Horsley, Richard A. "Consciousness and Freedom among the Corinthians: 1 Corinthians 8-10." *Catholic Biblical Quarterly* 40 (1978) 581–89.

Hurd, John Coolidge, Jr. *The Origins of 1 Corinthians*. New York: Seabury, 1965.

Jewett, Robert. *Paul's Anthropological Terms: A Study of Their Use in Conflict Settings*. AGJU 10. Leiden: Brill, 1971.

Murphy-O'Connor, Jerome. "Freedom or the Ghetto: 1 Cor viii, 1–13; x, 23–xi, 1." *Revue biblique* 85 (1978) 561–62.

Nanos, Mark D. "Intruding 'Spies' and 'Pseudo-brethren': The Jewish Intra-group Politics of Paul's Jerusalem Meeting (Gal 2:1–10)." In *Paul and His Opponents*, edited by Stanley E. Porter, 59–97. Pauline Studies 2. Leiden: Brill, 2005. (Available in volume 3 of this essay collection.)

———. *The Irony of Galatians: Paul's Letter in First-Century Context*. Minneapolis: Fortress, 2002.

———. *The Mystery of Romans: The Jewish Context of Paul's Letter*. Minneapolis: Fortress, 1996.

———. "The Polytheist Identity of the 'Weak,' And Paul's Strategy to 'Gain' Them: A New Reading of 1 Corinthians 8:1—11:1." In *Paul: Jew, Greek and Roman*, edited by Stanley E. Porter, 179–210. Pauline Studies 5; Leiden: Brill, 2009. (Available in this volume.)

Rudolph, David J. "A Jew to the Jews: Jewish Contours of Pauline Flexibility in 1 Corinthians 9:19–23." Ph.D. thesis, University of Cambridge, 2006.

Sandelin, Karl-Gustav. "Drawing the Line: Paul on Idol Food and Idolatry in 1 Cor 8:1—11:1." In *Neotestamentica et Philonica: Studies in Honor of Peder Borgen*, edited by David E. Aune *et al.*, 108–25. Leiden: Brill, 2003.

Schaff, Philip, ed. *A Select Library of the Nicene and Post-Nicene Fathers of the Christian Church. First Series. Vol. XII. Saint Chrysostom: Homilies on the Epistles of Paul to the Corinthians.* Grand Rapids: Eerdmans, 1978.

Smit, Joop. *'About the Idol Offerings': Rhetoric, Social Context, and Theology of Paul's Discourse in First Corinthians 8:1—11:1.* Contributions to Biblical Exegesis and Theology 27. Leuven: Peeters, 2000.

Theissen, Gerd. *The Social Setting of Pauline Christianity: Essays on Corinth.* Translated by John H. Schütz. Philadelphia: Fortress, 1982.

Theological Dictionary of the New Testament. (TDNT). 10 vols. Edited by G. Kittel and G. Friedrich. Translated by Geoffrey Bromiley. Grand Rapids: Eerdmans, 1964–76.

Thiselton, Anthony C. *The First Epistle to the Corinthians: A Commentary on the Greek Text.* NIGTC. Grand Rapids: Eerdmans, 2000.

Tomson, Peter J. *Paul and the Jewish Law: Halakha in the Letters of the Apostle to the Gentiles.* CRINT. Minneapolis: Fortress, 1990.

Willis, Wendell Lee. "1 Corinthians 8–10: A Retrospective after Twenty-five Years." *Restoration Quarterly* 49.2 (2007) 103–12.

———. *Idol Meat in Corinth: The Pauline Argument in 1 Corinthians 8 and 10.* SBLDS 68. Chico, CA: Scholars, 1985.

Zetterholm, Magnus. "Purity and Anger: Gentiles and Idolatry in Antioch." *Interdisciplinary Journal of Research on Religion* 1 (2005) 1–24.

3

Paul's Relationship to Torah in Light of His Strategy "to Become Everything to Everyone" (1 Corinthians 9:19–23)[1]

[106]¹⁹For though I am free with respect to all, I have made myself a slave to all, so that I might win more of them. ²⁰To the Jews I became as a Jew, in order to win Jews. To those under the law I became as one under the law (though I myself am not under the law) so that I might win those under the law. ²¹To those outside the law I became as one outside the law (though I am not free from God's law but am under Christ's law) so that I might win those outside the law. ²²To the weak I became weak, so that I might win the weak. I have become all things to all people, that I might by all means save some. ²³I do it all for the sake of the gospel, so that I may share in its blessings.[2]

---

1. I am grateful for comments from the conference attendees, and pre-conference reviews by Joel Willitts, Loren Rosson, Gerald McDermott, and Mark Given, as well as responses to variations delivered at the 2009 Society of Biblical Literature International (Rome) and Annual (New Orleans) Meetings.

2. NRSV translation. Lit.: "¹⁹For being a free one from everyone, I enslaved myself to everyone, so that I might gain [κερδήσω] the many. ²⁰And I became [ἐγενόμην] to the Jews/Judeans [τοῖς Ἰουδαίοις] as/like a Jew/Judean [ὡς Ἰουδαῖος], in order to gain Jews/Judeans; to the ones under law/convention [τοῖς ὑπὸ νόμον] as/like under law/convention [ὡς ὑπὸ νόμον], not being myself under law/convention, so that I might gain the ones under law/convention; ²¹to the ones lawless [ἀνόμοις] as lawless [ὡς ἄνομος], not being lawless of God but lawful/in-law [ἔννομος] of Christ, so that I might gain the ones

AFTER PAUL'S TURN TO Christ, what was his relationship to Torah? The traditional and almost undisputed answer is that he renounced Torah-observance for disciples of Christ—except to imitate Jewish behavior to evangelize among Jews. Yet to me it seems more logical that a Jew, such as Paul claims to be (2 Cor 11:22; Phil 3:5-6), who is seeking to convince [107] fellow Jews as well as gentiles to turn to Jesus as the one representing the ideals and promises of Torah, would uphold the quintessential basis of that message, that is, he would observe Torah (cf. Rom 1:1-5; 3; 9:32—11:36; 15:8-9; 1 Cor 15:1-28; Gal 3:19; 5:14).[3] Paul's rhetoric makes sense when approached from this perspective. Paul's arguments assume that his statements about Torah as well as criticism of some of his fellow Jews, which arise in letters full of appeal to the authority of Torah to support his positions, will be perceived to represent the views of a movement faithful to the Mosaic covenant, albeit maintaining some interpretations that are in rivalry with the interpretations of other Jewish groups. Moreover, these arguments seem to be targeted to gentiles (i.e., members of the nations other than Israel) who understand themselves to be participating in Judaism (i.e., Jewish communal life) by becoming Christ-followers, although remaining non-Jews.[4] For example, why would the non-Jews in Galatia want to become proselytes, and how would Paul expect his argument to be persuasive when declaring that proselyte conversion (circumcision) would thereafter oblige non-Jewish Christ-believers to keep the whole Torah (Gal 5:3), if they

---

lawless; [22]I became to the ones weak/impaired [as/like] weak/impaired [ἐγενόμην τοῖς ἀσθενέσιν ἀσθενής], in order that I might gain the ones weak/impaired. To everyone I become [γέγονα] everything, so that by all means I might save some. [23]Now I do everything because of the good news, so that I might have become [γένωμαι] a joint-sharer [συγκοινωνὸς] of it." It is also useful to note that the context that v. 23 ties back to is set in v. 18: "What therefore is my payment/reward? That proclaiming the good news without charge I might offer good news for which [I have] not made full use of my authority/power/rights in/with/by way of the good news."

3. How much sense would it make for Paul to proclaim Jesus to demonstrate the righteous ideals of Torah and to be its goal while seeking to convince Jews or non-Jews to turn to Jesus as Messiah/Christ if at the same time Paul either degraded Torah as ineffective or less than divine or even worthless, as many propose (e.g., when interpreting Rom 2; 3; 7; Gal 3; 4; Phil 3), or obsolete, as most do (e.g., when interpreting Rom 10; Gal 3), and to thus eschew any obligation to keep it as holy, and for Jews (which he claims to remain and represent the aspirations of), a responsibility to uphold in covenant faithfulness? Cf. Ellison, "Paul and the Law—'All Things to All Men'"; Jervell, *The Unknown Paul.*

4. Full bibliography is available at www.marknanos.com. Recent summary discussions include Nanos, "The Myth of the 'Law-Free' Paul Standing between Christians and Jews"; Nanos, "Paul and Judaism: Why Not Paul's Judaism?"

do not know him, a circumcised Jewish Christ-believer, to exemplify that obligation as logically concomitant?[5]

Based on these and other similar examples, it is probable that Paul approached his audience with this assumption if he imagined his arguments would be convincing. I find no reason to believe that the recipients of Paul's letters, who knew him personally, or knew others who did (in the case of Rome), would interpret his language in terms of later "Paulinism," a construction of Paul that operates around the proposition that the role [108] of Torah to express covenant faithfulness had ended for Christians—often applied to everyone else too—whether Jew or non-Jew.[6]

1 Corinthians 9:19–23, however, is widely perceived to support the traditional conceptualization of Paulinism (i.e., privileging of gentileness, freedom from Torah and Jewish identity) and to counter any challenges mounted against it, such as I propose, irrespective of the specific arguments made regarding the particulars of the other letters.[7] That interpretation is predicated on his audiences knowing that Paul did not observe Torah when among non-Jews, such as themselves. Just as importantly, it proceeds as if the meaning of this passage is self-evident for the later interpreter, without the hesitation one might expect in view of several suspect lexical and exegetical moves required to make that case, and the ethical compromises it must embrace as central to the character of Paul, and thus Christian ideology. For the Paul who is celebrated here for his passion to win for Christ everyone in everything he does adopts a highly questionable way of life. That Paul is deceitful and hypocritical in terms of the principles of choosing righteousness and suffering over expedience, which he otherwise teaches emphatically, and according to which standard he condemns others (e.g., Peter at Antioch in Gal 2:11–21).[8] He subverts his own teaching in this

---

5. Nanos, *The Irony of Galatians*, offers a sustained exegetical argument in this direction.

6. This perception is evident even at the level of popular culture: "Paulinism" is "the teachings of the apostle Paul, who believed that people should be emancipated from Jewish law and allowed to follow the faith and spirit of Christ," according to www.thefreedictionary.com/Paulinism (accessed on May 25, 2009).

7. The raising of objections based on this text has not only been my frequent experience when speaking or delivering papers, but is also a topic in discussions of my work, even among those sharing my view of a more Jewish Paul: Johnson Hodge, *If Sons, Then Heirs*, 122–25; Segal, "Paul's Religious Experience in the Eyes of Jewish Scholars," 341. I have briefly engaged this text when discussing the idol food context of the players, issues, and instructions of 1 Cor 8–10: Nanos, "The Polytheist Identity of the 'Weak,'" 209–10; Nanos, "Paul and Judaism."

8. Cf. Richardson, "Pauline Inconsistency: 1 Corinthians 9:19–23 and Galatians 2:11–14."

letter of his "rule for all the assemblies," which includes the principle that a circumcised one is to "remain in the state" of circumcision in which he was in "when called," not to mention the ultimate priority of "keeping the commandments of God" regardless of in which state it is that one remains (1 Cor 7:17-24). He misleads anyone responding positively to his message into a religious affiliation that represents convictions and lifestyles that are other than he or she supposed, including important propositions that are absolutely contrary to critical convictions that he or she believes to be central [109] to the proper worship of God (or gods).[9] It follows that he or she thereafter will be committed to adopting this same strategy of misleading others to win them to the gospel.

In addition to such serious moral compromises, the prevailing reading almost certainly involves Paul in an ineffective bait and switch strategy. While his disguising of his convictions is based on compromising truthfulness for expedience as he moves among different groups to successfully gain a hearing among each, this inconsistency will almost certainly result in failure, giving truth to the lie he lives. For each party will ultimately learn of his absolutely contrary behavior when among other parties subscribing to opposite propositional truths, whether by directly witnessing his flip-flopping, or by way of rumors.

Nevertheless, the prevailing readings have a long and powerful legacy. Peter Richardson perceptively observes that "rarely" is there "a passage that is as pregnant with implications—particularly for understanding his [Paul's] behavior—as 1 Corinthians 9.19-23."[10] Heikki Räisänen presents those implications in starkly simple terms with which Richardson's analysis also agrees: "1 Cor 9.20 f. is absolutely incompatible with the theory of an observant Paul."[11]

Already in the fourth century, Chrysostom sought to defend Paul from charges of inconsistency by non-Christian critics who developed the negative logical inferences of the Christian interpretation to demonstrate Paul's indifference to Torah as a central ideology that made him suspect. An anonymous apologetic work arguably preserving Porphyry's criticisms

---

9. Barclay, "'Do We Undermine the Law?'" 308, cleverly compares Paul's theology with "a Trojan horse which threatens the integrity of those who sought to live according to the law." The relevance of this comment is accentuated by the discussion below of Odysseus as *polytropos*.

10. Richardson, "Pauline Inconsistency," 347. The impact of this essay on Lloyd Gaston's interpretation of Paul is telling. The only comment I find for Gaston on this passage is Gaston, *Paul and the Torah*, 78-79, where he states that if Richardson is right, then "perhaps he [Paul] did not" keep the commandments.

11. Räisänen, *Paul and the Law*, 75 n. 171; cf. 73-76.

includes the accusations that it is neither reasonable, nor clear headed, nor healthy, nor independent, nor will it be effective, but corrupt and confused for Paul to claim to be free in 1 Cor 9:19 and call circumcision "mutilation" in Phil 3:2[12] while also circumcising Timothy in Acts 16:3;[13] moreover,

> [110] But anyone saying [both] "I am a Jew" and "I am a Roman" is neither, even if he would like to be.
>
> The man who hypocritically pretends to be what he is not makes himself a liar in everything that he does. He disguises himself in a mask. He cheats those who are entitled to hear the truth. He assaults the soul's comprehension by various tactics, and like any charlatan he wins the gullible over to his side.
>
> Whoever accepts such principles as a guide for living cannot but be regarded as an enemy of the worse kind—the kind who brings others to submission by lying to them, who reaches out to make captives of everyone within earshot with his deceitful ways. And if, therefore, this Paul is a Jew one minute and the next a Roman, [or a student] of the [Jewish] law now, but at another time [an enemy of the law]—if, in short, Paul can be an enemy to each whenever he likes by burglarizing each, then clearly he nullifies the usefulness of each [tradition] for he limits their worthwhile distinctions with his flattery.
>
> We may conclude that [Paul] is a liar. He is the adopted brother of everything false, so that it is useless for him to declaim, "I speak the truth in Christ, I do not lie" [Rom. 9.1]; for a man who one day uses the law as his rule and the next day uses the gospel is either a knave or a fool in what he does in the sight of others and even when hidden away by himself.[14]

The Christian apologist does not offer a satisfactory reply to the charges, including the duplicity, but simply seeks to justify this behavior.[15] Chrysostom also did not deny these problems, the criticisms of which he was acutely aware, but rather legitimated Paul's behavior as faithful to Jesus:

---

12. I have challenged this long-standing interpretation, and argued that Paul's reference to "mutilation" is likely to some "pagan" phenomenon rather than circumcision, in Nanos, "Paul's Reversal of Jews Calling Gentiles 'Dogs.'"

13. Macarius Magnes, *Apocritus* 3.30. See also e.g., Julian, *Against the Galileans* 106a-c, including Paul as responsible for Christians disregarding Torah and circumcision.

14. Macarius Magnes, *Apocritus* 3.31 (trans. Hoffmann, *Porphyry's Against the Christians*, 60–61).

15. 3.37 responding to 3.30, and 3.38 responding to 3.31: Crafer, *The Apocriticus of Macarius Magnes*, 101–3.

> Therefore Paul, in imitating his master, should not be blamed if at one time he was as a Jew, and at another as one not under the Law; or if once he was keeping the Law, but at another time he was overlooking it; . . . once offering sacrifices and shaving his head, and again anathematizing those who did such things; at one time circumcising, at another casting out circumcision.[16]

Elaborating an argument already made briefly by the author of the *Apocriticus*, Chrysostom also excused Paul's inconsistent and morally suspect behavior by appeal to a popular Greco-Roman topos of Paul's time, that of the physician who misleads a patient for the good of the patient, not that of the doctor.[17] The physician is expected to treat each patient differently [111] according to the needs of each, including changing treatments as the patient's level of illness or return to health progresses. This "condescending" behavior extends to lying to the patient, or play acting. That conduct is justified by the physician's overriding concern for the advantage of the patient, not of the doctor's own self. Thus Chrysostom explains: "as a physician rather, as a teacher, as a father, the one to the sick, the other to the disciple, the third to the son, condescends for his correction, not for his hurt; so likewise did he."[18] Chrysostom does not simply analogize the behavior of the doctor to Paul's rhetorical adaptability, but also to Paul's conduct: Paul "was variable and many-sorted not only in what he did, but also in what he said."[19] And what Paul did was based on indifference to Torah: "Therefore at one time he exalts the Law and at another he destroys it."[20]

---

16. *Laud. Paul.* 5.6 [SC 300.240], cited in Mitchell, "'A Variable and Many-sorted Man,'" 107.

17. On the physician topos, see Philo, *Unchangeable* 65–67; Philo, *Joseph* 32–34, 74–79; Stowers, "Paul on the Use and Abuse of Reason," 253–86; Glad, *Paul and Philodemus*, 21–22, 35–40, 53–98; Mitchell, "'A Variable and Many-sorted Man,'" 102–3; Mitchell, "Pauline Accommodation and 'Condescension' (συγκατάβασις)," 201–5.

18. Homily XXII.6, in Schaff, ed., *NPNF* XII, 129 [PG 61.185]; and see *Hom. in Gen.* 2.3 [PG 53.29]; *Hom. in Gal.* 2:11; 3 [PG 51.374]; *Hom. in 1 Cor.* 12.1 [PG 61.96]; *Hom. in 1 Cor.* 12.3–4 [PG 61.184–85]; *Hom. in 2 Cor.* 4.13; 2.2 [PG 51.283]; *Laud. Paul.* 5.7 [SC 300.242–44]; *Hom in Eph.* 6.3 [PG 62.46]; *Hom. in Tit.* 3.1–2 [PG 6.677–78]. Jesus provides Chrysostom with the precedent for this variation, for he both praised and rebuked Peter at various times (Mitchell, "Pauline Accommodation," 208–14). In Homily XX.8 on 1 Cor 8:7, he explains that the knowledgeable are approaching the impaired incorrectly: "they gained no ground by their refusing to condescend. For this was not the way to bring them in, but in some other way persuading them by word and by teaching" (Schaff, ed., *NPNF* XII, 115 [emphasis added]).

19. *Laud. Paul.* 5.6 [SC 300.242], from Mitchell, "'A Variable and Many-sorted Man,'" 111 n. 74.

20. *Laud. Paul.* 5.6 [SC 300.242], from ibid., 108.

In addition to failing to answer the criticisms, the topos does not actually correspond to Paul's language in 9:19–23, for it is based on becoming a physician to a patient, et al., whereas to correspond to Paul's language it would have to call for conduct like a patient to patients, student to students, and child to children. To the degree that Chrysostom understands Paul to be free of Torah and adopt variability in his behavior as well as his speech, his argument represents a variation on the focus of the traditional argument, but no serious challenge to it.[21] I do not see how it successfully explains this passage, or defends Paul of the charges made.

[112] In contemporary scholarship, the need for such apologies based on the prevailing interpretation of this passage continues unabated. Consider this example from Gordon Fee:

> [W]hen he [Paul] was among Jews he was kosher; when he was among Gentiles he was non-kosher—precisely because, as with circumcision, neither mattered to God (cf. 7:19; 8:8). But such conduct tends to matter a great deal to the religious—on either side!—so that inconsistency in such matters ranks

---

21. Augustine argued that Paul observed Torah because that was expected of the first generation of Jewish Christians, as long as they did not observe it for salvation (an early witness to the assumption of Jewish motives for Torah-observance as works-righteousness) (Augustine, *Letter* 40.4, 6, in Trigg, "Augustine/Jerome, *Correspondence*," 264–65. But he also argued that they did so only in order "to show them [Jews] what he thought he would need to be shown if he were still unconverted" (Augustine, *Letter* 40.6, in Trigg, "Augustine/Jerome, *Correspondence*," 266). In other words, Augustine denied that Paul was merely pretending, but his explanation was actually still based on pretense, yet ostensibly legitimate because of justifiable motives, namely, empathy. Augustine nevertheless sought to challenge the idea that Paul behaved like a Jew "out of any intention to mislead. Obviously the person who looks after sick people has to think like a sick person himself. I do not mean that he pretends to be sick, but he has to put himself in the place of the sick person in order to understand fully what he should be doing to help the sick person" (Augustine, *Letter* 40.4, in Trigg, "Augustine/Jerome, *Correspondence*," 264). Augustine was so concerned with the topos of the physician's lie being adopted, as it had been by Chrysostom, and before him Origen (Origen, *Hom in Jer.* 20.3 [PG 13.476]), that he wrote a treatise at about this time, *On Lying*, in which he challenged all lying, especially for the sake of religion, which effectively ended the perpetuation of the medicinal lie tradition in Western ethics (Trigg, "Augustine/Jerome, *Correspondence*," 252).

It is interesting to observe that Jerome strongly disagreed with Augustine, revealing his ideologically based disgust of the notion that Paul or any Christian would observe Torah for any reason other than pretense, and maintaining not only that Paul pretended to Jewish behavior to gain Jews (Jerome, *Letter* 104.17, in Trigg, "Augustine/Jerome, *Correspondence*," 289, and see Jerome, *Letter* 104.13 [285]), but also that Augustine's explanation actually supported behavioral pretense, regardless of the different motives for which Augustine argued, which Jerome also denied (Jerome, *Letter* 104.17, in Trigg, "Augustine/Jerome, *Correspondence*," 289–90).

among the greatest of evils. Paul's policy quite transcended petty consistency—and "religion" itself. . . . How can Paul determine to "become *like* a Jew"? The obvious answer is, in matters that have to do with Jewish religious peculiarities that Paul as a Christian had long ago given up as essential to a right relationship with God.[22]

[113] The apologies offered continue to seek to legitimate the infraction by denial of the problem or appeal to supposed superior values and noble motives, rather than attempting to actually eliminate the problem, which would, it seems, be accomplished by the exegetical approach to this passage that I seek to demonstrate, but that comes at the cost of eliminating the brush strokes supplied by this passage in the prevailing composite portrait of a Torah-indifferent Paul.

The virtually lone exception (of which I am aware) that proves the rule is stated by Wilfred Knox, who argues, against the consensus, that Paul did not "deny that the Jewish nation itself was still bound to the observance of the Law; indeed he himself kept it with all the rigour of a Pharisee." For his claim to be a Pharisee to be meaningful: "it is clear that S. Paul continued

---

22. Fee, *The First Epistle to the Corinthians*, 427–28 (emphasis his). Here we witness how this text is used not only to indicate that Paul was no longer a Jew in a religious behavioral sense, but that such identity and concomitant behavior was regarded now by Paul to be irrelevant to God; hence, that judgment is applied to everyone. Anyone who might criticize Paul on the basis that it ought to be relevant is simply being "religious," which is negatively valued, and not what Paul—on Fee's model of Pauline religion—is understood to represent. Rather, Paul is engaged in something superior; Fee is too, presumably, since no hermeneutical distance from this interpretation is expressed. Moreover, we learn that being religiously Jewish would also entail by definition participation in peculiarities that are not essential to a right relationship with God, including the concern for petty consistency. Yet Fee's assessment involves a logical double standard. For this Jewish behavior seeks to be consistent with observing the covenant obligations of Torah, which had originated from God according to the Jewish tradition (but Fee's argument presumes that is not so for Paul), and been articulated in the very Scriptures from which Paul drew his authority to speak of Jesus as Christ and to instruct his assemblies in the (peculiar) behavior that is consistent with God's will for them, which they are therefore to consistently observe.

Many other examples of this kind of reasoning to seek to resolve this matter could be provided. E.g., Hagner, "Paul as a Jewish Believer," 113, explains that "Paul regards himself as no longer under the law" since he "obeys it now and then. Paul thus feels free to identify with the Gentiles and not to remain an observant Jew. Incidentally, how remarkable it is that the Jew Paul can speak of himself as an outsider: 'To the Jews I became as a Jew'!" This implies a "break with Judaism," and "it is clear, furthermore, that observing or not observing the law is an unimportant issue before God. The position taken by Paul is one of complete expedience: he will or will not observe the law only in relation to its usefulness in the proclamation of the gospel." Also Paul Gooch, "The Ethics of Accommodation: A Study in Paul," 111–12.

60 Reading Corinthians and Philippians within Judaism

throughout his life to ractice Judaism, and that he expected Jewish converts to do so." Yet one passage stands in the way:

> [T]he only objection that can be brought against this view is the language of *1 Cor. ix.21*, where S. Paul seems to imply that when dealing with Gentiles *he behaved* as if not bound by the Law.... On the other hand *this interpretation* of the passage *is impossible*. S. Paul could not both behave as a Jew when dealing with Jews and as free from the Law when dealing with Gentiles, since apart from the *moral dishonesty* of pretending to observe the Law when in Jewish society and neglecting it in Gentile society, it *would be impossible for him to conceal* from Jews whom he hoped to convert the fact that he disregarded the Law when not in Jewish company.[23]

[114] It is difficult not to wonder if this interpretive conundrum does not result from an *a priori* driving the exegesis of this passage. For those who

---

23. Knox, *St. Paul and the Church of Jerusalem*, 103 (emphasis mine). Knox's solution is that Paul "means that in dealing with those outside the Law, he *behaves* as if he were free from the Law ... , not in the sense of refusing to recognize any divine Law, but as in fact obeying the Jewish Law in Christ, or *in a Christian sense*, as something which he is *more or less* bound to observe, but which others [i.e., gentiles (?)] are not. The rhetorical tone of the passage obscures the facts" (emphasis mine). In other words, Knox derives the opposite implication from the text: Paul was sincere and consistent when behaving jewishly among Jews, albeit "more or less" and adjusted to "a Christian sense," thus the mimicry of lifestyles was when modifying his Jewish behavior among non-Jews. It is unclear why this is not, inversely, still moral dishonesty, or how his Law behavior among Jews could be concealed from gentiles. Moreover, Knox undermines his solution, which already equivocated on Paul's level of Torah observance, when he states: "S. Paul is *not entirely consistent* with his own teaching, since he here denies that he is bound to keep the Law, whereas in vii. 18 he regards obedience to it as a duty.... It is, however, not surprising that his language is inconsistent. He was clear that it was necessary for Jewish Christians to continue to obey the Law; whether this was merely a matter of expediency, or a matter of principle, *he would hardly trouble to consider*. It must be noticed that on his own principles, if he obeyed the Law at all, *he was bound to obey it as a Pharisee.... Anything less was really worthless*" (122 n. 54; emphasis mine). However, if Paul would not "trouble to consider" whether obeying was motivated by expediency or principle, and if he sometimes obeyed it "more or less," he can hardly be observing Torah as a Pharisee.

Knox has raised an insightful objection, but in addition to compromising his own alternative with an inconsistent and non-Pharisaic portrayal of a more or less observant Paul, he has merely reversed which sensibilities to privilege, and thus failed to offer a satisfactory solution to the charges of inconsistency and moral dishonesty. And he has not explained how the strategy could have succeeded. Ellison, "Paul," 200, also objects, and insists that Paul observed Torah, but does not explain the proposition; and Jervell, *Unknown Paul*, 58, comments that 1 Cor 9:19–21 makes it "obvious that Paul lived as a pious Jew," although no argument is made, and it is clearly not obvious to the overwhelming majority of interpreters. Others objecting are listed in footnotes below.

look to Paul's life and teaching for guidance, the deeply troubling nature of the problems it creates require excusing or defending Paul, the hero of many disguises, and thereby, Christianity. But those defenses come up short on explanatory power for anyone else. In response, some Christians will develop hermeneutical distance: Paul was like that, yes, but in this behavior he should not serve as a model. For some others, the prevailing interpretation of this passage can be central to criticizing Paul and Christianity, for it provides legitimacy to, if not also cause for, dismissing him as immoral and incompetent.[24] This passage clearly stands in the way of improving relations between Christians and Jews—make that between Christians and non-Christians in general—because it undermines truthfulness as a core value, an essential element for the complete trust required in mutually respectful relationships. Is the prevailing interpretation of this passage really so clear, and is it so necessary that these many problems must be qualified or legitimated, go unrecognized or ignored, or left open to demonstrating the moral bankruptcy of Paul?

[115] For a Jewish interpreter of Paul and Christian-Jewish relations critic, this interpretive tradition is intriguing, including the way the problems that it generates are handled by Pauline scholars, while at the same time the obstacles these represent to advancing Christian-Jewish relations are troubling. Have my working hypotheses that Paul was probably Torah-observant, and his movement best approached as Judaism, been mistaken? Are the roots of Christianity far more discontinuous with Judaism, as sustained in the prevailing readings of Paul, than I have supposed?

The fact that this text is embedded in the rhetorical aims of a particular letter, combined with the fact that it deals specifically with how Paul seeks to win those who do not believe in Christ, makes it an unlikely text to turn to for ultimate proof that Paul was not Torah-observant, or that he upheld a Torah-free lifestyle to be the ideal for Christ-believing Jews. More importantly, I propose that this text has been misinterpreted.

This passage does not and cannot by itself demonstrate that Paul was or had to be Torah-observant, and that is not my objective in this study. Rather, I seek to show that it does not support the claim that he *cannot* observe Torah as an expression of covenant fidelity; for example, that he only practiced circumcision, dietary regulations, and calendrical celebrations

---

24. In addition to the kinds of "pagan" criticisms already discussed, see Jewish criticisms by Maccoby, *The Mythmaker*, 151–57, 166–67; Klinghoffer, *Why the Jews Rejected Jesus*, 106–10; and Levine, *The Misunderstood Jew*, 75–86. The history of this line of Jewish critique is discussed by Fuchs-Kreimer, "The 'Essential Heresy': Paul's View of the Law according to Jewish Writers," 63–82. See also the examples discussed in Langton, "The Myth of the 'Traditional View of Paul'"; Meißner, *Die Heimholung des Ketzers*.

such as Sabbath when judged expedient for the purpose of gaining a hearing among Jews, and then only as matters of indifference (*adiaphora*). The interpretation proposed not only challenges such conclusions, it also opens up for consideration other interesting matters relevant to Pauline studies, including several of concern to this book [i.e., Paul and Judaism]. Moreover, although I am not a Christian, I believe it offers many solutions to the ethical problems that must, or at least I would think should vex any Christian beholden to the prevailing interpretation of this serpent-like guile at the very heart of Paulinism, and thus Christianity itself.

First, I will focus on the topic of Paul's behavior as presented in prevailing views, and develop analytical categories to assess this matter. In the case of the consensus reading, Paul is describing his tactics in terms of "conduct" or "lifestyle adaptability." I will offer a different way to read Paul's language, suggesting instead that Paul was describing his "rhetorical adaptability." Then I will discuss examples from Acts 17 and Antisthenes' Odysseus that support my case. Throughout this essay, I note some of the problems that arise from the prevailing views, and how my reading avoids, solves, or problematizes them further, at the same time raising a few challenges of its own, certainly for anyone ideologically bound to the traditional "law-free" Paul.

1. THE PREVAILING INTERPRETATIONS

Central to the traditional and still prevailing readings is the proposition that Paul adapts his *behavioral conduct* to the different audiences he seeks to gain to Christ, as can be clearly seen in the citations already presented. Paul is understood to be describing his *lifestyle* in terms of Torah or Jewishness as [116] variable depending upon the social context in which he is operating. But it is specifically Jewish behavior that is primarily regarded to be compromised by Paul, for he is no longer Torah-observant, and therefore implicitly more aligned with non-Jewish behavior in principle, and thus involved in mimicking Jews more so than gentiles, whom he rather represents, because "gentileness" is the default setting for Pauline Christianity. Richardson states the prevailing view concisely:

> In 1 Corinthians 9 Paul describes his motivation for his *conduct*; the basic principle is that he adjusts his *conduct* to fit the immediate circumstances as long as this adjustment will help to win some to Jesus. This statement is found within a treatment of the problem of eating meat offered to idols (1 Cor 8.1ff.) in which he suggests that it is *acceptable to eat* such meat . . . .[25]

25. Richardson, "Pauline Inconsistency," 347 (emphasis added); see also the

The accusations in Acts 21 against Paul *are probably true*; he counsels certain kinds of non-observance of the customary practices of Judaism, even to the point of agreeing to suggestions that Jews might cease to circumcise their children.[26]

For Richardson, it is plain that it is eating behavior that Paul has in mind, and that Paul's theological position represents gentile (Christian) norms.[27] The subject of dietary behavior offers a good example to work around, since it represents a tangible expression of Torah-observance, or not, and one that involves different interpretations of certain elements from group to group, but one that never the less, however practiced, bears witness to the importance of seeking to live according to Torah as Jews, or not. We will return to this issue.

[117] Interpreters representing the New Perspective basically adopt the current consensus view that Paul was writing about adapting his behavioral *conduct* such as dietary practices to match that of the various audiences he addressed, with a Pauline Christianity based propositional bias towards gentileness, that is, toward norms that are not derived from an interpretation of Torah, but rather from its non-applicability for Christians, Jewish or gentile.[28] E. P. Sanders explains that,

> Paul is obviously attempting to formulate how he can live *outside* the law when evangelizing Gentiles and living among them, yet remain *within* the law of Christ and thus of God. He is attempting to formulate that possibility, yet the passage does not say how he can manage both. The truth is that he has no clear way of defining his own situation theoretically. When among Gentiles

---

interrelated essay by Gooch, "Ethics of Accommodation," 97, who states that "the passage clearly deals with Paul's behavior and not simply his methodology in mission or instruction." Given, *Paul's True Rhetoric*, 106–7, interprets Paul's reference to ἐγενόμην ("I became") to mean "temporarily assuming a different identity," and "refers to concrete, observable changes" (109). For a different view of Paul on idol food, that he instead teaches that no food known to be idol food can be eaten by Christ-believers or by Jews, implying also by himself as a Christ-believing Jew, as well as several other elements that challenge the consensus readings in these chapters, including the identity of the "weak," whom I propose to be idolaters who are not Christ-believers, see Nanos, "Polytheist Identity"; in agreement that Paul does not permit eating idol food per se, see also Tomson, *Paul and the Jewish Law*; Cheung, *Idol Food in Corinth*; Fotopoulos, *Food Offered to Idols in Roman Corinth*.

26. Richardson, "Pauline Inconsistency," 361.

27. Richardson, "Early Christian Sources of an Accommodation Ethic."

28. See Nanos, "Myth of the 'Law-Free' Paul," for a summary investigation of Paul's arguments about dietary matters challenging this consensus, and for more detail, see my *The Mystery of Romans*, 85–238; Nanos, *Irony of Galatians*; Nanos, "What Was at Stake in Peter's 'Eating with Gentiles' at Antioch?"; Nanos, "Polytheist Identity."

he does not observe the Jewish law: that is clear in Gal. 2:11–14.
. . . Christians, of whom Paul is here the example, are not *under* the law, but they are not thereby lawless toward God."[29]

Sanders interprets "became like" to mean "lived according to the law in order to win Jews," and not according to it to win gentiles.[30] He challenges the idea that this can be "a literal description of Paul's life and work," because it would not work for Paul to observe law when he goes to a synagogue and then not when he was with gentiles "*in the same church*."[31] For Sanders, this language is "hyperbolic," and the exception, when Paul practices Judaism, is only when Paul goes to Jerusalem: Paul lived like a Jew in Jerusalem, where that was expected in order not to give offence, but "in all probability, when he entered each city, he went to Gentiles, he preached to them with some success, and he lived like a Gentile."[32] In other words, Paul's lifestyle as far as

29. Sanders, *Paul, the Law, and the Jewish People*, 100 (italic emphasis his; underline emphasis mine). I challenge this reading of the Antioch Incident in Nanos, "What Was at Stake?"

30. Sanders, *Paul, the Law, and the Jewish People*, 185.

31. Ibid., 185 (emphasis his).

32. Ibid., 186. The comments on this passage by New Perspective critics are brief, and generally do not address the problems that this interpretation raises. Dunn, *The Theology of Paul the Apostle*, 576–78, observes: "His freedom as an apostle was freedom to adapt policy and practice to particular situations, even when that meant running counter to all precedent, and to both scriptural and dominical authorization" (577); Dunn, "Who Did Paul Think He Was?" Wright, *Paul for Everyone: 1 Corinthians*, 115, makes it plain that Paul could not describe himself becoming a Jew to Jews "if he regarded Christianity as simply a sub-branch of Judaism; it is a new thing, a fulfilment, no longer bound by ethnic or geographical identity." Paul was "prepared to observe customs and key commands of the law, presumably meaning by this that he would keep the Sabbaths and the food-laws" in order to win Jews to the gospel, with the caveat that Paul's "justification . . . didn't depend on these observances" (116). At the same time, Wright understands Paul to also become like non-Jews "without regard for the regulations of the Jewish law" in order to win them (116). Hays, *First Corinthians*, 153–54, views Paul as "free from the Law": "This sentence [9:21] states clearly what is abundantly apparent from many other bits of evidence: Paul not only resisted the imposition of Jewish Law on Gentiles but also himself adopted a casual attitude about Law observance (kosher laws, etc.) when he was among Gentiles."

Similar interpretations are mounted against the New Perspective, especially to accentuate Paul's discontinuity with Jewish observance and identity. Westerholm, *Perspectives Old and New on Paul*, 172, observes that, "Paul himself did not scrupulously adhere to the law. In 1 Corinthians 9:20–21 he notes that he behaves differently ('as one outside the law') in the presence of Gentiles than he does among Jews; nonobservance of the 'ritual' Torah must be meant." Carson, "Mystery and Fulfillment," 402, adds, "Perhaps the most startling passage is 1 Corinthians 9:19–23, . . . these [discontinuities] are of such a nature that Paul can think of himself, in this context, as not being a Jew . . . ." See also Carson, "Pauline Inconsistency," esp. 10–16, 37. Here we witness not only Paul discontinuous with Jewish behavior, but also with Jewish identity: Paul is no longer a

Torah [118] was concerned was like that of a gentile, and this was the direct result of having changed his convictions about Torah. Paul lived like a non-Jew when he worked in the Diaspora among non-Jews, which represented virtually all of his time, but he mimicked Jewish behavior on the few occasions he was in Jerusalem.

There are some minority interpretive approaches that are of interest for this discussion. But given the limits of this paper, and the fact that in the end these also lead to the same primary conclusions—that Paul no longer practiced Torah as a matter of covenant faithfulness, adopted a Torah-free lifestyle to the degree that he could do so in the Diaspora where he lived mainly among non-Jews, and that he varied his lifestyle to mimic Jewish and other groups of people, perhaps to a lesser degree, or in a supposedly less benign fashion, or with a different focus, or with more empathy or more admirable motives than are emphasized in the prevailing portrayals—they will not be presented here.[33] The few that point in the direction of my proposal will be discussed below.[34]

2. ANALYTICAL OPTIONS FOR INTERPRETING PAUL'S ADAPTABILITY

[119] The interpretations of Paul's language we have reviewed focus on Paul *adopting the lifestyle* of his audiences, *varying his conduct* to *imitate* or *mimic* the way that each of them *lives relative to Jewish halakhic practices* when he is among them. For analytical purposes I will refer to this as *"behavioral"* or *"lifestyle adaptability."*[35]

Jew; similarly, see also Paul Gooch, "Ethics of Accommodation," 96; Given, *True Rhetoric*, 103–17; Hagner, "Paul as a Jewish Believer," 113.

33. They are discussed below when rhetorical adaptability is introduced.

34. Knox, *St. Paul*; Ellison, "Paul"; and Jervell, *Unknown Paul*, have already been noted.

35. I am drawing on the suggestions of Paul Gooch, but with some modifications, including different labels for the categories. Gooch describes this category as "ethical accommodation," that which is "concerned not with the truth or transmission of beliefs, but with *behavior*. It is practised whenever one *adapts his pattern of living to the lifestyles of various groups*, having his *actions* dictated by the situations and circumstances in which he finds himself" (Gooch, "Ethics of Accommodation," 99 [emphasis mine]). Gooch places Paul in this category, and expresses the view that Paul has left Judaism and a Torah-defined way of life following his conversion to Christianity, in keeping with the prevailing views we have reviewed (107).

I do not find "ethical" helpful, since the behavior being described as duplicity is arguably not ethical but unethical, and "accommodation" has been used in ways that can confuse as much as clarify the issues, as his own discussion of the terminology

Adapting one's lifestyle to fit into the social context of another does not necessitate adopting *the propositional values* of the one whose behavior is imitated. One can pretend by mimicking behavior in an outward fashion in order to appear to share the values of the other, and thus to gain access and trust which might otherwise not be gained except by deception, with the intention of advancing one's own self-interests at the eventual expense of the other.[36] If one adopts the lifestyles of groups with contrary rational (or divine) bases for their very different behavior, such as Paul's language describes for the various referents, this by definition cannot represent adopting their propositional values.

Paul is interpreted to undertake this behavior solely in order to win each person or group to the Christian gospel's propositional values, which he believes to be superior. For interpreters who subscribe to and by way of Paul promote that ideology, the justification of this deceptive tactic is apparently self-evident. As noted, the charges of inconsistency and moral dishonesty are treated as if benign, generally discussed without offering explanations sufficient to those who do not share this ideological perspective. In less generous terms, for example, expressed by those not inclined to defend Paul, or instead toward demonstrating his faults, he is portrayed to ape the behavior of each in order to trick everyone into mistakenly believing that the message he proclaims does not subvert the rational basis or convictional value of living in the particular way that each lives.[37] In the case of non-Jews (idolaters or atheists), especially the lawless or weak, he appears to worship [120] their gods, or alternatively, to oppose any gods, when he believes in neither of these propositions. In the case of Jews, when Paul conducts himself like a Jew when among Jews, he is "misleading" Jews into thinking that he is a Jew whose message upholds the propositional conviction that Torah-based behavior is enjoined upon Jews by God, although he no longer shares that conviction. This policy obscures the fact that any Jews who valued Torah-observance enough for Paul to adopt it to gain their trust, would be, if they accepted his message, becoming members of a community characterized by the renunciation of Torah-faith, yet unbeknownst to them. It follows that if "converted," they too will adopt this chameleon-like expedient behavior thereafter on the same terms, i.e., only in order to trick other Jews. That creates a spiral of duplicity, with long-range deleterious results

---

demonstrates (Richardson, "Early Christian Sources of an Accommodation Ethic" and Paul Gooch, "The Ethics of Accommodation").

36. Cf. Josephus, *Ant.* 17.205.

37. Although not an example of imitating a person, treachery can be expressed in terms of becoming as if preparing to kiss a friend, when intending instead to stab the person after close access is thereby gained; Josephus, *Ant.* 7.284.

for their psychological and spiritual as well as social well-being should they remain "Christians" after finding out the truth.

In sharp contrast, one who adopts the lifestyle of another convinced of its superior value undertakes *"convictional adaptability."*[38] I am not aware of any interpretation of this passage that understands Paul to be describing convictional adaptation, and since he includes parties who uphold opposite propositional values, it would make little sense to do so.[39] But that is literally

38. Paul Gooch, "Ethics of Accommodation," 99, names this phenomenon "theological accommodation," and describes it as surrendering "some item or items of belief in order to be acceptable to some other party. What was formerly considered true is renounced and the other party's doctrine is substituted for it." According to Gooch, this could stretch from compromises on small matters of doctrine to achieve harmony to conversion to the doctrinal system of the other. I prefer to call this category *convictional* adaptability, because it is not merely imitating or mimicking the behavior of the target audience, but involves subscribing to their convictions for undertaking just such behavior, and not other kinds.

39. The exception to this would be cases of non-doctrinal practices among those who share the same core convictions, which is not what Paul is describing, but would apply to moving between different Jewish groups for a Jew, or between different Christian groups for a Christian. This falls under the category of lifestyle adaptability, but in the specific sense of locative adaptability (adapting to local custom variations that arise within a shared propositional set of overarching convictions).

Certainly, the idea of respecting the customs of one's hosts is ancient, reflected, for example, independent of any idea of compromising Torah-based norms, in R. Meir's maxim (*ca.* mid-second century CE), "If you come into a city, do according to their customs" (Gen. Rab. on 18.8; Exod. Rab. on 34.38), and in Jesus' instruction in Luke 10:7-8 to those he sent out throughout Israel to eat what was offered by their hosts (cf. Rudolph, "A Jew to the Jews," 138-43, 178-81, 185-87). Another parallel, although not about traveling, is Hillel's teaching about empathy and polite manners among one's peers: "Do not appear naked [where others go clothed], and do not appear clothed [where others go naked], and do not appear standing [where others sit], and do not appear sitting [where others stand] and do not appear laughing [where others weep] and do not appear weeping [where others laugh], because Scripture states, 'a time to weep, a time to laugh, . . . a time to embrace, a time to refrain from embracing' (Eccl 3:4-5)" (t. Ber. 2.21; trans. Neusner, *Tosefta* [p. 13]; cf. Let. Aris. 257, 267; Sir 31.1-2; Gen. Rab. 48.14; Exod. Rab. 42.5; Rom 12:9-18!). See also Daube, *The New Testament and Rabbinic Judaism*, 336-51 ["Missionary Maxims in Paul"], for a discussion of similarities with the rabbinic missionary practice of accommodation, although not from the same point of view on Paul's language, and with no evidence that this teaching parallels the kind of moral matters at issue if Paul was referring to lifestyle adaptability. The behavior enjoined is not against halakhic norms, but about living empathetically and politely in matters of halakhic indifference among fellow Jews.

In later Christian teaching, the case of Augustine's appeal to Ambrose's teaching on how to behave when attending a church other than one's own is instructive, albeit different than the case we are investigating, which would require a parallel concerning how a Christian should behave when in a pagan context, not another Christian one. In *Book I of Replies to Questions of Januarius [Letter 54]* 2.3, Augustine quoted Ambrose to uphold that one should seek to avoid giving offense on matters of "custom" that

[121] what "becoming like" (or, all the more, "becoming") someone of a particular persuasion such as Paul describes would mean.[40] In keeping with the many references just annotated, few would suppose that when Jesus is reported to tell his disciples in Matt 18:3 that they "should cause themselves to become like children [γένησθε ὡς τὰ παιδία]," that this meant to conduct themselves childishly in general, for example, in the sense of playing with toys, or teasing each other, and so on, or to pretend to be children; rather, they are to take on an unassuming humility of character that eschews the quest for greatness among peers, a characteristic that he attributes to a child (I assume not just [122] any child, either). It represents a call to undertake a particular change of behavior, and to do so wholeheartedly.

A third option for describing Paul's behavior is very different from either of the first two, focusing on his *argumentative* behavior, which can be undertaken without suggesting any adaptation of the practical lifestyles of others. Such *"rhetorical adaptability"* consists of varying one's speech to different audiences: reasoning from their premises, but not imitating their

---

were not of doctrinal significance, but instead reflected different local practices among Christians: "'When I visit Rome, I fast on Saturday; when I am here, I do not fast'" (trans. J. G. Cunningham, in Schaff [ed.], *NPNF, First Series*, Vol. 1); see also 2.2; 5.5–6; in 1.1, it is made clear that this does not include adopting any Jewish practices). Note that this citation of Ambrose was later developed into the famous slogan, "when in Rome, do as the Romans do," which no longer always expresses the same sentiment or limitations, but is just as likely to be appealed to as a warrant for escaping moral norms (a transitional development is witnessed in Justin Taylor, *Ductor Dubitantium, or the Rule of Conscience*, I.i.5 [1660]: "If you are at Rome, live in the Roman style; if you are elsewhere, live as they live there [*Si fueris Romae, Romano vivito more; / Si fueris alibi, vivito sicut ibi.*]"; cf. *Oxford Dictionary of Quotations*, 10.679.

40. See e.g., Gen 34:15; Num 23:10; Judg 16:11; 17:11; Ruth 4:12; 2 Sam 18:32; Sir 18:23; Hos 9:10; Matt 10:25; 15:28; Gal 4:12; Eph 5:1. In Jdt 12:13, γενηθῆναι . . . ὡς is used differently, to describe how Judith is received and told that she can join those serving the king by becoming a concubine in a way normally filled by Assyrian women. This usage is not about duplicity from their point of view, but actually taking on the role of another (she does not use this to describe her strategic behavior, although these terms could be used to describe her tactics as deceptive lifestyle adaptability). In the metaphorical sense of becoming like something or someone else in character qualities, destiny, etc., but not in terms of pretense, see LXX Pss 31:9; 77:8; 87:5; 108:19; 118:83; 125:1; 128:6; Sir 4:10; 32:8; Hos 5:10; 7:16; 8:8; Amos 4:11; Mic 7:1; Isa 1:9; 37:27; 48:18–19; 63:19; 64:6, 10; Jer 4:17; 12:8; 14:8; 15:18; 20:9; 23:9, 14; 31:28; Lam 1:1, 6; 2:5; Ezek 3:3; 16:31; 36:35; Dan 4:33; Matt 17:2; 18:3; Luke 22:26; 1 Thess 2:7; Rev 6:12. Given, *Paul's True Rhetoric*, 109, cites a few of these examples against the interpretation of Glad that Paul has in view association with these various people, but Given does not acknowledge that these examples also work against his own interpretation (which is that of the majority), that this language signifies behavioral as well as rhetorical pretense intended to create misleading perceptions about Paul's own propositional values.

conduct in other ways.[41] In fact, to uphold the ideals to which the argument calls the audience, it is far more likely that the propositionally driven differences between the speaker's lifestyle and that of his or her audience will be magnified.

This behavior arises when one seeks to express views in vocabulary and by way of models and examples that are calculated to persuade.[42] One thus works from the audiences' premises or worldviews, even though seeking to lead them to a conclusion that is based on another set of premises or worldviews. Teachers normally seek to relate to students in this way. It is highly useful for making a persuasive argument in any context, especially in philosophical or religious debates, including recruitment and discipleship, as well as for apologetical purposes.[43] That is just how

41. Paul Gooch, "Ethics of Accommodation," 99, describes this as "epistemological accommodation." Note that however unclear the parallel with language may be, Philo, QG 4.69, is about rhetorical behavior; cf. Rudolph, "A Jew to the Jews," 127–32. This must be distinguished from flattery and deceptive speech, which fall within the model of lifestyle adaptability as an extension of changed behavior only at the surface level in order to mislead the other into mistakenly supposing that one upholds a certain view or course of action as a matter of conviction (cf. Josephus, *Ant.* 16.301–4, for flattery and deceptive speech as well as actions).

There is another model of adaptability that is compatible with rhetorical adaptability, but not precisely the same, and does not align with what Paul describes here. This could be described as "hierarchical adaptability." It applies to cases where someone of superior status—such as an employer among employees, rulers among the ruled, and so on, inclusive of social position in arrangements such as parents with children—seeks to relate on equal terms by not pulling rank. It does not include compromising moral behavior, but rather is exemplified when a parent seeks to relate to a teenager on a fishing trip, becoming friends as far as possible apart from the role of parent/child. It is also relevant for how to gain the trust of others of inferior rank, or when among strangers. This kind of strategic adaptability for rulers is instructed in Sir 32:1–2: "If they make you master of the feast, do not exalt yourself; be among them as one of their number [γίνου ἐν αὐτοῖς ὡς εἷς ἐξ αὐτῶν]. Take care of them first and then sit down..." (NRSV). Paul's examples of referents for his adaptability here do not indicate that rank is the topic, but rhetorical adaptability can include this element of adapting in terms of rank, to which Paul appeals elsewhere.

42. Paul Gooch, "Ethics of Accommodation," 99: this is when "two parties operate with conceptual frameworks some distance apart and where one wishes to communicate with the other. The message needs to be accommodated to the epistemological conditions of the hearer, else it will be lost in ambiguity and misunderstanding."

43. Philo was troubled by the implications of anthropomorphisms in Scripture, in particular, that they could be exploited to argue that God had a body. He thus explained that God's "coming down" to meet people in their weak state in the various forms in terms of rhetorical adaptability: these expressed God's way of communicating with humans by words and revelations within the confines of their human limitations; see Mitchell, "Pauline Accommodation," 205–8. Note also a pertinent rabbinic parallel in Pesiq. Rab. Kah. 12.24–25 (trans. William G. Braude and Israel J. Kapstein, 223–24): "Moreover, said R. Jose bar R. Hanina, the Divine Word spoke to each and every person

Socrates approached his [123] interlocutors, starting from their premises in a way calculated to lead them step by step to conclusions they had not foreseen and might otherwise be unwilling to accept. For example, in order to explain the relation between knowledge and action, Socrates begins by articulating common assumptions about pleasure (*Protagoras* 352ff.). In order to win his interlocutor to a new understanding of *aretē* that conflicts with the conventional usage, Socrates works his argument beginning from the conventional usage (*Meno*).[44]

Moreover, this approach approximates much more closely the topos of physicians and patients, of teachers and students, of parents and children, but highlights a very different dynamic with far-reaching implications for modeling the case. For regardless of how empathetically the instructor relates to the one he or she instructs, and regardless of the highest of motives at work, it is more likely that he or she will appeal to the *differences in their lifestyles* to exemplify or prove the value of the instruction being offered, rather than adopting the conduct of the student, which would often run contrary to the instructional objective.

I propose Paul's self-description here refers entirely to his evangelistic tactic of rhetorical adaptability, and did not include the adoption of conduct representing his various audiences' convictional propositions, but not his own.[45] He could undertake this argumentative tactic as a Jew faithfully

---

according to his particular capacity." Origen analogized God's condescension to that of philosophers toward youths just taking up the study, not bodily, but in terms of speech (Mitchell, "Pauline Accommodation," 210).

44. Paul Gooch, "Ethics of Accommodation," 104.

45. The appeal to rhetorical adaptability is not entirely unprecedented, but as far as I am aware it has always been coupled with lifestyle adaptability, and almost always with Paul as Torah-free as a matter of principle. Aspects have been noted in Origen, Chrysostom, and Augustine. Knox, *St. Paul*, has been discussed; see also Chadwick, "'All Things to All Men' (1 Cor. IX.22)," 275; Chadwick, *The Enigma of St Paul*, 14; Chadwick, "St. Paul and Philo of Alexandria," 297–98; Longenecker, *Paul, Apostle of Liberty*, 244, addressing specifically pastoral rhetorical adaptability (230–44), but he does not discuss Torah observance, and the message of the monograph turns around freedom from Torah (see 153–55); Ellison, "Paul," 200, without caveat for speaking to Jews as a Torah-observant Jew (!), although not explaining how this works for the other referents (195–202); Gooch, "Ethics of Accommodation," 94, 95 n. 57, 107, but see also 105, 114; Bornkamm, "The Missionary Stance of Paul in 1 Corinthians 9 and in Acts," 199, but see 202–5; Mitchell, *Paul and the Rhetoric of Reconciliation*, 248, interprets Paul to call them "to be accommodating of one another in all things, but especially in regard to meat-eating practices," although she says that in addition to "Paul's *behavior*" attention should also be paid "to the *rhetorical strategy* in Paul's call for accommodation here in 1 Cor" (emphasis hers); Glad, *Paul and Philodemus*, 240, 273, 327, but see 1, 258; Smit, '*About the Idol Offerings*', 64–65; Barton, "'All Things to All People,'" 280, but see 285; Johnson Hodge, "*If Sons, Then Heirs*," 124–25; Rudolph, "A Jew to the

[124] observing Torah, even when speaking to lawless Jews, Jews upholding different halakhic standards, and non-Jews of any stripe. Thus Paul's behavior can be described as free of the duplicitous conduct that serves as the basis for the charges of moral dishonesty, inconsistency, and so on, that arise logically from the prevailing views.

3. PAUL'S RHETORICAL ADAPTABILITY

In the midst of the discourse of chapters 8–10, in which 9:19-23 is embedded, Paul seeks to show his "knowledgeable" addressees in Corinth how he exemplifies the behavior to which he calls them.[46] The context for 9:20-23 [125] begins with the comments in vv. 16-19, and illustrates Paul's tactic for convincing those who do not believe in Christ of the gospel message. He explains that this expresses a specific choice that he makes to be "enslaved" to all people without receiving payment for his proclamation of the gospel, even though theoretically free to choose to do otherwise, and therefore he expects to be rewarded.[47]

Earlier in the letter Paul explained how his approach to their instruction is limited by his audience's condition as "fleshly" or immature, although he would prefer to inform them differently if "spiritual" or mature (3:1). That this does not indicate Paul behaved in a fleshly or immature

---

Jews," 169-207, esp. 185-88, and see 130-32, maintains that Paul was Torah-observant, although his argument provides for some level of compromised behavior for tablefellowship. Fee, *First Epistle to the Corinthians*, 428 n. 36; and 432-33, and Given, *Paul's True Rhetoric*, 105-17, specifically reject arguments in this direction.

46. This approach to the purpose of ch. 9, to articulate how Paul embodies what he calls for the knowledgeable to do in ch. 8, rather than supposing it to be in the first instance a defense against charges brought against his apostleship by opponents, can be traced to at least Chrysostom, *Homily XXI*, in Schaff, ed., *NPNF XII*, 118, 129. Willis, "An Apostolic Apologia?"; Mitchell, *Paul*, 243-50, for detailed discussions. Note that throughout the letter, epistolary terms that relate to a discourse on adaptability are also attested: "*symphoros* (benefit, advantage), *euschemon* (proper, good order), and *kalos* (good, useful; 5:12; 7:1, 8, 26, 35, 37, 38; cf. 10:23; 12:7)" (Glad, "Paul and Adaptability," 31). See also Chadwick, "All Things," 268; Nasuti, "The Woes of the Prophets and the Rights of the Apostle"; Hall, "All Things to All People," 141-42; Martin, *Slavery as Salvation*, 78; Peter Gooch, *Dangerous Food*, 83-84; Eriksson, *Traditions as Rhetorical Proof*, 148-53, 154-73; Furnish, *The Theology of the First Letter to the Corinthians*, 23-24; Garland, "The Dispute Over Food Sacrificed to Idols," 185-97; Smit, 'About the Idol Offerings,' 64-65, 84-85, 153-54; Cheung, *Idol Food*, 115-17.

47. If confronting works-righteousness was as central to Paul as the traditional interpretations require, it is surprising that he is willing to admit to seeking to be rewarded for his choices and labor, as he does here, seemingly without caveat that the idea of earning something from God is anathema according to his most important theological teaching.

manner beyond the way he adapted his speech to them is readily evident to commentators. That is also how teachers adapt their speech to students at various levels, how parents adapt their speech to children at various levels (even baby talking), and so on. But specifically in view is *speech behavior*, how one relates to others discursively, not how one *behaves* in terms of conducting themselves like students, or children. The teacher or parent wants the students or children to recognize the very different behavior of the teacher or parent; they seek to provoke emulation, not confirmation of an immature status quo (cf. 4:8–17). This matter can also involve the obvious concern to speak pleasantly and respectfully. It is perhaps in this vein that *Acts of Paul* 3.1 begins the story of Thecla by describing Paul as having "sweetened them [ἐγλύκαινεν αὐτούς]" when declaring the gospel message to his traveling companions from loving intentions in contrast to their hypocritical treatment of Paul, entreating him as if they loved him, when they intended him harm.

In chapters 8–10, Paul's instructions to the knowledgeable to make lifestyle changes—in keeping with Christ-faith values, including learning to live in ways that take into consideration the best interests of others—actually exemplify Paul's rhetorical adaptability. Paul's "becoming" can be explained by examining the way that he relates to the "knowledgeable" at Corinth in this argument by becoming knowledgeable rhetorically:[48] although he disagrees with their thinking and approach, he tries to persuade them from their own premises. Paul does not eat like them (or how they propose to eat), or behave like them (or how they propose to behave), but his argument is based on their own premises (and proposals), at least at the start, in order to lead them to an entirely different set of conclusions that are in keeping with Scripture, and a different way of living than their own reasoning had led them to suppose followed from the renunciation [126] of idols.[49] Notwithstanding that Paul was probably citing sayings of

48. Cf. Horsley, *Wisdom and Spiritual Transcendence at Corinth*, 86–88 ["Gnosis in Corinth?"].

49. One of the interesting things about this argument in 1 Cor 8–10 is that it was necessary for Paul to make it. It appears that when he taught among them he did not anticipate where their logic would lead, in the very unjewish direction of supposing that because of renouncing the reality of the gods to which idol rites were devoted they were thus free to eat idol food or even participate in idol rites. They probably reasoned that this demonstrated that they regarded idols as merely profane, and also maintained the relationships that complete avoidance of such rites and food or meals would compromise if not destroy, with deleterious results for themselves. If Paul had anticipated this line of reasoning, it would seem that this exchange would not arise, or he would approach it by appeal to his earlier teaching among them. As a Jew, he would reason and likely suppose any Christ-believer would thus reason that regardless of the proposition that these were not gods as non-Jews supposed, that these gods and the rites and

the knowledgeable in 8:1, 4, rather than declaring his own point of view, he moves on to state the contradictory proposition that *not everyone* knows what they suppose to be self-evident now in vv. 7ff. And in chapter 9, Paul illustrates his very different lifestyle, including his rhetorical adaptability, to demonstrate the lifestyle they should now imitate. Although Paul does not explicitly call the Corinthians to proclaim the gospel to their families and neighbors as much as to seek to live with respect to one another, he does call them to imitate his lifestyle in order to gain others in 10:31—11:1, and elsewhere throughout the letter (e.g., 7:16; 10:24, 27–30; 14:22–25).[50] This brings up an interesting topic.

I join those who understand Paul to be explicitly describing his evangelizing tactics in 9:19–23, and my interpretation of the identity of the "weak" throughout these chapters as non-Christ-believing idolaters strengthens that case,[51] nevertheless, it would be surprising if Paul did not exemplify this rhetorical tactic in his pastoral approach to these Christ-believers.[52] In his [127] argument throughout chapters 8 to 10, Paul does

---

thus food dedicated to them were nevertheless anathema for worshippers of the God of Israel as the only God. Thus, even when Jews trivialized idols, they refrained from anything having to do with idolatry. As Paul represents the issue of marketplace food, the food is not designated idol food, but is rather assumed to be profane unless known to be otherwise (announcing this option implies that there was food available there that was not idolatrous; likewise it could be available at the home to which one might be invited). Rabbinic material is replete with discussions of the difference between interaction with things sold or used by idolaters and those which are specifically set apart to idols, the latter forbidden, while the former are often permitted (cf. m. Abod. Zar. 1.4–5; 2.3; 3.4; 4.3–6; 5.1; see Tomson, *Paul*, 151–77, 208–20; Cheung, *Idol Food*, 39–81, 152–64, 300–301; Smit, 'About the Idol Offerings,' 52–58, 65, *passim*; Zetterholm, "Purity and Anger," 15; Rudolph, "A Jew to the Jews," 97–104; Nanos, "Polytheist Identity."

50. For more discussion of the specifically polytheist orientation of the letter's message, see Nanos, "Polytheist Identity," esp. 203–9.

51. Ibid., 189–97, 200–202.

52. That Paul is approaching his addressees from their premises is evident throughout the letter, representing pastoral rather than evangelistic-oriented rhetorical adaptability. Chadwick, "'All Things,'" 268, 275; Chadwick, *Enigma of Paul*, 12, 14, notes that 1 Cor 7:1–6 similarly begins by hypothetical agreement in principle that it is good for a man not to touch a woman, but moves to a different conclusion that the wife controls whether that is good or not for the husband; Longenecker, *Paul*, 230–44; Paul Gooch, "Ethics of Accommodation," 114, observes that Paul does demonstrate epistemological accommodation in this letter: "if they were to reflect on the very things that Paul reveals to them about himself, they would discover interesting examples of his accommodation towards them," and although he includes examples of ethical accommodation based on interpretations of passages with which I disagree, he also notes: "he is willing to agree with the starting points of various groups in Corinth in order to move them from their extremes of liberty or asceticism or enthusiasm." Cf. Peter Gooch, *Dangerous Food*, 83–84, 93; Smit, 'About the Idol Offerings,' 64–65, 84, 153–54;

not become knowledgeable to the knowledgeable in the sense of lifestyle adaptability, but his rhetorical adaptation to the premises of the knowledgeable is based on empathy toward the weak as well as communicating this empathy to the knowledgeable. He calls the knowledgeable to change their lifestyle, to be sure, something he does not describe seeking among the recipients of his evangelistic tactics in 9:16–23. Paul also explains how he adapts his own lifestyle to accomplish various goals throughout chapter 9; but it is important to notice that he does not write that he mimics the behavior of others. Quite the contrary, he claims to do many things very differently than others do, including other apostles, in order to succeed in ways that he believes would be compromised otherwise, or less effective, or less able to gain him reward.

When engaging in pastoral adaptability, Paul relates to the knowledgeable from their premises at the beginning of his argument. He reasons from first principles that there is only one God and thus that idols are nobodies (8:4–6), and therefore the food offered to them can be eaten as profane (8:8; 10:19, 23, 25–26). But he grants this line of argument *only in theory*—even undermining it in the way it is first stated, for he includes the caveat that "*there are* many gods and many lords" (8:5)—thereafter seeking to lead them to a very different conclusion. For he explains that there are those who believe in these idols who will be encouraged to continue to believe in them, rather than coming to know what the knowledgeable know (vv. 7–13), and that there are such things as daemons represented by these idols (10:19–22). Thus, they are not to eat any food known to be dedicated to idols, just as Jews, who do not believe idols represent gods never the less do not eat idol food as if profane, but flee from anything that is associated with idolatry or pay the price for not doing so (10:1–23). In the end, the only food that can be eaten is food that they do not know to be idol-related, and even if they are guests and informed that certain food has been offered to idols previously, they are not to eat it (10:14–33).

Paul thus moves his addressees from non-Jewish premises, since they are not Jews, to very Jewish conclusions, since they are Christ-believers, which represents a Jewish (communal, philosophical, religious, moral, etc.) way of being in the world—even for non-Jews. Note that Paul leads these non-Jews to the same conclusions to which he would lead them if he was addressing Jews, arguing many of the same essential points (that God is One, that they must love their neighbor, that they cannot eat idol food if known to be [128] such, that idols represent daemons, that Scripture teaches these

---

Cheung, *Idol Food*, 115–17.

things[53]), and incorporating allusions to Torah, as in the rhetorical question of 10:22: "Or do we provoke the Lord to jealousy?" In this way, Paul has become like a non-Jew—rhetorically speaking, that is. If his addressees had been instead Jews, then I propose that we would have seen Paul appeal directly to Torah to discuss this matter, rather than begin with first principles or consideration of the other's sensibilities, or to the mere example of Israelites. We would have seen him instead becoming like a Jew, rhetorically, which would have been quite natural for him, since he was a Jew.

3.1 The Issue of "Becoming Like"

One of the interesting facets of the prevailing lifestyle adaptability viewpoint is that it is supposed to be a straightforward explanation of Paul's tactic of how he "became as/like [ἐγενόμην . . . ὡς]" the other, or in the case of the "weak," simply that he "became" weak.[54] But "becoming as" (and all the more "becoming") someone from some group according to their relationship to Torah or law are not lexical equivalents to the notions expressed by the prevailing lifestyle adaptability interpretation. For "imitating," "mimicking," "pretending to be," "aping," and so on, are actually descriptions of merely adopting the outward behavioral conduct of the other, but not at the propositional level that behavior is designed to express. There are Greek words for describing such behavior undertaken only at the surface level, including μιμέομαι (imitate, mimic, represent, portray), ὑποκρίνομαι (play a part; feign, pretend; hypocrisy), and δοκέω (seem, pretend, suppose, imagine, expect). In other words, the prevailing views are not based on what Paul has written, which does not describe a general case, but a specific one that revolves around the contrary behaviors to be expected among each of the referents named. Paul is not understood to have actually "become like" each of them, which would instead literally be represented by the convictional adaptability model, although this logical problem does not seem to be generally recognized.[55]

53. Cf. Deut 32:17; Ps 95:5 LXX; 106:37; Isa 65:3, 11.

54. Some variants do include the ὡς with this clause too, but even if omitted, this strikes me as another example of Paul's elliptical style and variation of language, probably an effort to be brief and get the readers/hearers attention, or simply variation. In other words, the missing ὡς is probably implied, although either way does not really effect my argument (note the poetic variation in Lam 5:3; and the reverse case of what is dropped in Matt 10:25). Note too that the verb ἐγενόμην is missing for two of the four referents, but the verb is understood to be implied.

55. See e.g., Philo, *Laws* 4.126. Pace Given, *Paul's True Rhetoric*, 105–17. Although I appreciate the argument against interpretations that seek to protect Paul's integrity,

[129] For example, interpreters do not read Paul to mean he actually *became* "under law," however defined (e.g., a proselyte),[56] or "lawless," which if read as "wicked" is even more difficult to imagine than that he *became* a Jew. And he could not actually "become *weak*" on the prevailing interpretations of the "weak," which suppose they are insecure about eating idol food as if such gods were thereby worshipped, or that he was overscrupulous when he resisted doing so, or did so under compulsion but with qualms about it.[57] To return briefly to the case of becoming like a Jew, taken literally, that would mean that Paul was not already a Jew, which he claims to have been, and still to be. Although many interpreters may work with the notion that Paul left behind Judaism and thus being a Jew in a religious sense, few claim that he left behind his ethnic identity as a Jew—albeit now defining him to be a "Christian," however described or labeled—even if it is not unusual to see perplexed references to this conundrum, as already

---

on 111, after Given concludes that Paul's "becoming like" signifies eating or otherwise behaving like each of the groups, Given's interpretation does not represent "the realm of being" rather than "that of seeming" anymore than do the viewpoints he criticizes (Glad in particular). On 112, Given uses "appearing as" synonymously with "becoming like." At the same time, I do not think that Given's reading need be far from the one I propose, if dropping *acting* like but keeping *speaking* like, for on 117 he concludes that Paul shapes his "insinuative rhetorical strategy similar to that imagined by Luke with respect to Jews and Gentiles." Paul Gooch, "Ethics of Accommodation," 104-5, also argues that, "He [Paul] does not say he adopted the language of those within law or outside of it; he does not present himself as agreeing with the basic premises of Jew or the weak. Instead he claims that he has *become* as one of those he is trying to win: he has adopted, not terminology, but ways of behaving" (emphasis his). But Gooch is interpreting "becoming" in a certain way, as "behaving." That "becoming as" does not equate to ethical accommodation in behavior as in mimicking others is not apparently noticed. Since Paul cannot become opposites at the propositional level, i.e., he cannot observe Torah as a matter of covenant conviction and also discard Torah as a covenantal behavioral norm because he is with a different audience, for Torah by definition involves a way of life that maintains different behavior in the midst of the other nations to bear witness to God's righteousness. Paul can but only "mimic" their behavior in the way that Gooch, with the consensus, proposes, and thus Gooch is translating "becoming" into "mimicking" without an argument that this is what Paul must mean by it. There is no proof that Paul ever, e.g., ate like an idolater, or alternatively, that he ever ate contrary to Torah-defined dietary norms. I am proposing herein that what Paul is doing in 1 Cor 8-10 is an example of the Socratic epistemology that Gooch identifies in 9:19-23 as Paul's tactic. Glad, *Paul*, 259-60, reads this as "Paul's willingness to *associate* with all" (emphasis added).

56. Chrysostom, *Homily* XXII.5, in Schaff, ed., *NPNF* XII, 128.

57. Thiselton, *First Epistle to the Corinthians*, 705, recognizes the problem, but does not resolve it. In view of such problems, many interpreters alter the identity of the "weak" here from representing those who are non-Christ-believers whom Paul seeks to win to Christ, to that of Christ-believers whom Paul seeks to win to a new way of expressing that faith (e.g., Willis, *Idol Meat in Corinth*, 37; Hays, *First Corinthians*, 155).

encountered. Thus, interpreters actually read this to connote that Paul *behaved* like a Jew, referring to *playing at* or *mimicking* or *pretending to* Jewish behavior, although not subscribing to the values of that Jewish behavior as a matter [130] of conviction, of faith, of loyalty to Torah. Similarly, when Paul describes in his own case being *"enslaved to"* everyone, interpreters do not suppose that Paul is an actual slave to the other, but he says he becomes one. It is not literal slavery, but signifies that he puts the concerns of the other above his own, that he serves them instead of himself. He is "like" a slave, which connotes his empathetic concern for the other.

In short, when Paul writes *behaved like*, his denotation is read with the connotation of *mimicked the behavior of*, because it defies logic that he *became* each of these contrary identities. In other words, short of postulating the unimaginable model of convictional adaptability, to actually coming over to another's way of life because one believes what the other believes, every interpreter has to fill out what Paul means by "I became," or "I caused myself to *become*," if the causative quality of the middle voice of this verb is emphasized.

Thus the prevailing interpretations of this passage are based on supposed connotations, but not denotation. And they have as central to their adoption of the lifestyle adaptability model the presupposition that Paul does not observe Torah, certainly not as a matter of covenant fidelity. As I have explained, and as the many problems that emerge not only from Christian interpreters but also from non-Christian critics of the prevailing lifestyle adaptability view (as well as the defenses offered to those criticisms) make obvious, there is good reason to consider another model, that of rhetorical adaptability.

I propose that instead of "behaving like" according to the model of lifestyle adaptability, this language signifies how Paul *reasons like* and *relates* his convictions *like*, how he *engages like*, how he rhetorically meets people where they are, according to their own worldviews and premises. Paul *reasons* with, *relates* to, or *engages* Jews as/like (in the manner of) a Jew, and so on. In this rhetorical, discursive sense Paul could actually *become like*—or even *become*—everything to everyone.

As a consequence, as interesting as it is to imagine who each of the specific referents represent and why Paul chose these referents to exemplify his tactics—Jews, those under law, the lawless, or the weak—or how any or all of these relate to Torah observance, or not, it is not necessary to do so on the interpretation I propose. Rhetorical adaptability can be undertaken by a Torah-observant Jew without the need to compromise those values by adopting outward behavior like that of the target audience, even if the audience does not similarly subscribe to Torah-defined behavior.

In fact, this difference in behavior may be emphasized or minimized, depending upon the audience and circumstance. What Paul is describing requires knowing how to communicate effectively, and within the limits of his objectives, respectfully.

Importantly, we have an example of Paul engaging in rhetorical adaptability by his earliest known biographer in Acts 17, regardless of whether this case accurately describes an historical event. It not only illustrates rhetorical adaptability in principle, but also that the author presumed it would be a persuasive example for his audience.

3.2 An Example of Paul's Rhetorical Adaptability from Acts 17

[131] In Acts 17:17-31, Luke relates the story of Paul's proclamation of the One God and Christ in Athens. Paul does not start with a denial of the reality of the gods in which the philosophers and other elites gathered at the Areopagus believe, although he does eventually criticize the effort to make representations of the divine.[58] Like a philosopher *becoming like*, as in *relating to*, fellow philosophers, he begins by recognizing them to be "very religious [δεισιδαιμονεστέρους]."[59]

Paul argues from within their propositional worldview towards declaring that the idol they have designated "To an Unknown God [Ἀγνώστῳ θεῷ]," need no longer remain unknown to them. He does not introduce a new god, which is a function of the judiciary meetings held at the Areopagus, but discloses the identity of the One true God in whom they should logically already believe.[60] Interestingly, Paul is described to say that which the Athenians worship is done "without knowledge/in ignorance [ἀγνοοῦντες]" (v. 23); he also refers to the "times of ignorance [χρόνους τῆς ἀγνοίας]" that his gospel declaration proposes to bring to an end (v. 30). Paul draws on Scrip-

---

58. Concerning Cynic and Stoic critiques of statues to represent gods, see Dio Chrysostom, *Orations* 12.52; 31.15; Ps.-Heraclitus 4.2.5; Antisthenes, in Clement, *Protreptikos* 6.71.1; 7.75.3; Epictetus, *Dissertation* 1.6.23-29; 2.30.26; Diogenes Laertius, *Lives* 7.147; Seneca, *Epistulae morales* 41.1; Downing, *God with Everything*, 27 n. 24 (20-42). See also Baltes, "Mixed Monotheism? The Areopagos Speech of Paul."

59. This can be translated also "superstitious," and arguably the speech plays with this ambiguity throughout, but here likely in language that the audience would hear in positive terms, to be expected in an introduction, although recognized to have a negative twist by Luke's Christ-believing reader: see Conzelmann, "The Address of Paul on the Areopagus," 220; Given, *Paul's True Rhetoric*, 68-74, discusses the double, ironic language choices throughout this section.

60. Kauppi, *Foreign but Familiar Gods*, 83-93, discusses the possibility that Paul draws on an allusion to Aeschylus' *Eumenides* here. See also Gill and Gempf, eds., *The Book of Acts in its Graeco-Roman Setting*, 446-48.

tural concepts throughout his speech, and could have offered many prooftexts for his argumentative points. But Paul does not cite any scriptures. Rather, the only explicit citations he incorporates include the inscription to the unknown deity on the altar, and a line from "some of your own poets": τοῦ γὰρ καὶ γένος ἐσμέν ("for we also are his offspring"; v. 28).[61]

[132] I submit that Luke's example represents the rhetorical strategy of "I became (i.e., reasoned) to the idolaters as [in the manner of] an idolater." Paul related his message to them—inclusive of challenges to their concepts, conclusions, and behavior—from within their own premises in order to gain them to Christ.

This example from Acts was similarly drawn upon to interpret 1 Cor 9:19-23 by Origen and Chrysostom, *mutatis mutandis*, that is, granting that they were not seeking to make the overarching case that I propose for rhetorical in sharp contrast to lifestyle adaptability, and they interpreted Paul to be free of Torah as a matter of policy, indeed, to be free of Judaism. Nevertheless, Origen referred to the example in Acts 17:23, 28, to explain how Paul adapted his speech "to the lawless" by becoming "lawless": Paul "did not use either prophetic or halakhic terms, but if he had a memory of some Greek learning from his preparatory instruction he *spoke* about it to the Athenians," and he did not uphold that Paul behaved lawlessly in doing so.[62] In addition, Origen provided examples for two of the other referents in terms of adaptability, one rhetorical and the other lifestyle: in rhetorical terms when he spoke to the weak as weak in 1 Cor 7:6; and in lifestyle terms when he behaved as a Jew by circumcising Timothy because of the Jews (Acts 16:3), and taking the Nazarite vow (Acts 21).[63] Commenting on 9:21, Chrysostom notes that others before him had already made the point: "But some say that he hints at his *discourse* with the Athenians from the inscription on the altar, and that so he saith, 'to them that are without law, as without law.'"[64] He concludes that in Athens Paul "was *speaking* to pagan

---

61. Apparently from the Cretan poet Epimenides, and Paul's usage perhaps draws on criticism of some Cretans pointing to a tomb for Zeus to undermine his immortality, so that Paul may be playing off of a commonly known dispute about whether a statue undermines the reality of the deity to which it is built to point: Lake, "'Your Own Poets': Note XX"; Bruce, *The Acts of the Apostles*, 384-85.

62. *Comm. in 1 Cor.* 3.43 (emphasis mine), ed. C. Jenkins, "Origen on 1 Corinthians," *Journal of Theological Studies* 9 (1907-8), 513 (231-47, 353-72, 500-514); cited by Mitchell, "Pauline Accommodation," 208.

63. Origen apparently did not provide an example of becoming under law to those under law, which he took to mean non-Jews who placed themselves under law, but he was sure there were examples; from ibid., 208, 306 n. 58, referring to SC 157.400-402.

64. *Homily XXII.5*, in Schaff, ed., *NPNF XII*, 128 (emphasis mine).

Greeks, who believed in none of our sacred books, and *so he used arguments from their own beliefs* to subdue them."[65]

An example of Paul's rhetorical adaptability in terms of becoming to Jews as a Jew is illustrated just prior to his arrival in Athens among the idolaters. In [133] Acts 17:1–3, Paul is described proceeding immediately to the synagogue upon his arrival in Thessalonica:

> [1]After Paul and Silas had passed through Amphipolis and Apollonia, they came to Thessalonica, where there was a synagogue of the Jews. [2]And Paul went in, as was his custom, and on three sabbath days *argued* with them *from the scriptures,* [3]*explaining* and *proving* that it was necessary for the Messiah to suffer and to rise from the dead, and saying, "This is the Messiah, Jesus whom I am proclaiming to you." (NRSV, emphasis mine)

Such an argument would have made little to no sense to non-Jews, for example, among the philosophers at the Areopagus. He would have to describe why he appealed to Scripture as proof, what a messiah is or why that should be of concern to them, especially his suffering and rising from the dead. And that is just the point that Luke makes about the problems that emerge for Paul among the philosophers. For even though these Jewish premises are not the place from which Luke portrays Paul to begin his argument with the philosophers, as already discussed, these are nevertheless the kinds of topics to which his speech drives, even if Luke also describes the results encumbered by this propositional gap. The philosophers are puzzled by some of his premises, and elements of the conclusions to which he seeks to move them. Paul does not make as clear a case for the relevance of these matters as he can among Jews, because he (or Luke) is unaware of adequate analogies from their non-Jewish culture, or does not know how to prepare an argument that will effectively bridge the cultural divide between them.

Thus, in two almost immediately concurrent examples, the author of Acts describes two cases of variability in terms of the rhetorical adaptability model. And note that in the synagogue example, Luke presents it to be "his custom" to argue in this manner at Sabbath meetings (17:10–12 continues this pattern in Beroea, and in v. 17 it is implied that he argues thus in the synagogues of Athens, but it is not the way he is shown to argue in the marketplace with the philosophers; immediately after Athens, it is still the way Paul is presented to proceed in the synagogue of Corinth in 18:4–5, and throughout ch. 18 as he moves from place to place).[66]

---

65. *Adv. Jud.* 5.3.2 (emphasis mine); trans. from Harkins, *Saint John Chrysostom*, 105; see also Chrysostom's comments on speaking to Jews differently, in *Adv. Jud.* 5.3.3.

66. Cf. Jervell, *Luke and the People of God*, 41–74.

Luke's example of rhetorical adaptability among philosophers seeking to win each other to their positions or schools is not the only example of the discussion or presentation of this model among Paul's contemporaries.[67]

3.3 Antisthenes on Odysseus as *Polytrope*

[134] The tactic Paul describes can be compared to that of Odysseus as interpreted by Antisthenes, a student of Socrates. The similarities are not exact, and there is a tendency in the discussions of Homer's passage on Odysseus to blur the lines between lifestyle and rhetorical adaptability just as arises in discussion of Paul's passage, where I am trying to draw a sharp line between these models for the sake of clarifying what I propose Paul meant. Moreover, the few interpreters discussing this parallel (of whom I am aware), conclude that Antisthenes' Odysseus model stands in contrast to Paul's message; but that is largely based on their view of Paul's language in the direction of the consensus lifestyle adaptability model, including that he was indifferent to Torah, if not opposed to it in principle.[68] From the perspective I propose, the dynamics are much more suggestive of similarity, although the frequent blending with figures such as that of the physician

---

67. Other examples, not discussed here for the sake of space, include at least the philosopher Aristobulus, and Philo, the latter overlapping with Paul, and exemplifying rhetorical adaptability while declaring commitment to Torah observance. In addition, *The Letter of Aristeas* expresses Jewish views of God and righteousness (including topics like dietary regulations) in Hellenistic philosophical terms argued from within Greek premises when among non-Jews in Egypt, including to the king and his representatives, which involved respectful analogies drawn to Egyptian practices and even worship (e.g., 16, where worship of Zeus and Jove is likened to worship of God, but under different names). Following the introductory arguments made to his scholarly brother, Philocrates, similar arguments are delivered in conversation with the king and his guests during the time when philosophical conversation normally took place according to symposium conventions, that is, following the shared meal with these non-Jews, which was served according to Jewish halakhic norms, albeit by the king's (non-Jewish) servants. The kind of Jewish men Eleazar, the High Priest in Jerusalem, is said to have selected to travel to Alexandria, is of interest: "they had not only mastered the Jewish literature, but had made a serious study of that of the Greeks as well. . . . [T]hey had a tremendous natural facility for the negotiations and questions arising from the Law, with the middle way as their commendable ideal; they forsook any uncouth and uncultured attitude of mind; in the same way they rose above conceit and contempt of other people, and instead engaged in discourse and listening to and answering each and every one, as is meet and right" (121–22; trans. Shutt).

68. For application to Paul, from which I learned much, albeit taken to different conclusions, see Stanford, *The Ulysses Theme*, 91; Malherbe, *Paul and the Popular Philosophers*, 100, 118–19; Glad, *Paul and Philodemus*, 97–98, 251, 272–73; Reis, "Flip-Flop?: John Chrysostom's Polytropic Paul."

to patient (which is not the same as patient to patient), and discussions of motives rather than simply tactics, lead to an examination that must be carefully nuanced and critical of every example discussed.

The simplest way to interpret the opening line of the *Odyssey*, "Tell me, Muse, of the *polytropic* man," is that he will wander on his journey home rather than taking a direct course.[69] However, by the fifth century BCE, the image of Odysseus had taken on the negative ethical connotation of "often changing one's character, hence unstable, unprincipled, unscrupulous," a chameleon-like quality that moralists condemned among party politicians of the period.[70] After all, with Odysseus, the innovator of the Trojan horse and many other cunning disguises, it does not take much to get to a model [135] of lifestyle adaptability in the negative sense of duplicity and expedience over principle, and this had been the subject of philosophical discussion for some time.[71] Already Achilles had declared the moral depravity of the man who compromises his character for expedience: "For hateful in my eyes as the gates of Hades is that man who hides one thing in his mind and says another" (*Iliad* 9.312–13; trans. Murray and Wyatt). Many Athenians found fault with Odysseus and Homer, especially in the context of the stricter ideals of morality and truth following from Pythagoras and Xenophanes versus the style of the Sophists, who were unscrupulous to achieve their ends, since this kind of model was used to justify political exploitation by those who relished self-aggrandizement and ambition over truth, and debased moral values along the way, just as they did the Athenian coinage, according to Thucydides.[72] Political victory became associated with the immoral expedience, to success at all costs, and thus, with Homer's trickster hero.[73] The Sophists, ironically, were also critical of Odysseus's character, including his clever use of language.[74]

Antisthenes countered this interpretive tradition with a controversial reading of Odysseus according to the model of rhetorical adaptability. It stands in stark contrast to the prevailing readings, which were based on the model of lifestyle adaptability:

> And what then? Are we perhaps to believe that Odysseus is wicked because he is called *polytropos*? Nevertheless, the poet

---

69. Porphyry's scholion on *Odysseus* 1.1, begins the epic with Homer's request: "Tell me, Muse, of the man of many devices [πολύτροπον] . . . ."

70. Stanford, *Ulysses Theme*, 99.

71. Ibid., 95–99.

72. Ibid., 100–101.

73. Ibid., 101.

74. Ibid., 95–96, 146.

has called him that at a point where he is thought wise (*sophos*). Perhaps, in fact, the word *tropos* is not applied to moral character (*ethos*), as much as to his <u>skill in speaking</u> (*logou khresis*)? One is called *eutropos* if one has a moral character that is "turned" (*tetrammenon*) toward the good, and in <u>discourse</u> *tropoi* are called diverse styles (*hai poiai plaseis*). Homer has also adopted the word *tropos* with regard to the voice and variety of melodies, as in the case of the nightingale: ". . . changing (*troposa*) it over and over again, she pours forth her many-toned voice" (Odyssey 19.521). Therefore, if wise men are skilled in <u>speaking</u> and know how <u>to express the same thought in many ways</u> (*kata pollous tropous*), those who know many ways of expression concerning the same thing can rightly be called *polutropoi*. The wise men are therefore also excellent men (*hoi sophoi kai agathoi eisin*). For this reason Homer bestows upon Odysseus, as a wise man, the epithet *polutropos*: because he can <u>speak with men in many ways</u>. So it is also said that Pythagoras, having been invited <u>to speak</u> with children, <u>used the language</u> of children; in <u>speaking</u> with women, <u>the language appropriate</u> to women, in <u>speaking</u> with rulers, <u>the language of</u> rulers; in <u>speaking</u> with youths <u>the language of</u> youths. For it is a mark of wisdom to discover <u>a form of wisdom appropriate to each person</u>, and a mark of ignorance to use only <u>one form (*monotropo*) of speech</u> with dissimilar people. This is a specialty which also belongs to medicine, in a case that is well treated. For the care of the ill ought to be *polutropos*, because of <u>various predispositions</u> of the cured. *Tropos* is therefore that which changes, that which is variable in the human spirit. The <u>multiplicity of the ways of speaking</u> [136] (*polutropia logou*) and the <u>use of varied speech for various ears</u> becomes a single type (*monotropia*) of speech. For <u>one thing is appropriate for each person</u>. Thus, that which is <u>adapted to each person</u> reduces <u>variety of speech</u> to one thing—that which is <u>suitable</u> for each person. But that which is uniform and unadapted to different ears renders <u>a speech</u> (which is rejected by many) *polutropos*, because it has been rejected by them.[75]

Antisthenes begins his appeal by reference to the fact that the context of Homer's language usage calls for a challenge to the prevailing interpretation of it because of the logical inconsistency it creates between Odysseus' words and the moral character of Odysseus that Homer is otherwise seeking to communicate, which sets up a very close parallel to the problem under

---

75. *Antisthenis Fragmenta* 51 (Fernanda Decleva Caizzi, ed., 43); trans. by Rostagni, 25–26 (underline emphasis mine).

discussion about Paul's language. Antisthenes thus argued that this description of Odysseus exemplified rhetorical rather than lifestyle adaptability.[76]

He maintained that *polytropos* does not refer to Odysseus adapting his lifestyle in duplicitous ways, with the concomitant ethical problems of the lifestyle model, but to Odysseus as the example of the virtuous man who adapted his *figures of speech* ("*tropes*") to his various audiences ("*poly*") in order to persuade each of them in terms to which they could relate. Antisthenes linked Odysseus' adaptability to that which was exemplified and taught by the austere Pythagoras, famed for his commitment to moral fidelity and truth, but who never the less recommended rhetorical adaptation to one's various audiences: the right word for the right person at the right time is the way of the wise.[77] The concern to match different verbal styles of rhetorical presentation to suit different character types to enhance persuasion became a focus of rhetorical theorists seeking to match various speaking styles to different famous orators.[78]

Paul need not be a student of Homer to expect his readers to understand him to be describing the practice of rhetorical adaptability. He and his audiences were products of a Greco-Roman culture in which debates about adaptability were lively and included the topics of rhetorical versus lifestyle and the ethical consequences thereof, witnessed in the works of Philo, Plutarch, Maximus of Tyre, Philodemus, Horace, Dio Chrysostom, Epictetus, and Lucian, among others.[79] Antisthenes and his Odysseus became [137] the heroes and models for the Cynics and Stoics—or the heroes and models to oppose—including in the matter of rhetorical adaptability.[80] Diogenes Laertius writes that "of all the Socratics Antisthenes alone

76. Cf. Stanford, *Ulysses Theme*, 99; Glad, *Paul and Philodemus*, 272.

77. Rostagni, "New Chapter," 30–31.

78. Worman, *The Cast of Character*, 33.

79. Glad, "Paul and Adaptability," 21–22, 26, 28–29. Glad, *Paul and Philodemus*, 273, notes that "By Paul's time versatility and charges of cunning focused both on behavior and speech; one could adapt both by conforming to different manners as well as being discriminating in speech. Discrimination in speech is already seen in Pythagoras' practice of teaching his disciples to speak to children in childlike terms, to women in women-like terms. Such concerns are also present in the moralists' focus on character portrayal. Because of this, and in light of the intricate connection between the philosopher's *schema* and *logos*, we should be careful not to focus solely on adaptation in behavior when explicating Paul's statements on adaptability." See also Reis, "Flip-Flop?" 10–12.

80. Malherbe, *Paul and the Popular Philosophers*, 35–48, 95–119, discusses the conflicting views of Odysseus among Cynics, whether he was the father of Cynicism or not, including the range from more rigorous to more moderate Cynic practices. The cloak is an issue: Odysseus wore it once, while Diogenes who wore it all the time, etc. Thus Diogenes is upheld as the father by the more rigorous such as Ps.-Crates and Ps.-Diogenes. But rigorous Cynics rejected his adaptability of speech (109–12). Stoics

is praised by Theopompus, who says he had consummate skill and could by means of agreeable discourse win over whomsoever he pleased" (6.14; trans. Hicks). Diogenes was famous for "a wonderful gift of persuasion, so that he could vanquish anyone he liked in argument" (*Diog. Laertius* 6.75–76; Loeb). Crates became famous for *philanthrōpia*, nicknamed "'the Door Opener'—the caller to whom all doors fly open—from his habit of entering every house and admonishing those within" (*Diog. Laertius* 6.86; Loeb). In an epigram echoing funerary epithets, Meleager expressed his cosmopolitan variability, bidding each in their own language: "Be you Phoenician, *naidios*! Be you Syrian, I bid you *salam*! Be you Greek, *chaire*!—and you respond in kind" (*Anth. Gr.* 7.419.7–8).[81] Dio Chrysostom maintained that the philosopher must teach "sometimes by persuasion and exhortation, at other times by abuse and reproach, [hoping] he may rescue some from folly, . . . taking them on one side on their own but also admonishing them together, whenever the opportunity arises, with gentle words at times, [and] at other [times] harsh" (*Or.* 77/78.35–38).[82]

Paul's competitive metaphors in verses 24–27, immediately following our passage, resemble those closely associated with Antisthenes and the Cynics, and there are many other similarities throughout the Corinthian correspondence, from word usage to concepts. The Pythagorean and Antisthenean traditions focused on finding the right word for each circumstance, and Paul is engaged in explaining the variable of the theoretical "good" in terms of food and eating, adapted to variable factors and social circumstances. In fact, Abraham Malherbe goes so far as to suggest that Paul may have thought of himself within the Antisthenic model.[83] That Odysseus is portrayed as the wise man [138] who plays the fool, which is how Paul also describes himself in this letter, may also suggest further comparisons at work.[84]

The tradition of interpreting Odysseus in terms of rhetorical rather than lifestyle adaptability represents a minority position, to be sure.[85] Moreover, whether it accurately characterizes Odysseus as Homer and the

---

celebrated Odysseus as an example of virtue and wisdom, as sensible, in control of his passions, adaptable, courteous, and affable to everyone in his every word (cf. Cicero, *De Off* 1.113–14).

81. Luz, "Salam, Meleager!"

82. Citation from Reis, "Flip-Flop?" 16.

83. Malherbe, *Paul and the Popular Philosophers*, 118–19; cf. Funke in "Antisthenes bei Paulus"; Desmond, *Cynics*, 106–7.

84. And Socrates is the classic rhetorical "fool" in ironic terms; cf. Welborn, *Paul, the Fool of Christ*, 149–51, 158.

85. Stanford, *Ulysses Theme*; Navia, *Antisthenes of Athens*, 39–52.

Homeric tradition intended remains an open question. But the tradition bears witness to a deep awareness of the moral problems that arose from the prevailing interpretations of the great-hearted sacker of cities as a morally compromised chameleon who expediently disguised his true convictions by mimicking the lifestyle of different people in order to gain victory when he might otherwise risk failure—and thus the place for challenging that interpretation in terms of rhetorical adaptability. Surprisingly, that stands in sharp contrast to the apparently unchallenged tradition of interpreting Paul's language in 1 Cor 9:19–23 in terms of lifestyle adaptability, modified occasionally by the addition of rhetorical adaptability, even though it yields morally reprehensible results for Paul's character, significantly effects the interpretation of other texts, and plays a profound role in larger constructions of Paul, and thus Christianity.

I do not propose Odysseus to be a perfect analogy for Paul. But the tradition for reading Odysseus in terms of *rhetorical* adaptability is suggestive and parallels my own effort to read Paul here, *mutatis mutandis*. It certainly legitimates the direction of this challenge to the prevailing view, which proceeds to read Paul's language here as if self-evidently bearing witness to a variation of *lifestyle*, just as did the prevailing interpretation of Odysseus. Quite unlike the clever "Nobody" of many disguises, I submit that Paul was easily recognizable as somebody Torah-observant and willing to suffer misunderstanding and much more to announce a controversial if not dangerous interpretation of his nation's ruler as the savior of the world. At the same time, and in keeping with the universal aspirations of that message, like one enslaved to ply the wine-dark seas, Paul cleverly turned every phrase in every way he could to make it intelligible to everybody.

CONCLUSION

Since the earliest commentators on Paul, 1 Cor 9:19–23 has been explained in terms of compromising his behavior according to the model of lifestyle adaptability. Central to that interpretation is the overarching concept that Paul no longer expressed covenant faithfulness in terms of Torah observance, but rather taught indifference to and freedom from Torah (i.e., gentileness) [139] as the norm for those who believe in Christ, although he did intermittently pretend to Torah observance in order to evangelize among Jews. A few interpreters recognize rhetorical adaptability as at least a facet of the tactic Paul describes. They draw attention to Paul's motives as noble, and modify the degree to which he would adapt his conduct to facilitate association. Some have even objected to the prevailing view that Paul adopted a gentile ideological view of the value of Torah and its observance. However, these arguments have generally not been developed in detail and primarily appear designed to defend Paul from charges of moral dishonesty arising from the lifestyle model, to which they still fundamentally subscribe.

As demonstrated, 1 Cor 9:19–23 can be understood very differently, with a working hypothesis that Paul was Torah-observant as a matter of covenant fidelity, and known to be halakhically faithful by the audience to which he addressed this text. When approached from this perspective, there is no reason to suppose that his addressees would imagine Paul's language signified *lifestyle* adaptability. Rather, it would immediately be recognized that Paul was explaining his evangelistic tactic of adapting *rhetorically*, a discursive strategy they had witnessed themselves, and one that is also evident in his pastoral approach to them in this letter. A similar interpretation of Paul's tactics can be demonstrated at points in Luke's interpretation of Paul, and it is mirrored in the interpretation of Odysseus by Antisthenes, which was developed among the Cynics and Stoics of Paul's time.

Reading this passage in terms of rhetorical adaptability yields a coherent and productive interpretation. It also significantly impacts the interpretation of critical elements for overall constructions of Paul. It offers many other important benefits too. Reading Paul's text this way eliminates the charges against Paul, at least on the basis of this text, of moral dishonesty, hypocrisy, misrepresentation, trickery, inconsistency, subversion of principles for expedience, and practical shortsightedness, all of which ineluctably result from the traditional and still prevailing interpretations. A thorny obstacle to improving Christian-Jewish relations is thereby removed. At the same time, a different concern is raised. This passage could be used as a warrant and guideline for how to conduct the evangelizing of Jews in addition to other people.

I respectfully hope that, in view of the history of Christian pronouncements about and policies and actions toward Jews (and others), such adaptability will be hermeneutically qualified as unwarranted and unreasonable in evangelistic terms. Jews have had more than enough opportunity to be made aware of Christian propositional truths, including by coercion, and have suffered enough for them. Christianity is no longer Judaism, unlike the case was for Paul. Alternatively, inter-faith dialogue also involves learning the premises and cultural worldview of the other, but for very different reasons. It seeks to understand the other on their own terms, and to successfully explain one's own premises and worldview in cross-culturally intelligible terms in order to advance mutual respect and beneficial relationships going forward. These are goals to which one can hardly object.

[140] Any historical-critical interpretation of this passage implicitly carries ideological freight. The results offered here come with a challenge to several longstanding elements central to the interpretation of Paul and thus Paulinism, including a challenge to important ideological elements in the constructions of Christianity and in its conceptualizations of Jews and Judaism as the "other" by which to ostensibly define superior difference. At the same time, it eliminates elements central to ideological criticisms by non-Christians developed in reaction to these traditional Christian interpretations of Paul. Thus, the implications have the potential to challenge Jewish (mis)perceptions of Christianity as much as Christian (mis)perceptions of Judaism where Paul's voice is concerned, and thereby to advance Christian-Jewish relations. This is perhaps a strange approach to that desirable outcome for a Jewish investigator to support, and should not be understood to express approval of Paul's objectives; nevertheless, I find this to be the most historically probable reading of his text and of the contribution it makes to understanding Paul.

In view of such desirable possibilities, is it wrong to hope that rosy-fingered dawn might rise on a different Pauline tradition in years to come, including new perspectives on Paul and the Jews?

BIBLIOGRAPHY

Antisthenis Fragmenta 51. Edited by Fernanda Decleva Caizzi. Milan: Instituto Editoriale Cisalpino, 1966.

Baltes, Matthias. "Mixed Monotheism? The Areopagos Speech of Paul." In *With Unperfumed Voice: Studies in Plutarch, in Greek Literature, Religion and Philosophy, and in the New Testament Background*, edited by Frederick E. Brenk, 1–25. Stuttgart: Steiner, 2007.

Barclay, John M. G. "'Do We Undermine the Law?': A Study of Romans 14.1—15.6." In *Paul and the Mosaic Law*, rev. ed., edited by James D. G. Dunn, 287–308. Grand Rapids: Eerdmans, 2001.

Barton, Stephen C. "'All Things to All People': Paul and the Law in the Light of 1 Corinthians 9.19–23." In *Paul and the Mosaic Law*, edited by James D. G. Dunn, 271–85. Grand Rapids: Eerdmans, 2001.

Bornkamm, Günther. "The Missionary Stance of Paul in 1 Corinthians 9 and in Acts." In *Studies in Luke-Acts*, edited by Leander E. Keck and J. Louis Martyn, 194–207. Philadelphia: Fortress, 1980.

Bruce, F. F. *The Acts of the Apostles: The Greek Text with Introduction and Commentary*. 3rd rev. and enlarged ed. Grand Rapids: Eerdmans, 1990.

Carson, D. A. "Mystery and Fulfillment: Toward a More Comprehensive Paradigm of Paul's Understanding of the Old and the New." In *Justification and Variegated Nomism: Vol. 2: The Paradoxes of Paul*, edited by D. A. Carson et al., 393–436. Tübingen: Baker Academic, 2004.

Carson, David. "Pauline Inconsistency: Reflections on 1 Corinthians 9.19–23 and Galatians 2.11–14." *Churchman* 100 (1986) 6–45.

Chadwick, Henry. "'All Things to All Men' (1 Cor. IX.22)." *New Testament Studies* 1 (1954–55) 261–75.

———. *The Enigma of St Paul*. London: University of London, Athlone, 1969.

———. "St. Paul and Philo of Alexandria." In *History and Thought of the Early Church*, edited by Henry Chadwick, 286–307. London: Variorum Reprints, 1982.

Cheung, Alex T. *Idol Food in Corinth: Jewish Background and Pauline Legacy*. JSNTSup 176. Sheffield, UK: Sheffield Academic Press, 1999.

Conzelmann, Hans. "The Address of Paul on the Areopagus." In *Studies in Luke-Acts*, edited by Leander E. Keck and J. Louis Martyn, 217–30. Philadelphia: Fortress, 1980.

Crafer, T. W. *The Apocriticus of Macarius Magnes*. Translations of Christian Literature Series 1: Greek Texts. London: SPCK, 1919.

Daube, David. *The New Testament and Rabbinic Judaism*. 1956. Reprint. Peabody, MA: Hendrickson, 1990.

Desmond, William D. *Cynics*. Ancient Philosophies. Berkeley: University of California Press, 2008.

Downing, Francis Gerald. *God with Everything: The Divine in the Discourse of the First Christian Century*. The Social World of Biblical Antiquity, Second Series 2. Sheffield, UK: Sheffield Phoenix, 2008.

Dunn, James D. G. *The Theology of Paul the Apostle*. Grand Rapids: Eerdmans, 1997.

———. "Who Did Paul Think He Was? A Study of Jewish-Christian Identity." *New Testament Studies* 45 (1999) 174–93.

Ellison, H. L. "Paul and the Law— 'All Things to All Men.'" In *Apostolic History and the Gospel: Biblical and Historical Essays Presented to F. F. Bruce on his 60th Birthday*, edited by W. Ward Gasque and Ralph P. Martin, 195–202. Grand Rapids: Eerdmans, 1970.

Eriksson, Anders. *Traditions as Rhetorical Proof: Pauline Argumentation in 1 Corinthians*. CBNT 29. Stockholm: Almqvist & Wiksell, 1998.

Fee, Gordon. *The First Epistle to the Corinthians*. NICNT. Grand Rapids: Eerdmans, 1987.

Fotopoulos, John. *Food Offered to Idols in Roman Corinth: A Social-rhetorical Reconsideration of 1 Corinthians 8:1—11:1*. WUNT 2.151. Tübingen: Mohr Siebeck, 2003.

Fuchs-Kreimer, Nancy. "The 'Essential Heresy': Paul's View of the Law According to Jewish Writers: 1886-1986." Ph.D. diss., Temple University, 1990.

Funke, Hermann. "Antisthenes bei Paulus." *Hermes* 98 (1970) 459–71.

Furnish, Victor Paul. *The Theology of the First Letter to the Corinthians*. New Testament Theology. Cambridge: Cambridge University Press, 1999.

Garland, David E. "The Dispute over Food Sacrificed to Idols (1 Cor 8:1—11:1)." *Perspectives in Religious Studies* 30.2 (2003) 173–97.

Gaston, Lloyd. *Paul and the Torah*. Vancouver: University of British Columbia Press, 1987.

Gill, David W. J. and Conrad H. Gempf, eds. *The Book of Acts in its Graeco-Roman Setting*. Book of Acts in Its First Century Setting. Grand Rapids: Eerdmans, 1994.

Given, Mark Douglas. *Paul's True Rhetoric: Ambiguity, Cunning, and Deception in Greece and Rome*. Emory Studies in Early Christianity 7. Harrisburg, PA: Trinity, 2001.

Glad, Clarence E. "Paul and Adaptability." In *Paul in the Greco-Roman World: A Handbook*, edited by J. Paul Sampley, 17–41. Harrisburg, PA: Trinity, 2003.

———. *Paul and Philodemus: Adaptability in Epicurean and Early Christian Psychagogy.* NovTSup 81. Leiden: Brill, 1995.

Gooch, Paul W. "The Ethics of Accommodation: A Study in Paul," *TynBul* 29 (1978) 93–117.

Gooch, Peter David. *Dangerous Food: 1 Corinthians 8–10 in its Context.* SCJ 5. Waterloo, ON: Wilfrid Laurier University Press, 1993.

Hagner, Donald A. "Paul as a Jewish Believer—According to his Letters." In *Jewish Believers in Jesus: The Early Centuries*, edited by Oskar Skarsaune and Reidar Hvalvik, 97–120. Peabody, MA: Hendrickson, 2007.

Hall, Barbara. "All Things to All People: A Study of 1 Corinthians 9:19–23." In *The Conversation Continues: Studies in Paul & John In Honor of J. Louis Martyn*, edited by Robert T. Fortna and Beverly R. Gaventa, 137–57. Nashville: Abingdon, 1990.

Harkins Paul W., trans. *Saint John Chrysostom: Discourses Against Judaizing Christians.* The Fathers of the Church: A New Translation 68. Washington, DC: Catholic University Press of America, 1979.

Hays, Richard B. *First Corinthians.* Interpretation. Louisville, KY: John Knox, 1997.

Hoffmann, R. Joseph, trans. *Porphyry's Against the Christians: The Literary Remains.* New York: Prometheus, 1994.

Horsley, Richard. *Wisdom and Spiritual Transcendence at Corinth: Studies in First Corinthians.* Eugene, OR: Cascade, 2008.

Jervell, Jacob. *Luke and the People of God: A New Look at Luke-Acts.* Minneapolis: Augsburg, 1972.

———. *The Unknown Paul: Essays on Luke-Acts and Early Christian History.* Minneapolis: Augsburg, 1984.

Johnson Hodge, Caroline. *If Sons, Then Heirs: A Study of Kinship and Ethnicity in the Letters of Paul.* New York: Oxford University Press, 2007.

Kauppi, Lynn Allan. *Foreign but Familiar Gods: Greco-Romans Read Religion in Acts.* Library of New Testament Studies 277. London: T. & T. Clark, 2006.

Klinghoffer, David. *Why the Jews Rejected Jesus: The Turning Point in Western History.* New York: Doubleday, 2005.

Knox, Wilfred L. *St. Paul and the Church of Jerusalem.* Cambridge: Cambridge University Press, 1925.

Lake, Kirsopp. "'Your Own Poets': Note XX." In *The Acts of the Apostles: Part 1, Vol. 5*, edited by Kirsopp Lake and Henry Joel Cadbury, 246–51. The Beginnings of Christianity. London: Macmillan, 1920.

Langton, Daniel R. "The Myth of the 'Traditional View of Paul' and the Role of the Apostle in Modern Jewish-Christian Polemics." *Journal for the Study of the New Testament* 28.1 (2005) 69–104.

Levine, Amy-Jill. *The Misunderstood Jew: The Church and the Scandal of the Jewish Jesus.* New York: HarperSanFranscisco, 2006.

Longenecker, Richard Norman. *Paul, Apostle of Liberty.* New York: Harper & Row, 1964.

Luz, Menahem. "Salam, Meleager!" *Studi italiani di filologia classica* 6 (1988) 222–31.

Maccoby, Hyam. *The Mythmaker: Paul and the Invention of Christianity.* New York: Harper & Row, 1986.

Malherbe, Abraham J. *Paul and the Popular Philosophers.* Minneapolis: Fortress, 1989.

Martin, Dale B. *Slavery as Salvation: The Metaphor of Slavery in Pauline Christianity.* New Haven: Yale University Press, 1990.

Meißner, Stefan. *Die Heimholung des Ketzers: Studien zur jüdischen Auseinandersetzung mit Paulus.* WUNT 2.87. Tübingen: Mohr Siebeck, 1996.

Mitchell, Margaret Mary. *Paul and the Rhetoric of Reconciliation: An Exegetical Investigation of the Language and Composition of 1 Corinthians.* Louisville: Westminster/John Knox, 1992.

———. "Pauline Accommodation and 'Condescension' (συγκατάβασις): 1 Cor 9:19–23 and the History of Influence." In *Paul beyond the Judaism/Hellenism Divide*, edited by Troels Engberg-Pedersen, 197–214. Louisville, KY: Westminster John Knox, 2001.

———. "'A Variable and Many-sorted Man': John Chrysostom's Treatment of Pauline Inconsistency." *Journal of Early Christian Studies* 6.1 (1998) 93–111.

Nanos, Mark D. *The Irony of Galatians: Paul's Letter in First-Century Context.* Minneapolis: Fortress, 2002.

———. *The Mystery of Romans: The Jewish Context of Paul's Letter.* Minneapolis: Fortress, 1996.

———. "The Myth of the 'Law-Free' Paul Standing Between Christians and Jews." *Studies in Christian-Jewish Relations* 4 (2009) 1–21. Online: http://escholarship.bc.edu/scjr/vol4/iss1/4/. (Available in volume 1 of this essay collection.)

———. "Paul and Judaism: Why Not Paul's Judaism?" In *Paul Unbound: Other Perspectives on the Apostle*, edited by Mark Douglas Given, 117–60. Peabody, MA: Hendrickson, 2009. (Available in volume 1 of this essay collection.)

———. "Paul's Reversal of Jews Calling Gentiles 'Dogs' (Philippians 3:2): 1600 Years of an Ideological Tale Wagging an Exegetical Dog?" *Biblical Interpretation* 17 (2009) 448–82. (Available in this volume.)

———. "The Polytheist Identity of the 'Weak,' and Paul's Strategy to 'Gain' Them: A New Reading of 1 Corinthians 8:1—11:1." In *Paul: Jew, Greek, and Roman*, edited by Stanley E. Porter, 179–210. Pauline Studies 5. Leiden: Brill, 2008. (Available in this volume.)

———. "What Was at Stake in Peter's 'Eating with Gentiles' at Antioch?" In *The Galatians Debate: Contemporary Issues in Rhetorical and Historical Interpretation*, edited by Mark D. Nanos, 282–318. Peabody, MA: Hendrickson, 2002. (Available in volume 3 of this essay collection.)

Nasuti, Harry P. "The Woes of the Prophets and the Rights of the Apostle: The Internal Dynamics of 1 Corinthians 9." *Catholic Biblical Quarterly* 50 (1988) 246–64.

Navia, Luis E. *Antisthenes of Athens: Setting the World Aright.* Contributions in Philosophy 80. Westport, CT: Greenwood, 2001.

The Oxford Dictionary of Quotations. Edited by Angela Partington. 4th ed. Oxford: Oxford University Press, 1992.

Räisänen, Heikki. *Paul and the Law.* Philadelphia: Fortress, 1986.

Reis, David. "Flip-Flop?: John Chrysostom's Polytropic Paul." *Journal of Greco-Roman Christianity and Judaism* 4 (2007) 9–31. Online: http://jgrchj.net/volume4/JGRChJ4-1_Reis.pdf.

Richardson, Peter. "Early Christian Sources of an Accommodation Ethic—From Jesus to Paul." *Tyndale Bulletin* 29 (1978) 118–42.

———. "Pauline Inconsistency: 1 Corinthians 9:19–23 and Galatians 2:11–14." *New Testament Studies* 26 (1979): 347–62.

Rostagni, Augusto. "A New Chapter in the History of Rhetoric and Sophistry." In *Rhetoric and Kairos: Essays in History, Theory, and Praxis*, edited by Phillip Sipiora and James S. Baumlin, translated by Phillip Sipiora, 23–48. Albany, NY: State University of New York Press, 2002.

Rudolph, David J. "A Jew to the Jews: Jewish Contours of Pauline Flexibility in 1 Corinthians 9:19–23." Ph.D. thesis, University of Cambridge, 2006.

Sanders, E. P. *Paul, the Law, and the Jewish People*. Philadelphia: Fortress, 1985.

Schaff, Philip, ed. *A Select Library of the Nicene and Post-Nicene Fathers of the Christian Church. First Series. Vol. I.* Buffalo, NY: Christian Literature Publishing Co., 1887

———. *A Select Library of the Nicene and Post-Nicene Fathers of the Christian Church. First Series. Vol. XII. Saint Chrysostom: Homilies on the Epistles of Paul to the Corinthians.* Grand Rapids: Eerdmans, 1978.

Segal, Alan F. "Paul's Religious Experience in the Eyes of Jewish Scholars." In *Israel's God and Rebecca's Children: Christology and Community in Early Judaism and Christianity: Essays in Honor of Larry W. Hurtado and Alan F. Segal*, edited by David B. Capes et al., 321–43. Waco, TX: Baylor University Press, 2007.

Smit, Joop. *'About the Idol Offerings': Rhetoric, Social Context, and Theology of Paul's Discourse in First Corinthians 8:1—11:1*. Contributions to Biblical Exegesis and Theology 27. Leuven: Peeters, 2000.

Stanford, W. B. *The Ulysses Theme: A Study in the Adaptability of a Traditional Hero.* Dallas: Spring, 1992.

Stowers, Stanley K. "Paul on the Use and Abuse of Reason." In *Greeks, Romans, and Christians: Essays in Honor of Abraham J. Malherbe*, edited by David L. Balch et al., 253–86. Minneapolis: Fortress, 1990.

Theissen, Gerd. *The Social Setting of Pauline Christianity: Essays on Corinth.* Translated by John H. Schütz. Philadelphia: Fortress, 1982.

Thiselton, Anthony C. *The First Epistle to the Corinthians: A Commentary on the Greek Text*. NIGTC. Grand Rapids: Eerdmans, 2000.

Tomson, Peter J. *Paul and the Jewish Law: Halakha in the Letters of the Apostle to the Gentiles*. CRINT. Minneapolis: Fortress, 1990.

Trigg, Joseph W. "Augustine/Jerome, Correspondence." In *Biblical Interpretation*, edited by Michael Glazier, 250–95. Message of the Fathers of the Church 9. Wilmington, DE: 1988.

Welborn, L. L. *Paul, the Fool of Christ: A Study of 1 Corinthians 1–4 in the Comic-Philosophic Tradition*. Early Christianity in Context. London: T. & T. Clark, 2005.

Westerholm, Stephen. *Perspectives Old and New on Paul: The "Lutheran" Paul and his Critics.* Grand Rapids: Eerdmans, 2004.

Willis, Wendell Lee. "An Apostolic Apologia? The Form and Function of 1 Corinthians 9." *Journal for the Study of the New Testament* 24 (1985) 33–48.

———. *Idol Meat in Corinth: The Pauline Argument in 1 Corinthians 8 and 10*. SBLDS 68. Chico, CA: Scholars, 1985.

Worman, Nancy Baker. *The Cast of Character: Style in Greek Literature.* 1st ed. Austin: University of Texas Press, 2002.

Wright, Tom. *Paul for Everyone: 1 Corinthians.* London: SPCK, 2003.

Zetterholm, Magnus. "Purity and Anger: Gentiles and Idolatry in Antioch." *Interdisciplinary Journal of Research on Religion* 1 (2005) 1–24.

4

Was Paul a "Liar" for the Gospel?
The Case for a New Interpretation of Paul's "Becoming Everything to Everyone" in 1 Corinthians 9:19–23

> [592] "I have become all things to all people, that I might by all means save some. I do it all for the sake of the gospel so that I may share in its blessings."
>
> 1 Cor 9:22b–23, NRSV

IN SPITE OF THE high moral price required to maintain Paul's explanation that he adapted his conduct to mimic Torah-observance when evangelizing among Jews ("to the Jews, a Jew") and at the same time to engage in "lawless [ἄνομος—*anomos*]" behavior when evangelizing among non-Jews ("to the lawless, lawless"), the interpretative tradition continues to read Paul's strategy to "become everything to everyone" in terms of chameleon-like *conduct* that misrepresents his convictions about how a Christ-follower should otherwise behave. When the compromise of moral integrity this interpretation requires is recognized (it is not always acknowledged or discussed), it is variously rationalized, for example, by being dismissed as less important than the expedient objective of successfully winning everyone to the gospel message.

One of the reasons the interpretive tradition appears to be willing to accept and seek ways to downplay or justify this deceptive behavior is simply the result of the exegetical decision that by referring to how he "became as/like [ἐγενόμην ... ὡς / egenomēn ... hōs]" each group he sought to win to Christ, Paul was describing changes in his *lifestyle*. Interpreters do not mean literally that Paul "became like" them in the sense that actually became them or shared their convictions about the value of such behavior; they mean Paul "became (in outward appearance/in pretense) like" them in the sense of play-acting. In other words, interpreters work from what this phrasing is supposed to connote, not denote. It involves an inherent interpretive move because the words themselves cannot be taken literally to describe Paul's behavior in convictional terms: he cannot become both a Jew and a non-Jew, a law-observer and lawless, and so on.

The connotations drawn relate to a web of other assumptions and conclusions about Paul, and they include among them the widely held view that Paul renounced the observance of Torah as a matter of covenant fidelity, changing his religious affiliation from Judaism to Christianity. Even when [593] described by interpreters less anachronistically—e.g., without reference to "Christianity," and recognizing that Paul described more of a "calling" than a "conversion"—Paul's change of course is not conceptualized or explained *within* Judaism.[1] He is thus assumed to regard Torah-derived behavioral standards with *indifference* as a matter of theological conviction. Paul, therefore, would only behave jewishly to (mis)lead Jews into giving him an audience to proclaim the gospel because it "appeared" to be a message in continuity with Jewish norms (when actually it was not, according to this interpretive trajectory). Otherwise, Paul is assumed by default now to behave according to non-Jewish norms (as if that represented "neither Jew nor Greek," when it instead represents "not Jew, but Greek"), albeit like a non-Jew who believes in Jesus. Paul's new religious affiliation (Paulinism) is understood in essence, then, to be a form of gentilized Christianity, regardless of the specific language used to describe the phenomenon. He and it are set in contrast to Jewish Christianity, and to Judaism in general.

The matters these decisions raise are many. In this essay I can only briefly address the moral imperative to reconsider exegetically whether Paul was describing a strategy involving the way he *behaved* when among Jews or non-Jews, specifically related to Torah-defined behavior or its abandonment, or alternatively, a strategy involving the way that he *argued* with Jews versus with non-Jews, which allows for the understanding that he continued to behave consistent with his convictions, however those might be defined.[2] To make this case, I will first discuss the charge

1. For fuller discussion of this matter, see Nanos, "Paul and Judaism: Why Not Paul's Judaism?"

2. This essay draws on exegetical and other arguments worked out in much more detail in Nanos, "Paul's Relationship to Torah in Light of His Strategy 'to Become

of deception that the interpretation of this text plays in the traditional portrayal of Paul and how it has failed to solve the problems raised; I will then explain the alternative interpretation proposed, and follow with an outline of the benefits this alternative provides in comparison to the problems the prevailing view perpetrates.

My own interest in this topic and the challenge to find a new solution was raised by my working hypothesis that Paul remained Torah-observant as a matter of covenant fidelity. Since he remained a Jew, it logically follows that he would regard his convictions about Jesus to be promoting the ideals of Judaism. My solution does not prove or require that Paul was actually Torah-observant, but it does demonstrate that this text, often cited as if "absolutely [594] incompatible with the theory of an observant Paul,"[3] does not in fact represent the obstacle widely supposed. Regardless of one's assumptions about or convictions on that topic, the interpretation offered here may be appealing to many because it offers a way to exegete this passage without proposing that Paul lived a lie, along with a web of other negative implications that could follow.

The reading proposed has the additional benefit of being useful for advancing Christian-Jewish relations as well as relations between Christians and all non-Christians. At the same time, because the topic deals with defining Paul's strategy for evangelizing, it can be (mis)understood to support the evangelizing of Jews by Christians. The situation today is not an intra-Jewish one, as it was for Paul, involving a change of viewpoint *within* Judaism for those Jews who were convinced by him about the meaning of Jesus as Messiah (a completely Jewish issue!). Instead, the proclamation of Jesus Christ by Christians involves promoting a change of religion for Jews. I hope readers will appreciate that I do not think that is appropriate to promote, and, along with most Jews, I do not support efforts to bring about a change of religious affiliation in the opposite direction. Ideally, we should learn to have mutual respect for each other's decisions as expressions of faithfulness to what each person believes has been revealed for him or her to uphold.

As a Jew, as well as a historian and interpreter of Paul and Christian as well as Jewish origins, I am committed to exegeting this text as well as the rest of the Pauline corpus as accurately as is possible. I want to get Paul (as) right (as I can). Whether the proposed interpretation offers a higher degree of probability, as well as the degree to which it solves what seems to me to be an important challenge to the integrity of Christian prepositional values, is for the reader to decide.

Everything to Everyone' (1 Corinthians 9:19–23)."
   3. Räisänen, *Paul and the Law*, 75 n. 171; cf. 73–76.

THE MORAL CHALLENGE TO THE PREVAILING VIEW

The negative implications of Paul's language in 1 Cor 9:19–23 were immediately recognized by those who did not share the worldview of the Christians who shaped this interpretive tradition. We see these implications spelled out in the late third century by the non-Christian philosopher Porphyry:

> The man who hypocritically pretends to be what he is not makes himself a *liar* in everything that he does. He disguises himself in a mask. He cheats those who are entitled to hear the truth. He assaults [595] the soul's comprehension by various tactics, and like any charlatan he wins the gullible over to his side.
>
> Whoever accepts such principles as a guide for living cannot but be regarded as an enemy of the worst kind—the kind who brings others to submission by *lying* to them, who reaches out to make captives of everyone within earshot with his deceitful ways. And if, therefore, this Paul is a Jew one minute and the next a Roman, [or a student] of the [Jewish] law now, but at another time [an enemy of the law]—if, in short, Paul can be an enemy to each whenever he likes by burglarizing each, then clearly he nullifies the usefulness of each [tradition], for he limits their worthwhile distinctions with his flattery.
>
> We may conclude that [Paul] is a *liar.* He is the adopted brother of everything false, so that it is useless for him to declaim, "I speak the truth in Christ, I do not lie" [Rom. 9.1]; for a man who one day uses the law as his rule and the next day uses the gospel is either a knave or a fool in what he does in the sight of others and even when hidden away by himself.[4]

Christian apologists did not really counter the charges of lying and deception so much as justify the behavior they attributed to Paul as legitimate, since the criticisms were seen to stem from correct inferences about how Paul behaved tactically to win everyone to Christ.[5] Chrysostom even upheld that Paul was justified because he was simply following the way of Jesus himself, thereby logically also portraying Jesus to be guilty of a policy of deception:

> Therefore Paul, in imitating his master, should not be blamed if at one time he was as a Jew, and at another as one not under the Law; or if once he was keeping the Law, but at another time

---

4. Macarius Magnes, *Apocritus* 3.31 (trans. R. Joseph Hoffmann, *Porphyry's Against the Christians*, 60–61; emphasis added).

5. *Apocritus* 3.37 responding to 3.30, and 3.38 responding to 3.31: Crafer, *The Apocriticus of Macarius Magnes*, 101–3.

he was overlooking it; . . . once offering sacrifices and shaving his head, and again anathematizing those who did such things; at one time circumcising, at another casting out circumcision.[6]

[596] Little has changed over the centuries. In contemporary scholarship, Paul's chameleon-like strategic effort to misrepresent his own convictions by way of the behavior he temporarily adopts for evangelical expedience continues to be justified (when not simply avoided), rather than denied or challenged. Endless examples could be provided from every tradition. Consider this representative example from Gordon Fee, who proceeds to dismiss the value of Judaism for Jews as mere religion and even "the greatest of evils," which is concerned with matters such as inconsistency of practicing the convictions one holds to be given from God (which are but "peculiarities")! Moreover, Fee does so at the risk of no longer regarding Paul to be a Jew:

> [W]hen he [Paul] was among Jews he was kosher; when he was among Gentiles he was non-koher—precisely because, as with circumcision, neither mattered to God (cf. 7:19; 8:8). But such conduct tends to matter a great deal to the religious—on either side!—so that inconsistency in such matters ranks among the greatest of evils. Paul's policy quite transcended petty consistency—and "religion" itself. . . . How can a Jew [Paul] determine to "become *like* a Jew"? The obvious answer is, in matters that have to do with Jewish religious peculiarities that Paul as a Christian had long ago given up as essential to a right relationship with God.[7]

Besides questionable decisions about the lexical and exegetical details themselves, the prevailing view raises a host of ethical issues, including ethical misrepresentation of what Paul actually believes by way of his behavior, which include duplicity, inconsistency or hypocrisy, and the privileging of expedience over principle. These hardly make for a sound strategy. Non-Christians can see they are being duped into believing something other than what the gospel is represented to be. This strategy raises justifiable criticism of Christian principles and legitimate suspicion of motives and tactics,

---

6. *Laud. Paul.* 5.6 [SC 300.240], cited in Mitchell, "'A Variable and Many-sorted Man': John Chrysostom's Treatment of Pauline Inconsistency," 107.

7. Fee, *The First Epistle to the Corinthians*, 427–28 (emphasis his). One wonders if similar Christian practices and rites, such as baptism, communion, marriage, and so on, are similarly valued, or is inconsistency of treatment across religious lines so as to privilege one's own according to different standards also upheld as superior and desirable?

including endeavors ostensibly represented as undertaken to encourage mutual respect and good will, such as those involving interfaith dialogue.

[597] Moreover, it raises practical issues, such as whether such a strategy would or even could eventually prove effective. Once we have surveyed the dynamics involved in the prevailing exegetical model and proposed an alternative model, we will return to these topics in a bit more detail to consider how the model proposed answers or avoids them, as well as several other benefits that result.

THE PREVAILING MODEL: *LIFESTYLE* ADAPTABILITY

Since the earliest commentators, Christian interpreters have unanimously understood Paul to be explaining that he temporarily adopts the *lifestyles* of his audiences. Their working model is developed around the idea that Paul *alters his conduct* to *imitate* or *mimic* the way that each of his audiences *lives relative to Jewish halakhic practices* when he is among them. This approach can be classified as *"lifestyle adaptability"* (or *"behavioral adaptability"*). In general, adapting one's lifestyle to fit into the social context of another does not necessitate adopting the *propositional values* of the one whose behavior is imitated. One can mimic behavior outwardly in order to appear to share the inner values of the other, and thus to gain access and trust which might otherwise not be gained. If one adopts the lifestyles of groups with contrary rational (or divine) bases for their very different behavior, such as Paul's language describes for the various referents, this lifestyle by definition cannot represent adopting their propositional values.

According to this model, Paul undertakes this behavior solely to order to win each person or group to the "Christian" gospel's propositional values, which he believes to be superior. As noted, it appears that the justification of this deceptive tactic is self-evident to interpreters who subscribe to, and by way of Paul, promote that ideology. To others, however, it will appear that Paul is aping the various behaviors of others in contrary ways depending upon which group he is among in order to trick everyone in every group into mistakenly believing that the message he proclaims does not subvert the rational bases or convictional values of living in the particular way that each lives. In the case of non-Jews (idolaters or atheists), especially the lawless or weak, this view upholds a Paul who appears to worship their gods, or alternatively, to oppose any gods, although he believes in neither of these propositions. In the case of [598] Jews, when Paul conducts himself like a Jew when among Jews he is "misleading" Jews into thinking that he is a Jew whose message upholds the propositional conviction that Torah-based behavior is enjoined by God, although he no longer shares that conviction. This policy obscures the fact that any Jews who value Torah-observance enough for Paul to adopt it to gain their trust, would be, if they accept his message, becoming members of a community characterized by the renunciation of Torah-faith as inferior, if not also entirely obsolete, although unbeknownst to themselves until afterwards. It follows that if "converted," they too will adopt this chameleon-like expedient behavior thereafter on the same terms, i.e., only in order to trick other Jews. Such a bait-and-switch strategy by definition creates a spiral of duplicity, with long-range deleterious results for their psychological and spiritual as well as social well-being should they remain "Christians" after finding out the truth.

THE PROPOSED MODEL: *RHETORICAL* ADAPTABILITY

I propose a very different way to understand Paul's language. Instead of interpreting his explanation of his strategy in terms of adapting the lifestyles of others, Paul is describing his *argumentative* strategy. He seeks to *argue* for the propositional truth of the gospel beginning from the premises of each kind of person and group among which he finds himself. This approach represents *"rhetorical adaptability,"* that is, varying one's speech to different audiences by reasoning from their premises.[8] The implications for behavior are completely different.

It is far more likely, regardless of how empathetically an instructor relates to the one he or she instructs, and regardless of the highest of motives at work, that he or she will appeal to the *differences in their lifestyles* to exemplify or prove the value of the instruction being offered, rather than adopting the conduct of the student, which would often run contrary to the instructional objective. In other words, if one upholds, as does Paul, "not to associate with anyone who bears the name of brother or sister who is sexually immoral or greedy, or is an idolater, reviler, drunkard, or robber," (1 Cor 5:11), or that those who practice "the works of the flesh, . . . fornication, impurity, licentiousness, idolatry, sorcery, jealously, anger, quarrels, [599] dissensions, factions, envy, drunkenness, carousing, and things like these, . . . will not inherit the kingdom of God" (Gal 5:16–22), then it would be logically unlikely that he would *conduct* himself in such ways in order to

---

8. Cf. Philo, *QG* 4.69. Although Paul's examples of referents for his adaptability here do not indicate rank as a matter of consideration, rhetorical adaptability can include the element of adapting in terms of rank (cf. Sir 32:1–2). For discussion of other interpretive approaches and even models, including a few suggestions of rhetorical adaptability while retaining lifestyle adaptability and thus undermining the insight (e.g., Chrysostom), see Nanos, "Paul's Relationship to Torah," 119–30.

relate his convictions about Christ to non-Christ-followers who so behave! Similarly, would anyone propose that when Jesus eats with prostitutes and tax collectors that this action in some way suggests that he behaved like them to do so, or quite the opposite, that he exemplified a very different way of life, one that welcomed sinners but did not involve sinning similarly in order to do so?[9]

"Rhetorical adaptability" involves seeking to relate to an audience's worldviews and premises in order to persuade them to very different conclusions than they had heretofore likely drawn. This is the way that philosophical argumentation proceeds, as exemplified in the Socratic method. Socrates started from his interlocutor's premises in a way calculated to lead them step by step to conclusions they had not foreseen and might otherwise be unwilling to accept (cf. *Protagoras* 352ff.; *Meno*). According to this model, in 1 Cor 9:19–23 Paul describes his evangelistic tactic of rhetorical adaptability; it did not include the adoption of conduct representing his various audiences' convictional propositions. He could undertake this argumentative tactic as a Jew faithfully observing Torah even when speaking to: (1) lawless Jews; (2) Jews upholding different halakhic standards; and (3) non-Jews holding any kind of convictional and behavioral values. Thus, Paul's behavior can be described as free of the duplicitous conduct that serves as the basis for the charges of moral dishonesty and inconsistency that arise logically from the prevailing views. It is simply the way one expects persuasive speakers to proceed.

THE MODEL OF RHETORICAL ADAPTABILITY AS EXEMPLIFIED IN 1 COR 8–10 AND ACTS 17

Paul's "becoming like" in the sense of "arguing from the premises of" each kind of person can be explained by examining the way that he relates to the "knowledgeable" at Corinth in the argument he makes in chapters 8–10, in which this passage on adaptability arises.[10] Although Paul disagrees with their thinking and approach, he tries to persuade the Corinthians from their own premises. Paul does not eat like them (or how they propose to eat), or [600] behave like them (or how they propose to behave), but his argument is based on their own premises (and proposals), at least at the start. Paul leads them to an entirely different set of conclusions that are in keeping with Scripture, and a different way of living than their own reasoning had led them to suppose followed from the renunciation of idols.

9. Cf. Rudolph, *A Jew to the Jews*.
10. For more detail, see Nanos, "Why the 'Weak' Were Not Christ-believers."

Paul begins his argument by reasoning from the knowledgeable ones' premises that there is only one God and thus that idols are nobodies (8:4-6), and therefore the food offered to them can be eaten as profane (8:8; 10:19, 23, 25-26).[11] He grants this line of argument, however, only in theory—even undermining it in the way it is first stated, for he includes the caveat that *"there are* many gods and many lords" (8:5)—thereafter seeking to lead them to a very different conclusion. He explains that some who believe in these idols will be encouraged to continue to believe in them rather than coming to know what the knowledgeable know (vv. 7-13), and that there are such things as demons represented by these idols (10:19-22). Thus, they are not to eat any food known to be dedicated to idols, just as Jews, who do not believe idols represent gods, are careful not to eat idol food as if profane, but instead flee from anything that is associated with idolatry or pay the price for not doing so (10:1-23). In the end, the only food that can be eaten is food that they do not know to be idol-related; even if they are guests and informed that certain food has been offered to idols previously, they are not to eat it (10:14-33).

In this argument, Paul moves his addressees from non-Jewish premises, since they are not Jews, to very Jewish conclusions, since they are Christ-followers, which represents a Jewish (communal, philosophical, religious, and moral) way of being in the world, even for non-Jews. Note that Paul leads these non-Jews to the same conclusions to which he would lead them if he were addressing Jews, arguing many of the same essential points (God is One; they must love their neighbor; they cannot eat idol food if known to be such; idols represent demons; Scripture teaches these things[12]), and incorporating allusions to Torah, as in the rhetorical question of 10:22: "Or do we provoke the Lord to jealousy?" In this way, Paul has *become like* a non-Jew—rhetorically speaking, that is. If his addressees had been instead Jews, I propose we would have seen Paul appeal directly to Torah to discuss this matter, rather than begin with first principles or consideration of the other's sensibilities, or to the mere example of Israelites. We would have seen him instead becoming like a Jew, rhetorically, which would have been quite natural for him, since he was a Jew.

[601] In addition to the context of the passage in which this language arises, we have an example of Paul engaging in rhetorical adaptability related by his earliest known biographer. In Acts 17:17-31, Luke presents Paul beginning from the premise of his non-Jewish audience by logically

---

11. A full discussion of the identity of the weak and the situation in Corinth is available in Nanos, "The Polytheist Identity of the 'Weak' and Paul's Strategy to 'Gain' Them."

12. Cf. Deut 32:17; Pss 95:5 LXX; 106:37; Isa 65:3, 11.

acknowledging the reality of the gods in which the philosophers and other elites gathered at the Areopagus believed (although he will eventually criticize the effort to make representations of the divine). Like a philosopher *becoming like*, as in *relating to* fellow philosophers, Paul begins by recognizing them to be "very religious."[13]

Paul argues from within their propositional worldview towards declaring that the idol they have designated "To an Unknown God" need no longer remain unknown to them. Paul is described as stating that the Athenians' worship is "without knowledge/ in ignorance" (v. 23); he also refers to the "times of ignorance" that his gospel declaration proposes to bring to an end (v. 30). Paul does not cite any Scriptures; instead, the only explicit citations he incorporates include the inscription to the unknown deity on the altar, and a line from "some of your own poets": "for we also are his offspring" (v. 28).

Luke's example represents the rhetorical strategy of "I became (i.e., reasoned) to the idolaters as [in the manner of] an idolater." Paul related his message to them—inclusive of challenges to their concepts, conclusions, and behavior—from within their own premises in order to gain them to Christ, but he did not in any way *behave* like an idolater to do so!

In contrast to this example of rhetorical adaptability among non-Jews, in the same chapter in vv. 1–3, Luke presents Paul adapting rhetorically to Jews as a Jew. Upon his arrival in Thessalonica, he went first to the synagogue to proclaim his message. As is the case throughout Acts, this action is explained as Paul's "custom." He proceeded to argue with them "from the Scriptures" about the message he bore of Jesus as Messiah, just as one would expect a fellow Jew to do.

In these two almost immediately concurrent examples, we witness the author of Acts describing two cases of variability in terms of the rhetorical adaptability model, one wherein Paul becomes (rhetorically adapted) to (persuade) Greek Jews like a Greek Jew, and another wherein Paul (rhetorically adapted) to (persuade) non-Jewish Greeks as a non-Jewish Greek. In neither case does Paul behave other than according to his own [602] convictional values, thereby avoiding entirely the charge of "lying" that has rightfully beset readings based on the model of lifestyle adaptability.

13. Discussion of the parallel tradition of interpreting Odysseus according to a rhetorical adaptability model in contrast to the lifestyle adaptability model that dominated the tradition is available in Nanos, "Paul's Relationship to Torah," 134–38.

CONCLUSION: COMPARING THE ISSUES AND IMPLICATIONS OF THE TWO MODELS FOR INTERPRETING PAUL'S ADAPTABILITY

The following comparisons are offered in a summary fashion in order to illustrate the issues and implications arising from each interpretive model with respect to Paul's strategy of adapting either his lifestyle or alternatively his rhetoric to seek to persuade everyone about the gospel.

Ethical Issues

Ethical misrepresentation

Ethical misrepresentation arises from the traditional interpretation because Paul is not portrayed as sharing the propositional values upon which the conduct of these various groups is based, but he merely pretends to do so in order to gain their (mistaken) trust that he is like them in ways that he is in fact not. Paul is even seen to mimic behavior that springs from convictions that he diametrically opposes.

Lifestyle Model: In order to win different groups, Paul is represented engaging in conduct that can be variously described as "mimicking," "imitating," "deceiving," "tricking," or "aping" the conduct of the other in Torah-defined terms, e.g., observing Torah among Jews and idol-related activity among non-Jews, but without sharing the others' propositional convictions in either case. That representation of Paul is by definition not Torah-observant consistently or as a matter of conviction; instead, he implicitly if not explicitly shares the propositional values of non-Jews who do not observe Torah, although perhaps for different reasons, as in the case of idolaters. In both the cases of Jews and idolaters, he misrepresents his convictions and those concomitant with the message he delivers to them. Paul is, in short, open to the charge of hypocrisy as well as to being a liar.

Rhetorical Model: Paul is not describing lifestyle adaptability, so his language does not imply any kind of moral behavioral compromise. Rhetorical adaptability can be morally neutral and is to be expected of one seeking to be persuasive in speech. However, because Paul's motive is to bring others to a change [603] of propositional beliefs and concomitant lifestyle changes, it is not a good model for interfaith dialogue today, unless that motive is altered, and mutual effort to understand and respect the worldview of the other participants is also made one's goal. I assume Paul agrees with the propositional bases of Torah-observant Jews, and the motive of covenantal fidelity, regardless of probable interpretive and halakhic differences between each person and group. My understanding of this matter, however, is not required by the rhetorical adaptability model.

Ethical duplicity

Ethical duplicity also arises from the prevailing model because the result of undertaking the course to which Paul seeks to persuade is not evident to the ones being persuaded; thus Paul has masked this implication by his own behavior when among different groups.

Lifestyle Model: On the one hand, non-Jews who are idolaters are not made aware that becoming Christ-believers in response to Paul's message will result in no longer behaving in the manner Paul has appeared to behave, presumably in keeping with his own convictions while among them. Rather, they will find that they must withdraw from idol rites and idol food known to be associated with it, at least when observed by the "weak," regardless of how they are defined. This same consequence can be applied to many different referent categories.

On the other hand, Jews, especially Torah-observant Jews, are not made aware that becoming Christ-believers in response to Paul's message will result in no longer behaving in the manner he has appeared to observe himself when among them. Rather, they will be later taught to value withdrawal from Torah-observance as a way of life, as no longer an appropriate expression of covenant loyalty for Christ-followers. To the degree that Jews who follow Jesus continue to practice Torah "habits," this will represent a "weak" and "immature" expression of faithfulness to Christ (see the usual interpretations of Rom 14–15 on this).[14] The exception for them will be in the case of mimicking other Torah-observant Jews in order also to dupe them in the same way, generating a spiral of duplicity. This whole phenomenon is more reminiscent of a central negative value of the deceiver who is the opposite of godliness, the serpent in the garden misrepresenting the outcome of eating the fruit, a strange parallel for the apostle upheld to be the quintessential model of the truth of the gospel of Christ.

[604] *Rhetorical Model:* No duplicity is involved in arguing from an interlocutor's premises to a conclusion they had not presumably foreseen, and thus no similar moral compromise is involved. One would be led to a new set of perceptions and convictions and concomitant behavior, but that

---

14. For discussion of this phenomenon and an alternative reading, see Nanos, *The Mystery of Romans*, 85–165.

is all part of the conclusion of the argument made, which is understood to be undertaken to move one from a set of convictions to another set.

Ethical inconsistency and hypocrisy

Ethical inconsistency and hypocrisy arise for the prevailing model because Paul is understood to change his behavior as he switches from one group to another, at the same time masking the behavior that would exemplify his own convictions from all of them.

Lifestyle Model: Paul's ostensibly inconsistent or hypocritical behavior is defended to be in the service of a higher cause. Justifying the motives does not remove the problem, however. It does not demonstrate equality or fair play or respect for free will, and it does not result in one recognizing the truth to which one is asked to subscribe. On the one hand, this approach reveals supersessionism and superiority at work, for seeking to justify it in this manner emphasizes that the other is not equally entitled to regard his or her cause as equal if not superior. On the other hand, it does not respect the right of the other to know that one's own cause is being subverted instead of challenged outright, so that a defense can be mounted.

Rhetorical Model: None of these problems result; quite the contrary, each party has an opportunity to understand the message in their own terms, by one who represents in his lifestyle the propositions that the message upholds, and to challenge the arguments, if they so choose, or to proceed to be convinced by them, aware of the cost (to some degree, at least). Often the very different lifestyles of the speaker will be evident, even emphasized as such in order to illustrate the proposition for which one argues, such as Paul regularly does when calling his audiences to imitate him, or Jesus, or the values of the kingdom of God, rather than those of their neighbors, of unbelievers, or of the ways of the flesh.

Expedience versus principle

[605] Lifestyle adaptability raises the additional ethical problem for the prevailing views of making a strategy of putting expedience above principle.

Lifestyle Model: If Paul gives priority to expedience above principle in this matter, it brings up at least two other problems for the assessment of his character in terms of hypocrisy. One is that this contradicts his own insistence for his audiences to put principle above expedience, which include many appeals to himself as an example of that teaching, in spite of suffering as a result of doing so (e.g., 1 Cor 4:10–16; 6:7, 12–20; 8:7–13; 9:1–27;

11:27-34; 15:30-34; 16:13-14). The other involves his accusations against others for putting expedience above principle. This includes accusations of the motives and conduct of third parties when addressing his audiences, e.g., writing about the influencers in Galatia (Gal 1:6-10; 4:17-18; 5:7-12; 6:12-13), and accusations made directly to others, e.g., Peter at Antioch, at least as he reports it to his addressees in Galatia (Gal 2:10-21).[15]

Rhetorical Model: The rhetorical model does not have these problems. Moreover, it actually eliminates problems and discussions about the tensions, if not contradictions between this passage and texts such as Galatians 2.

Tactical and Practical Issues

Level of effectiveness

It is difficult to understand how Paul supposed that this tactic would succeed as it is developed in the prevailing views.

Lifestyle Model: If Paul conducts himself in opposite ways in terms of Torah and other convictional matters in the same community or even when he moves between communities, it would soon become evident to members in each group, whether by observation or rumor, that he was guilty of duplicity. A tactic undertaken for expedience would undermine its own legitimating principle of ends justifying means, because the means would become known and thus reveal the implicit but undisclosed ends. To Torah-observant Jews, Paul would in effect become like the opposite, like a non-Jew, even an idolater. Likewise, in reverse, he would become like a Torah-observant Jew to non-Jews and idolaters. In the same congregation, for those who argue that this is a pastoral as well as evangelistic tactic, the problem is all the greater. Besides alienating rather than attracting interest, it simply would not work.

[606] *Rhetorical Model*: This problem does not arise. Any philosopher or rhetorician should be able to make his or her case in various ways to various people, even when speaking to one group made up of a variety of people. One is arguably less effective and wins less respect if unable to rhetorically adapt.

---

15. See Nanos, "What Was at Stake in Peter's 'Eating with Gentiles' at Antioch?"

Additional practical problems

Problems arise for the prevailing views depending upon how one defines the referents.

Lifestyle Model: As we have seen, to understand Paul becoming a Jew in terms of behavior infers that he does not actually behave like a Jew otherwise, leaving him only with ethnic descent from birth. Some take this view to the next logical stop by suggesting that Paul no longer considered himself a Jew at all. In addition, how could Paul behave lawlessly to the lawless without compromising basic values he otherwise enjoins as essential to those who are affiliated with Jesus Christ? To do so would involve moral decadence. If one takes *anomos* to refer instead to non-Jews in general (a very questionable decision), and thus to idolaters, rather than lawlessness in general or with respect to Torah, the problem remains: How could Paul conduct himself like those who worship the gods of other nations?

The case of relating to the "weak" is even more complicated. If "weak" refers to those whose eating (or not eating) is defined in terms of their sensibilities based on believing that the gods represented are real, in keeping with the beliefs of those conducting those rites, how could Paul actually share those sensibilities? In other words, how could Paul respect those gods or their food as holy, or become ambivalent, insecure, or over-scrupulous?[16]

Rhetorical Model: In the rhetorical model, these problematic questions do not arise. One can explore various identities for the referents, whether Jews or non-Jews observing Torah or not, the lawless or those without the Torah, or the "weak" (or: "impaired") whether they are defined as Christ-followers or non-Christ-followers (as I suggest). Paul can argue beginning from the premises of any person or group, attentive to their convictions and [607] sensibilities without in any way behaving like them; of course, he would behave like those who share his convictions, but he would not behave like those who do not!

BIBLIOGRAPHY

Crafer, T. W. *The Apocriticus of Macarius Magnes*. Translations of Christian Literature Series 1: Greek Texts. London: SPCK, 1919.

Fee, Gordon D. *The First Epistle to the Corinthians*. NICNT. Grand Rapids: Eerdmans, 1987.

Hoffmann, R. Joseph, trans. *Porphyry's Against the Christians: The Literary Remains*. New York: Prometheus, 1994.

---

16. Pace Thiselton, *The First Epistle to the Corinthians*, 705.

Mitchell, Margaret M. "'A Variable and Many-sorted Man': John Chrysostom's Treatment of Pauline Inconsistency." *Journal of Early Christian Studies* 6 (1998) 93–111.

Nanos, Mark D. *The Mystery of Romans: The Jewish Context of Paul's Letter.* Minneapolis: Fortress, 1996.

———. "Paul and Judaism: Why Not Paul's Judaism?" In *Paul Unbound: Other Perspectives on the Apostle*, edited by Mark D. Given, 117–60. Peabody, MA: Hendrickson, 2010. (Available in volume 1 of this essay collection.)

———. "Paul's Relationship to Torah in Light of His Strategy 'to Become Everything to Everyone' (1 Corinthians 9:19–23)." In *Paul and Judaism: Crosscurrents in Pauline Exegesis and the Study of Jewish-Christian Relations*, edited by Didier Pollefeyt and Reimund Bieringer, 106–40. London T. & T. Clark, 2012. (Available in this volume.)

———. "The Polytheist Identity of the 'Weak' and Paul's Strategy to 'Gain' Them: A New Reading of 1 Corinthians 8:1—11:1." In *Paul: Jew, Greek, and Roman*, edited by Stanley E. Porter, 179–210. Pauline Studies 5. Leiden: Brill, 2008. (Available in this volume.)

———. "What Was at Stake in Peter's 'Eating with Gentiles' at Antioch?" In *The Galatians Debate: Contemporary Issues in Rhetorical and Historical Interpretation*, edited by Mark D. Nanos, 282–318. Peabody, MA: Hendrickson, 2002. (Available in volume 3 of this essay collection.)

———. "Why the 'Weak' Were Not Christ-believers." In *Saint Paul and Corinth: 1950 Years Since the Writing of the Epistles to the Corinthians: International Scholarly Conference Proceedings (Corinth, 23-25 September 2007)*, edited by C. J. Belezos, et al., 385–404. Athens: Psichogios, 2009. (Available in this volume.)

Räisänen, Heikki. *Paul and the Law.* Philadelphia: Fortress, 1986.

Rudolph, David J. *A Jew to the Jews: Jewish Contours of Pauline Flexibility in 1 Corinthians 9:19–23.* WUNT 2, 304. Tübingen: Mohr, 2011. (2nd ed., Eugene, OR: Cascade, 2016.)

Thiselton, Anthony C. *The First Epistle to the Corinthians: A Commentary on the Greek Text.* Grand Rapids: Eerdmans, 2000.

PART II

Philippians

5

Paul's Reversal of Jews Calling Gentiles "Dogs" (Philippians 3:2)

1600 Years of an Ideological Tale Wagging an Exegetical Dog?

Phil 3:2–3a:
[449] βλέπτε τοὺς κύνας,   Beware of the dogs;
βλέπτε τοὺς κακοὺς ἐργάτας,   Beware of the evil workers;
βλέπτε τὴν κατατομήν.   Beware of the mutilation.
ἡμεῖς γάρ ἐσμεν ἡ περιτομή   For we are the circumcision . . .

CHRISTIANS I KNOW WOULD not call Jews dogs. Historically, however, that has not been the case, and it is not the case everywhere today.[1] As a Jewish person engaged in Pauline studies, I have discovered that it is not the case in commentaries on Philippians, where in Paul's name Jews are repeatedly called "dogs."

Regardless of intent, the prevailing interpretations perpetuate the notion that Paul's unspecified reference to "dogs"—along with "evil workers" and "the mutilation"—are aimed at Jews and the values of Judaism without denunciation of this language as inappropriate, if not also mistaken.[2] Many

---

1. See Stow, *Jewish Dogs*.

2. Exceptions known to me include Schmithals, *Paul & the Gnostics*, 83–84, who argues that "for the Jews the Gentiles particularly were regarded as dogs," but he finds it "inconceivable" that Paul would use this epithet to "describe strict law-observing Jews" or Jewish Christians of the Jerusalem church—rather it is aimed at Jewish

interpreters would qualify that these apply only [450] to Jews who promote their faith to Christ-believing non-Jews (i.e., "Christians"), and even more specifically, that they refer to Christian Jews who do so. The latter are commonly labeled "Judaizers," because they are imagined to be promoting proselyte conversion. The implicit negative valence of this common labeling technique apparently does not need to be explained to readers, since promoting Jewish values among Christians has been valued negatively in Christian tradition in the strongest terms.[3] Indeed, the perception that Paul is attacking the promotion of conversion into Judaism as entirely unthinkable is so [451] common that it is reflected in the NRSV translation of the

---

Christian gnostics; Grayston, "The Opponents in Philippians 3," 170–72, although he nevertheless understands Paul's concern to be with opposing circumcision, it is gentiles who promote it as an initiation rite based on a "semi-magical belief in ritual blood-shedding"; Ulonska, "Gesetz und Beschneidung," 318–21, does not see how the name-calling that Jews reserved for non-Jews would have been understood by Jews to apply to themselves; instead Paul is applying this to pagans who have been castrated in various orgiastic religions (e.g., Cybele cult), but think of this as comparable to circumcision among Jews, although not with any interest in Torah, but in becoming part of the Agape-cult of Paul's followers; de Vos, *Church and Community Conflicts*, 268 n. 124; Bateman, "Were the Opponents at Philippi Necessarily Jewish?" 54–56, 60–61, tentatively suggests Christian Gentile Judaizers.

3. One preliminary matter of terminology to get out of the way before proceeding concerns the use of the terms "judaizing" and "judaizers" so common in discussions of Philippians, drawing on Cohen, *The Beginnings of Jewishness*, 175–97; Nanos, *The Irony of Galatians*, 115–19; Nanos, "What Was at Stake in Peter's 'Eating with Gentiles' at Antioch?" 306–12.

"Judaizing" in the Greek texts upon which this terminology is based does not refer to something that Jews do, such as Jews who promote the practice of Judaism or conversion. The referent for the verb "to judaize" is non-Jews. It refers reflexively to behavior that a non-Jew undertakes when seeking to become a Jew (a proselyte), or to behave like a Jew. A proselyte is a judaizer, one who has judaized (proselytized). It could perhaps apply to Jews who had abandoned Judaism and returned (in this case actually "re-judaizing"), but otherwise it simply does not properly refer to the actions of Jews toward seeking non-Jewish converts, or to persuading non-Jews to behave more Jewishly.

Moreover, the way this language is commonly used in Pauline studies is objectionable on ideological grounds. It plays to an assumption that the reader shares the writer's (non-Jewish) viewpoint that there is something inherently negative about a Jew (including a Christian Jew or practitioner of Judaism, or even a "judaized" gentile) promoting their faith to someone not Jewish, which does not need to be explained to the reader (hence, at work at an ideological level). Note that at the same time the writer and presumed reader often uphold that there is something desirable about a Christian promoting their faith to someone not Christian, or at least a benign attitude toward such behavior. Christians (like Paul!) are described as missionaries or evangelists, not as missionizing or Christianizing, while (supposed) similarly motivated and behaving Jews are described as judaizing or judaizers, which involves an inherently negative valuation within the grammatical construction, as Shaye Cohen has shown ("izers/izing" endings implicitly carry a negative valence).

third clause: "beware of those who mutilate the flesh!"—even though the Greek does not refer to mutilators but to "mutilation." *The HarperCollins Study Bible* refers the reader to a note "p" that admits the Greek is literally "the mutilation," but in the explanatory footnote, it nevertheless informs the reader that, "*Those who mutilate the flesh* is a harsh rejection of literal circumcision of Christians."[4] In other words, interpreters subscribe to the notion that it is the continued positive valuation of the covenantal norms of Judaism—upholding identity in Jewish terms as an expression of faith, whether Christ-believers or not[5]—that provides the foundation for Paul's polemical language.[6] This understanding of Paul is an essential element of the traditional "Pauline" worldview, in other words, of Paulinism, as normally defined.

This study does not share that point of view on Paul, but that larger issue is not the topic to be addressed here. Under investigation is the interpretive tradition's claim that because Jews commonly referred to gentiles contemptuously as dogs, Paul is simply reversing the invective. Even when other bases for Paul's language are provided, the nature [452] of his rhetoric as retaliatory is apparently supposed to provide sufficient legitimation to persist in this caricature of the Jewish "other" without reservation, hermeneutical distance, or censure being expressed.[7]

---

4. Meeks et al (eds.), *The HarperCollins Study Bible*, 2207. There is also a cross reference made to Gal 5:12, without any explanation. I do not believe that text constitutes a case of analogizing circumcision to mutilation (castration, in particular), but a sarcastic comment that betrays just how profoundly different the two topics are in Paul's thought and vocabulary in order for the polemic to communicate effectively; it also probably conceptualizes the knife slipping to cut the one doing the cutting, the *mohel*, not the one receiving it, the proselyte candidate; see Nanos, *Irony of Galatians*, 204–5.

5. For further explanation of this issue, see Nanos, "How Inter-Christian Approaches to Paul's Rhetoric Can Perpetuate Negative Valuations of Jewishness."

6. E.g., Lightfoot, *St. Paul's Epistle to the Philippians*, 53, reads this as "a stern denunciation of Judaism," and 143, as "much more serious" than "social dissensions actually prevalent among the Philippians" is "the infection of Judaism."

7. This Christian polemical tradition, including its basis in a reversal of accusation, can be traced at least to the comments on 3:2 in *Homily X* of Chrysostom, *Homilies on the Epistle of St. Paul to the Philippians*. I have yet to find a straightforward case undermining these suppositions, but some who take exception to the usual views expressed are noted above. It is universal enough to generalize that every interpreter of Philippians believes this, but a listing of some cases beyond the long list of commentaries includes: Strack and Billerbeck, *Kommentar zum Neuen Testament aus Talmud und Midrasch*, 1.722–24; 3.621–22; Michel, κύων, *TDNT* 3.1101–4; Koester, "The Purpose of the Polemic of a Pauline Fragment," 319 n. 7; Garland, "The Composition and Unity of Philippians," 167 n. 92, 168; DeSilva, "No Confidence in the Flesh," who on p. 34 specifically notes his disagreement with Grayston's objection; Tellbe, *Paul between Synagogue and State*, 259–60; Snyman, "A Rhetorical Analysis of Philippians 3:1–11,"

It will be shown that although this conclusion is doggedly repeated from interpreter to interpreter, it is not confirmed by the texts upon which this supposed reversal would have to be based—a tale that can be traced back at least to Chrysostom (discussed below). For in order for Paul to be reversing this epithet toward Jews, there would have to be evidence that Jews had called gentiles dogs prior to Paul's text. Yet there is no evidence predating Paul that Jews called gentiles dogs. And it is also not used in the later rabbinic tradition to describe gentiles, or Christians, or Christianity, where it would perhaps be understandable (though still not commendable) for a suffering minority community enduring such name-calling and concomitant destructive policies—even that anachronistic evidence does not exist.

CALLING JEWS DOGS

[453] It is important to recognize how often Christian interpreters have called Jews dogs in Paul's name. One finds the following language used by Gerald F. Hawthorne, in the current *Word Biblical Commentary* on Philippians 3:2. It represents concepts at work generally in Philippian commentaries, variously phrased:

> The Jews were in the habit of referring contemptuously to Gentiles as dogs—unclean animals with whom they would not associate if such association could be avoided. . . . Paul now hurls this term of contempt back "on the heads of its authors."[8]

For Hawthorne the implications are unmistakable:

> to Paul the Jews were the real pariahs that defile the holy community, the Christian church, with their erroneous teaching.[9]

---

esp. 267–69.

8. Hawthorne, *Philippians*, 125, who refers the reader to Matt 15:21–28; Michel, *TDNT* 3.1101–4; Str.-B. 1.724–25; 3.62–22, as the basis for this observation.

9. Hawthorne, *Philippians*, 125, who refers to Jewett, "Conflicting Movements in the Early Church as Reflected in Philippians," 386. The reach of this interpretation is evident when it does not even need to be spelled out in scholarly essays about Philippians, but merely stated: cf. Hooker, "Philippians: Phantom Opponents and the Real Source of Conflict," 377, who, when engaged in arguing that there are not real opponents in Philippi in view in ch. 3, but a general warning should such teachers arrive, nevertheless concludes: "In 3:2 Paul issues a peremptory warning against 'the dogs', who were clearly Judaizers of some kind . . . ."

Some recent interpretations which do not otherwise find Christ-believing Jews, or Jews of any kind for that matter, in the context of the implied situation in Philippi (outside of this and some other language in ch. 3, which is equally cryptic, with no clear referent named), instead focus on the Roman political and Greek cultural contexts;

[454] The interpretive tradition represented in Hawthorne's language to describe Jews and Judaism is not confined to Philippian commentaries. Since no later than the fourth century, the dogs interpreted to be Jews in Philippians 3:2 have been conflated in Christian tradition with Matthew 15:26, to communicate "an image of Christian children hungering for the Eucharist, which 'Jewish dogs' incessantly plot to steal, consume, savage, or pollute."[10] Chrysostom put it this way in his homilies on Philippians:

> But whom does he style "dogs"? There were at this place some of those, whom he hints at in all his Epistles, base and contemptible Jews, greedy of vile lucre and fond of power, who, desiring to draw aside many of the faithful, preached both Christianity and Judaism at the same time, corrupting the Gospel. As then they were not easily discernible, therefore he says, "beware of the dogs": the Jews are no longer children; once the Gentiles were called dogs, but now the Jews. Wherefore? because as the Gentiles were strangers both to God and to Christ, even so are these become this now. And he shows forth their shamelessness and violence, and their infinite distance from the relation of children, for that the Gentiles were once called "dogs," hear what the Canaanitish woman says, "Yea, Lord: for even the dogs eat of the crumbs which fall from their masters' table" (Matt. 15:27).[11]

---

nevertheless, on the basis of v. 2, understand Paul to be opposing a group promoting proselyte conversion (circumcision) of Paul's addressees: see e.g., Oakes, *Philippians*, 111–12, 117–18; de Vos, *Community Conflicts*, 263–75; Sandnes, *Belly and Body in the Pauline Epistles*; Heen, "Phil 2:6–11 and Resistance to Local Timocratic Rule"; Ascough, *Paul's Macedonian Associations*, 203–5.

10. Stow, *Jewish Dogs*, xiv–xv; Stow's ideological-critical discussion of the Christian tradition's development of the notion of "Jewish dogs" starts from the consensus view that Paul in Phil 3:2 was referring to "judaizing" Christian-Jews as dogs.

11. *Homilies on the Epistle of St. Paul to the Philippians*, X, in Schaff (ed.), *NPNF First Series*, vol. 13, 230. Chrysostom goes on to ensure that his reader knows that the Jews are not to even have the "advantage" the Canaanite woman's appeal affords to the dogs. Citing Matt 15:27, he writes: "But that they might not have this advantage, since even dogs are at the table, he adds that, whereby he makes them aliens also, saying, 'Beware of the evil workers'; he admirably expressed himself, 'beware of the evil workers' . . . ." See also Chrysostom, "Introductory Discourse 3"; Chrysostom, *Homilies Against the Jews* 1.11.1–2. See also Augustine, *A Treatise Against Two Letters of the Pelagians* ("In Four Books Written to Boniface, Bishop of the Roman Church, in Opposition to Two Letters of the Pelagians, A.D. 420, or a Little Later"), Book III, chapter 22: "For from the place in which he undertook to say these things, he thus began, 'Beware of *dogs*, beware of evil workers, beware of the concision. For we are the circumcision, who serve God in the Spirit,'—or, as some codices have it, 'who serve God the Spirit,' or 'the Spirit of God,'—'and glory in Christ Jesus, and have no confidence in the flesh.' Here it is manifest that he is speaking against the *Jews*, who, observing the law carnally, and going about to establish their own righteousness, were slain by the letter, and not made

[455] Note that the only evidence presented for Jews calling gentiles dogs is from the lips of Jesus in a document that post-dates Paul (an approach followed in some commentaries to this day). And although Chrysostom here is writing of Christ-believing Jews, he elsewhere extends this to all Jews since the continued participation with non-Christian Jews in the synagogues and festivals brought the polluting influence into the church and the Eucharistic meal:

> Tell me, then: How do you Judaizers have the boldness, after dancing with demons [i.e., Jews], to come back to the assembly of the apostles? After you have gone off and shared [bread or ritual] with those who shed the blood of Christ, how is it that you do not shudder to come back and share in his sacred banquet, to partake of his precious blood? Do you not shiver, are you not afraid when you commit such outrages? Have you so little respect for that very banquet? (*Eight Homilies Against the Jews*, 2.3.5).[12]

The perception of Jews as a threat to the sacred institution of the Eucharist eventually developed into an element in accusations of blood libel, resulting in pogroms and the murder of Jews. The fear of pollution extended to Christians in general, the "Body of Christ," so that mere interaction with Jews was to be avoided as corrupting.[13] Even synagogue prayers were maligned as "barking." It is little wonder that in Hitler's Germany (occasionally attested even in the U.S.) signs would read "No Jews or Dogs Allowed," which had not only church history on which [456] to draw but, ostensibly, the New Testament itself. Apparently certain Palestinians and some other Muslims chant to this day, "the Jews are our dogs" ("Al Yahud Kelabna").[14]

For those interested to learn more, the unsavory Christian legacy of calling Jews dogs, and the harmful treatment this legitimated, is traced in Kenneth Stow's 2006 monograph, *Jewish Dogs: An Image and Its Interpreters: Continuity in the Catholic-Jewish Encounter*. Stow does not himself challenge the prevailing interpretation of Paul's language or discuss the modern

---

alive by the Spirit, and gloried in themselves while the apostles and all the children of the promise were glorying in Christ" (P. Schaff [ed.], *NPNF* [trans. B. B. Warfield], vol. 5, 413 [emphasis added]).

12. Citation from Stow, *Jewish Dogs*, 14. The link between the Eucharist and the saying of Matt 7:6 to keep what is holy from the dogs is made as early as Didache 9.5, to articulate an injunction that prohibits the unbaptized from participation.

13. Stow, *Jewish Dogs*, 6–8, 13–36, *passim*.

14. *The New York Sun*, August 22, 2006: Online: http://64.233.167.104/search?q=cache: RrEz_3Th48IJ:www.hsje.org/pdf/'Jews%2520Are%2520Our%2520Dogs%27.pdf+dogs+hitler+jew&hl=en&ct=clnk&cd=30&gl=us&client=safari (accessed March 2007).

commentary tradition and its claim of reversal, but instead draws on Paul and Matthew as if they have been properly interpreted to refer to Jews as dogs. It appears that nothing in his research gave him cause to question the accuracy of the interpretation of the texts or traditions upon which this legacy depends.

Anyone who understands how prejudice and racism is perpetuated, how it is communicated in the slightest gesture or turn of phrase uttered to a child, or even whispered in their presence, will immediately understand how important it is to challenge this interpretive tradition, which otherwise will continue to inform the development of Bible study and church materials produced for every level of readership. In addition to the concern for historical and rhetorical accuracy in the task of interpretation, one should always expect the exegete to exhibit ideological-critical warrant for investigating whether Paul had in view Jews or some expressions of Judaism with the epithet "dogs," and likewise with the other negative monikers he enlists. Although these other epithets are significant and the subject of my research as well, space does not permit detailed discussion of them, or the broader context of Paul's language in the rest of the chapter, including the relevant polemical language in vv. 18–20. My focus here is on the fact that Paul was not engaged in reversing toward Jews an invective supposedly common for Jews to express toward non-Jews, analogizing them to dogs; moreover, it is not probable that Paul has in view Jews in his warning about dogs. This is [457] an epithet that most likely indicated to Paul's audience in Philippi some kind of "pagan" entity or threat.

"DOGS" IN GENERAL POLEMIC

"Dog" or "dogs," and associated epithets and descriptions of dog-like behavior, are so universal in metaphors and polemic that the usage in any given case is itself unremarkable and unlikely to provide specific information about the referent. Appeal to "dogs" and dog-like behavior is employed to make polemic graphic, usually in negative strokes, although sometimes it is used positively too.

In one direction, dogs are portrayed in positive terms, as watch-dogs, shepherd-dogs, hunting hounds, and companions.[15] They have keen senses, tenacity, and legendary loyalty. This characterization can also be used metaphorically for people who function as guardians. Dogs are natural hunters, and can be trained to assist in the hunt, so metaphorically, writes Philo,

---

15. Ancient Greek examples of many of these characterizations are listed in Liddell, et al., *A Greek-English Lexicon*, 1015 (κύων).

the "lover of instruction *tracks out* the sweet breeze which is given forth by justice."[16] Ostensibly negative traits can be turned to positive ends, such as the aspect of scavenging endlessly, which was appreciated in ancient cities as providing street-cleaning services. This feature was apparently also utilized in certain sacrificial rites, in which impurities were soaked up by a dog, which was then removed from the space, carrying away the transferred impurities.[17] At the same time, this [458] characteristic has a negative side, for example, when a corpse is eaten by dogs instead of being properly buried.[18]

Sometimes quintessential positive traits are inverted in polemic. One's loyalty can be degraded as dog-like, meaning, typically, cute, but without proper thought, failing to realize it is inappropriate in this case. When someone says "he is like a dog with a bone," the positive attribute of tenacity and commitment is communicated. But if delivered with or communicating an edge, as if it would actually be appropriate by this point to leave matters alone, then the usefulness is no longer as important as the nuisance the persistence represents. This can take on an additional twist when it is delivered by a party who will eventually be implicated if the dogged behavior persists. It is then actually a good trait being characterized as bad from their concerned perspective,[19] which is evident to the third party hearing the exchange, who is consoled by the hope that this persistence is a guarantee of eventual justice. What one person or group celebrates as a positive trait in dogs can be turned into a negative direction, for example, as discussed below, if Paul was referring negatively to groups whose iconography incorporated dogs, including Silvanus, Diana, Hecate, and Cybele, or those who

---

16. Philo, *Dreams* 1.49 (emphasis added): "for as it is said that those dogs which are calculated for hunting can by exerting their faculty of smell, find out the lurking places of their game at a great distance, being by nature rendered wonderfully acute as to the outward sense of smell; so in the same manner the lover of instruction tracks out the sweet breeze which is given forth by justice . . ." (trans. Yonge). For an ancient source extolling the virtues of hunting dogs, see Phillips and Willcock (eds.), *Xenophon & Arrian, On Hunting (ΚΥΝΗΓΕΤΙΚΟΣ)*.

17. Scholz, *Der Hund in der griechisch-römischen Magie und Religion*, 13; a Hittite purification rite for restoring fertility includes a small black dog which is held above the head of the supplicant, and later apparently taken away and burned (Götze, and Sturtevant, *The Hittite Ritual of Tunnawi*, 5, 11, 17).

18. 1 Kgs 14:10–11; 16:4; 21:19, 24; 22:38; 2 Kgs 9:35–37; Jer 15:3; cf. Michel, *TDNT* 3.1101 n. 2

19. They wish for the tenacious one "to let sleeping dogs lie," to add another metaphorical example here. Metaphor upon metaphor, with both positive and negative implications mixed, exemplify just how commonly this particular language group is employed, and can be mined to communicate even complicated interactions and multiple perspectives.

Paul's Reversal of Jews Calling Gentiles "Dogs" (Philippians 3:2) 119

used dogs as part of their activities, including sacrifices and magical potions, or in the case of the philosophical group known as Cynics (i.e., "dogs").

In the other direction, negative characterizations of dogs and dog-like traits are extremely common in polemic. Dogs are associated with voracious appetites, with eating anything that can be eaten, including human flesh, gluttonous to the point of making themselves sick, and [459] then even eating what they eliminate.[20] They are scavengers. They search out any food left exposed, including that which is involved in sacrificial offerings. This brings up the negative characteristic of dogs defiling that which is holy, as discussed above in the Christian tradition's polemic toward Jews defiling the host. This topic predates Scriptural texts, for it is expressed in an ancient Hittite text that dogs were not permitted near the temple doors because of fear that they will defile the altar and sacrifices: "since a dog approached the table and consumed the daily bread, they 'consume' the table."[21] In Deut 23:18, the wages of dogs are excluded from the temple service, which has been traditionally interpreted to be a euphemistic reference to temple prostitution.[22]

Because dogs parade about naked, defecate, conduct sexual behavior, and generally carry on without regard for human conventions of modesty or prudence, they are characterized to be shameless in terms of the prevailing social terms for proper conduct in human society. Anecdotally, while engaged in research for this paper, I overheard an adult (French-American) woman lamenting the lack of manners common in American culture; for example, the failure to open or hold the door for the elderly or crippled, as well as to offer a seat on public transport to the same, with the following quip: "We are humans, not dogs." Surely this represents no more than the general stereotype of dogs as unaware of proper decorum for humans, that they are, in those terms, impolite, base, expressing the desire to satisfy their own appetites and carnal pleasures without regard for good manners. They are noisy, barking sometimes for what seems to be eternity. And dogs arouse fear by growling, barking, and charging. They can travel in packs that roam the streets or countryside and even the lone watchdog poses a threat to the [460] passerby, a warning not to trespass that strikes fear when the fangs are

---

20. In Prov 26:11, a dog returning to eat its own vomit is used metaphorically for "a fool who repeats his folly."

21. Wright, *The Disposal of Impurity*, 105–6.

22. Thomas, "Kelebh 'dog': Its Origin and Some Usages of It in the Old Testament," in addition to recognizing the possibility of referring to temple prostitution, discusses the possibility that this was a positive reference among Israel's neighbors to priests who served the gods like faithful watchdogs in the temple, and thus were called "the dogs of god" (423–26).

bared, with angry barking and charging motions.[23] They are the stereotypical aggressor in polemic, such as when the Psalmist cries out: "For dogs are all around me; a company of evildoers encircles me" (Ps 21:17 LXX).[24]

In a very real sense, calling someone or group a dog or dogs or referring to dog-like behavior is simply name-calling. It does not make clear precisely who is in view in other definable terms, but functions as a word of reproach, commonly understood without being spelled out. In our case, we may make too much of a general put down when we seek for specificity. Nevertheless, although not the focus of this study, it is a task that must be undertaken by the interpreter of Philippians; thus, some suggestions are offered below.

"DOGS" IN JEWISH LITERATURE PRIOR TO AND AFTER PAUL

To make the argument that Paul is referring to Jews or Judaism or so-called "Judaizers" in 3:2, most commentators appeal to the example of Jesus and the Canaanite woman of Matt 15:21-28; Mark 7:24-30 (Syro-Phoenician), in addition to texts from the Tanakh. One of my first surprises when beginning to research Phil 3:2, was failing to find—before it was attributed to Jesus—the term [461] "dogs" used in any Jewish texts to denounce non-Jews as non-Jews per se, that is, to equate gentileness with doggishness. As you will see, upon examination, I was further surprised to find that it may not be the case with Jesus either, but if it is, he (or the Gospel writer) is apparently the inventor of this rhetorical trope against gentiles.

Some modern commentaries additionally point to several rabbinic texts; more often, actually, reference is made to Strack-Billerbeck's *Kommentar zum Neuen Testament aus Talmud und Midrasch* or Michel's entry

---

23. MacMullen, *Roman Social Relations, 50 B.C. to A.D. 284*, 2, 26–27.

24. Philo, *Moses* 1.130–31: "The remaining punishments are three in number, and they were inflicted by God himself without any agency or ministration of man, each of which I will now proceed to relate as well I can. The first is that which was inflicted by means of that animal which is the boldest in all nature, namely, the dog-fly (*kynomuia*) which those person who invent names have named with great propriety (for they were wise men); combining the name of the appellation of *the most impudent* of all animals, a fly and *a dog*, the one being *the boldest of all terrestrial*, and the other the boldest of all flying, animals. For they approach and run up fearlessly, and if any one drives them away, they still resist and renew their attack, so as never to yield until they are sated with blood and flesh. And so the dog-fly, having derived boldness from both these animals, is a biting and treacherous creature; for it shoots in from a distance with a whizzing sound like an arrow; and when it has reached its mark it sticks very closely with great force" (trans. Yonge; emphasis added).

for κύων in the *Theological Dictionary of the New Testament*. German works of the early twentieth century, which list rabbinic texts, are also supposed to indicate Jews regularly referred to non-Jews as dogs. Not content to let a sleeping dog lie, I checked the rabbinic texts listed and I was again surprised to find yet another tale. How likely is it that Paul was involved in reversing invective if the supposed initial invective against gentiles is without any literary witness? A review of the sources is in order.

"DOGS" IN THE TANAKH

In the case of the Tanakh, the term "dogs" is employed occasionally as a general put-down for rivals of various sorts, for sinners and fools, including fellow Jewish (or better: Israelite) ones (e.g., Deut 23:19; Judg 7:5; 1 Sam 17:43; 2 Sam 3:8; 9:8; 16:9; 2 Kgs 8:13; Pss 22:16; 59:6, 14; Prov 26:11; Isa 56:10–11; also Sir 13:18). In the case of Israelite "dogs," it refers to "other" Israelites, those who do not behave like Israelites should, usually political rivals.

There are actually only a few references to dogs that are typically construed to refer to gentiles from the lists in Strack-Billerbeck, *TDNT*, or in commentaries. In 1 Sam 17:43, a Philistine Goliath snarls ironically, "Am I a dog?" He does so because he is insulted by the appearance of a mere boy sent to battle him, armed only with a stick. It is not his own non-Israeliteness that provokes this ironic bark. The appearance of a mere shepherd boy represents to him an insult to his power as an imposing soldier, against whom one would expect the appearance of the most threatening soldier that Israel could put forth. He is further dishonored by the advancing of this mere youth, David, with [462] but a shepherd's staff (hence, the metaphorical trope of sticks and dogs), not an arsenal to rival his own. This is not a reference to gentiles as dogs. Note that in a slightly later incident, David asks Saul if Saul is chasing "a dead dog," referring to himself (1 Sam 24:15), and further, whether he is after "a single flea." Such language is playfully derogatory, but not associated with gentileness; this case is quite the opposite!

In the same vein, the gentile Hazael of Aram refers to himself as Elisha's "servant," and thus "a mere dog, that he should do this great thing," in response to hearing Elisha's prophecy that he will become the king of Aram, which will lead to horrible destruction for Israelites (2 Kgs 8:7–13). The point is not that he is a gentile but that he is the present King Benhadad's mere servant sent to bring word to the king, not in line to become the king himself.[25]

25. Similarly, Galán, "What is He, the Dog," 175, discusses how the term "dog"

The Psalmist writes: "For dogs are all around me; a company of evildoers encircles me. My hands and feet have shriveled" (Ps 22:16 [LXX 21:17] NRSV). It is common to interpret this text to refer to non-Jews, but that is far from certain (here, or as applied by the Gospel writers to Jesus; cf. Matt 27:39-44; Mark 15:29-32; Luke 23:35-37). This psalm lacks sufficient specificity to identify the opponents. Many psalms focus on rivalries with fellow-Israelites, especially David's rivalries, for example, with Saul (cf. Ps 59; cf. Josephus, *Ant.* 7.207-10) or Absalom (cf. 2 Sam 16:9). Dogs and lions are used to colorfully communicate how savage is the attack upon the Psalmist, not to identify someone specifically as dogs, or lions, for that matter. If not directed at Israelite rivals, at most, it is a political polemic toward the surrounding kingdoms and their armies which threaten his own, but not gentiles or even gentile nations per se. The Psalmist does not call gentiles dogs.

It is interesting to note that in the rabbinic tradition's Midrash on Psalms (*Tehillim*), Ps 22:17 (in comment 26 on Ps 22),[26] this language is interpreted to refer to the story of Esther and the persecution [463] under Haman and his sons. In the following comment on the verse about the hands and feet being made repulsive, they are understood to be guilty of sorcery upon the Psalmist, who is Esther. Although appeal to this midrash in any direction is of course not relevant to the background of Paul's usage, since it post-dates him by centuries, it is nevertheless to be observed that the rabbis did not indulge the opportunity to call gentiles dogs, as commonly supposed. It should also not go without mention that this psalm concludes with a positive expectation that there will be those who seek the Lord from all the nations who will enjoy the Lord's rule. This positive outcome is also reflected later in the Midrash on Ps 22 (comments 29 and following). This psalm does not offer a foundation for interpreting Paul's language in the direction that commentators have claimed.

There are no cases to discuss based on an Accordance[27] search of the usage of "dog(s)" in the Old Testament Pseudepigrapha. Sometimes Enoch 89.42-49 is cited, but it is an allegory with several wild animals representing kingdoms that oppress the sheep, and not a case of gentiles being called dogs because they are not Jews (90.4 does not apply either). Although I have not seen anyone appeal to the Dead Sea Scrolls to legitimate any claims (it was of course not referred to in Strack and Billerbeck or Michel in *TDNT*),

---

when applied to people in Egyptian correspondence and in the Amarna letters was used to stress "someone's status as inferior, sub-ordinate and dependent."

26. To which Strack and Billerbeck, *Kommentar zum Neuen Testament* 1.724-25, refers, to argue that gentiles are equated to dogs.

27. Version 7.1 (Oak Tree Software, Inc.).

a search of an electronic reference library turned up very few references to dogs, and none that could be construed as support.[28] There are no references to gentiles per se as dogs in Philo, or in Josephus.[29] No literary evidence predating Philippians sustains the charge that Paul was engaged in a reversal of invective.

DOGS IN RABBINIC LITERATURE

[464] Some modern commentators have appealed to rabbinic literature to indicate that non-Jews are called dogs in Jewish texts, although this evidence post-dates the usage of Paul and the Gospels, so Paul cannot be supposed to be reversing it.[30] Moreover, if fair-play is invoked, if there were any cases where gentiles were called dogs, these would have to be regarded as potential rejoinders to Christian invective in the first place, and thus would not legitimate Paul's behavior in the way supposed. A brief investigation of the texts listed in Strack and Billerbeck's *Kommentar zum Neuen Testament aus Talmud un Midrasch,* and Michel's article in *Theological Dictionary of the New Testament,* to which interpreters appeal, proves interesting.[31]

Mishnah Nedarim 4.3 does not call non-Jews dogs, in fact, it differentiates between non-Jews and dogs to make its point that one under a vow could either profit in the case under discussion from selling something to non-Jews, or even to use it as dog-food. This represents an exaggerated way to emphasize that one under a vow may do whatever one might wish to do with the carcass of an unclean animal: "For if he wants, lo, he can sell it to gentiles or feed it to dogs" (Neusner trans.). At issue is the productive use of the dead animal: one can either profit from its sale or feed the carcass to

---

28. Tov (ed.), *The Dead Sea Scrolls Electronic Reference Library* 2.

29. Paul's contemporary, Philo (*Laws* 4.91; *Contemp* 40), refers to gluttonous banquet behavior in collegia. In *Free* 89–91, Philo uses dogs metaphorically to refer to hypocritical oppressors to make the point that such had never prevailed against the Essenes, because of their great virtue. In *Gaius* 139, Philo derides the Egyptians for various animal idols, including dogs. Josephus, *Apion* 2.85, writing at the end of the first century CE, does use it once in a derisive way toward his Egyptian accuser, Apion, which includes a slam on Egyptians having dogs among the gods ("unless he had himself had either an ass's heart or a dog's impudence; of such a dog I mean as they worship").

30. Modern commentators refer the reader to Strack and Billerbeck, *Kommentar zum Neuen Testament* 1.724–25; 3.621–22; Michel, *TDNT* 3.1101–4.

31. Occasionally interpreters include the references in Strack and Billerbeck, *Kommentar zum Neuen Testament* 1.722–24 (esp. in notes a–d), which have to do with mention of dogs, but even Strack and Billerbeck does not suggest these references have to do with equating gentiles to dogs.

dogs. Gentiles and dogs are two very different referents and not equated.[32] The dogs are real dogs. The term is not metaphorically applied to humans; real dogs are fed. This aligns with the reward dogs receive according to rabbinic legend: because they protected Israel during the escape from Egypt by not barking at them, the dogs receive food that is forbidden to Israelites to eat. Moreover, [465] even their excrement is honored by being used in the tanning of the hides on which the Torah scrolls are made, as well as phylacteries and Mezuzot.[33]

Likewise, Mishnah Bekorot 5.6 does not call gentiles dogs, but distinguishes between them in a discussion about how payment is to be made when a firstborn animal was sold inappropriately: "[If] they sold it to gentiles or tossed it to the dogs, they return to him the value of the *terefah* [meat, which is cheap, and he repays the difference between what they paid and what they received]" (Neusner trans.). The topic is what to do when meat was sold without proper inspection to ensure that it was unfit to be dedicated and thus available to sell. The argument does not conflate gentiles with dogs, and is not a metaphorical use of this language. Rather, it explains that if the food was not sold to a Jew, but to a non-Jew, and thus cannot be reclaimed with full restitution of payment made (including for the part already eaten, which would be the case for a fellow Jew), the payment is nevertheless to be made to the non-Jew for the balance of the animal that can be repurchased.

Strack and Billerbeck refer to y. Šabbat 9, 11d, 23.[34] The text of y. Šabbat 9 deals with Israelites calling what idolaters refer to as the "Face of God," instead to be the "Face of Dog." Tosefta Avodah Zarah 6.4, explains that places named for idols are to be given negative epithets; hence, "what is named Face of the Goddess [*pny 'lh*] is called Face of the Dog [*pny klv*]."[35] This is but one of several examples discussed to explain what it means in practice

---

32. *Contra* Garland, "Composition and Unity of Philippians," 167 n. 92: "The two are thus almost synonymous," which he also writes about m. Bek., discussed below; *contra* Bockmuehl, *The Epistle to the Philippians*, 186, who says it is metaphorically applied here to "pagans, who also did not know how to distinguish between pure and impure, sacred and profane."

33. Ginzberg (ed.), *The Legends of the Jews*, 3.6 and n. 4 (in 6.1, he cites Mekilta Mishpatim 20, 98a [cf. Mekilta de R. Ishmael Exod. 22:30–31 (Kaspa 2)]; Shem. Rab. 31.9 [cf. Exod. Rab. 31,9]; Tg. Yer. Exod. 22.30 [cf. Tg. Ps.-J.: Exod. 22:30]); see also Deut. 14:21; Tg. Ps.-J.: Exod. 11:7; Tg. Onq. to Exod. 11:7. Note that Tg. Neof. 1: Exod. 22:30, however, negatively compares gentiles to dogs in the sense that unlike Israelites, they can eat the flesh torn from a living animal, as can dogs.

34. 11d=9 in a different edition; I did not locate 23.

35. See also 3.6; Tanḥ. Tem. 6, refers to where it is called "Face of Molech," it should be called the derogatory term instead, "Face of a Dog."

to detest idols. It is not a reference to gentiles as dogs, but to their idols, or to a specific idol. It is possible that the real-life example involved a god or goddess associated with [466] dogs, such as the Egyptian jackal-headed god Anibus, for example, or the dogs on Assyrian-Babylonian monuments who accompanied the Sun-god Merodach,[36] or the goddess Hekate (Trivia), to whom idols were constructed and sacrifices commonly made at three-way intersections, and one of the three heads of the goddess, which were on three poles, was sometimes a portrayal of the head of a dog.

After surveying the Mishnaic and Talmudic texts mentioned in Strack and Billerbeck and Michel in *TDNT*, and by an Accordance search of the Mishnah, I find no texts that refer to gentiles as dogs, or that can be understood to do so. One interesting case to note is that the obstinacy of dogs is a characteristic used *positively* to distinguish Israel among the nations, that is, *that Israelites are like dogs*. In b. Beṣah 25b,[37] in a discussion of why the Torah was given to Israel rather than the other nations, R. Simeon b. Lakish explained: "There are three distinguished in strength [fierce]: Israel among the nations [footnoted: 'but the Law tempers their strength'], the dog among animals, [and] the cock among birds."[38] Ironically, there is no corresponding negative example equating gentiles with dogs. In this case, the gentile nations are decidedly *un*like dogs![39]

Let us consider even later rabbinic texts to which reference is made in Strack and Billerbeck. In the case of Tanḥuma Terumah 3, on Exodus 25.2, Akiba relates a dream to Tinneius Rufus, the Roman governor of Judea at the start of the Bar Kokba Revolt, wherein he named his dogs Rufus and Rufina. This insult is directed toward a political foe, if indeed also a non-Jew or a non-Judean, to keep salient the political context of the slur.[40] It is not a general equation of gentiles or even gentile rulers per se as dogs. Contrary to the comments in Strack and Billerbeck, [467] Midrash on Psalms, Psalm 4 (comment 11), does not equate gentiles with dogs.[41] It refers to fellow Israelites who are so wicked and greedy in their prosperity that they are lik-

---

36. Ginzberg (ed.), *Legends of the Jews* 4.275 and n. 82 (in 6.368).

37. Noted by Strack and Billerbeck, *Kommentar zum Neuen Testament* 1.723, repeated in Michel, *TDNT* 3.1101–2.

38. Ginsberg (ed.), *Hebrew-English Edition of The Babylonian Talmud, Seder Mo'ed, Bezah*.

39. In another case, Israel is metaphorically represented by the "unfortunate dog," in that Moab and Midian team up to destroy their enemy Israel like a weasel and cat team up to destroy their enemy the dog (Ginzberg [ed.], *Legends of the Jews* 3.353–54 and n. 721 [in 6.123]).

40. Strack and Billerbeck, *Kommentar zum Neuen Testament* 1.725.

41. Ibid., 1.724–25.

ened to dogs who eat well in the parable of the king's banquet. The midrash does so in order to signify how much more abundant the banquet that God makes for the blessed of Israel will be in the age to come.

This political kind of usage is also the context for many of the other rabbinic texts noted in Strack and Billerbeck, including Leviticus Rabbah 33.6. These do not equate gentiles with dogs, but constitute put downs of royal figures. Note also that Genesis Rabbah 81.3, is not about gentiles, but a Samaritan. The only text I have found in some way equating gentiles with dogs is in an edition of the medieval Pirqe Rabbi Eliezer 29, where eating with the uncircumcised *slave* in the house of Israel is likened theoretically to eating with a dog which also has not had the foreskin circumcised.[42] It is not present in all editions.[43] The example is part of a discussion of why the Abrahamic covenant called for slaves of his house to also be circumcised, since unlike proselytes, who choose in freewill to be circumcised, slaves are compelled to be, and are thus not regarded in this argument to be true converts. Even in this case, it is neither gentiles, nor Christians that are named, but gentile slaves in a theoretical sense. This text is obviously far too old (after the founding of Islam) to be used as background for Paul, representing centuries of suffering under Christians calling the circumcised Jews dogs who defile, with whom Christians were thus prohibited from eating.

In sum, it is exegetically mistaken, as far as the sources that have been referred to by commentaries to date, or on the basis of the searches I have been able to conduct, to continue to approach Phil 3:2 claiming that Paul is turning a well-known and common Jewish slur of gentiles on its head so that it refers to Jews. There are certainly no [468] grounds in Jewish literature for the interpretive tradition to conclude with Michel that the term dogs is "a *common* term to express *Jewish* contempt for other peoples"![44] The usage of dogs is multifaceted in rabbinic literature, just as it is in general, with both positive and negative examples. When we deal with metaphors, we need to be cautious about making too much out of any image that is used in a particular way, as if it is considered intrinsically so, and limited to only that meaning.

---

42. Börner-Klein, *Pirke de-Rabbi Elieser*, 322–23.

43. According to Friedlander, *Pirke de Rabbi Eliezer*, 208, the Vienna manuscript of the twelfth to thirteenth century reads: "as though he were eating flesh of abomination," and does not have the next sentence with the reference to dogs.

44. Quoting from Michel, *TDNT* 3.1103 n. 11, where he attributes this language to Lohmeyer, *Kommentarz. Apokalypse*, 177 (by which he presumably refers to *Offenbarung des Johannes*) (emphasis added), in other words, in comments on the NT book of Revelation.

Thus, contrary to the claim of Markus Bockmuehl in his recent commentary on Philippians, that the "Jewish background, then, offers a clue to Paul's usage," it does *not* do so.[45] Paul does not "attack . . . those who, from the imagined superiority of their Jewish status and practice, reject fellowship with Gentile Christians whose indifference to the purity laws makes them like dogs." It is not the case that "[f]rom this perspective, the Gentiles cannot become part of the people of God without converting to Judaism: only full Jews can be full Christians; others are 'dogs.'" If this is what Paul meant, it will have to be determined apart from his language about dogs.

Ostensibly, it is in a saying attributed to Jesus that dogs first arises as a negative reference to non-Jews, in other words, gentiles as gentiles per se (Matt 15:21–28; Mark 7:24–30).[46] Since it has been shown that there is no evidence Jews called gentiles dogs before Jesus, which interpreters of the Gospels as well as Paul have consistently claimed, assuming that Jesus was simply repeating a common prejudice (and [469] often not reflecting on the implication that Jesus would engage in such an endeavor anyway) this logically makes Jesus, or the Gospel writer, the inventor of this polemical development. Or does it?

"DOGS" IN JESUS' ENGAGEMENT WITH THE CANAANITE (OR SYRO-PHOENICIAN) WOMAN

Although this text represents language written after Paul's letter, as we have seen, it has repeatedly been employed by interpreters to indicate Jewish attitudes and language predating it. An appeal to this incident in the Gospels alone to make the case must presume not only that the language of Jesus recorded in the Gospels predates Paul's usage here, but that Paul was aware of it, and that so too were his addressees in Philippi.[47] Disregarding these

---

45. Bockmuehl, *Philippians*, 186, and for the following citations.

46. An exemplary case of this common view is witnessed in the note to 15:22 in the HarperCollins Study Bible (1993 version): "*Canaanite*, a scriptural term for ancient Israel's pagan enemies (see, e.g., Deut. 7.1; cf. Mk. 7.26) here used to designate a Gentile" (p. 1886).

Matt 7:6, when stating, "Do not give what is holy to dogs," is likely based on the notion not to distribute sacrificial food improperly, including not to seek to profit from an animal dedicated to the priests, perhaps also not to use the carcass to feed the dogs, that is, to eschew all utilitarian purposes for that which is set apart. In its context, it seems to be about intra-communal behavior (how to treat neighbors), not directed toward non-Israelites in particular, perhaps not at all, if Jesus is understood to be involved at this point entirely in an intra-Jewish context.

47. Jewett, "Conflicting Movements," 382–87, adopts the usual view, nevertheless perceptively observes: "How would the Gentile Philippians know that the Jews used

historical problems, not least that the Philippians would not have these Gospels from which to interpret Paul's language,[48] let us investigate whether this case can support the weight it is required to bear in Pauline scholarship.

According to Matthew, when Jesus was in ("withdrew to" or "retired to") the district of Tyre and Sidon, on the border of the ancient Israelite northern tribal territory, a Canaanite women seeking relief from a demon for her daughter hounded them, shouting at Jesus for mercy, hailing him as "Lord, son of David" (Matt 15:21–28; Mark 7:24–30).[49] This declaration suggests respect for Judahide dynastic aspirations in a way that Canaanites, and arguably, some Israelites of the Northern tribes since the divided kingdom days, would be stereotypically expected to [470] instead deny.[50] Jesus is portrayed as ignoring her: he "did not answer her at all." When the disciples urged Jesus to send her away, he responded to them, not to her directly, with the enigmatic phrase that he was "sent only to the lost sheep of the house of Israel."

This case is thus also set in a particular political context, and not a general Jews/gentiles one, as supposed by those who point to it as support for the claim that Paul is reversing a Jewish practice of calling gentiles dogs. In fact, Jesus' response may suggest an intra-Jewish (among and between Israelites and Judahites) context rather than a Jewish/non-Jewish (or Judean/non-Judean) one. Jesus is specifically concerned with the lost sheep of the house of Israel, which may well refer to members of the Northern tribes. They had been deported or intermixed with other peoples by the Assyrians in the eighth century and might be expected to populate the area to which Jesus is depicted here as withdrawing, regardless of how indistinguishable from other people in the area they might be after these many centuries. The question is, is she entitled to reap what Jesus intends to sow among the lost Northern tribes?

Jesus' response would seem to suggest an opening for her approach, rather than rejection, although expressed indirectly. It perhaps plays to the chance that she is a descendent of those from the Northern tribes who

---

'dog' to refer to 'foreigners' and that this is the connotation here?" (385).

48. The reach of the consensus view is exposed when, in the opposite direction, Tagawa, *Miracles et Évangile*, 118–19, argues circularly that one cannot be certain that dogs refers to non-Jews except by the context (noting in Mark that the woman is called a Greek specifically) because in Phil. 3:2 one sees it applied to Jewish Christians.

49. The variations between Mark and Matthew, or the probable textual histories of either, do not require discussion for the matters under review here.

50. Cf. Horsley, *Archaeology, History, and Society in Galilee*. On the other hand, many Judeans had settled in the northern areas during the Hasmonean period, so the dynamics of the intra-communal tensions are not clear; see Chancey, *The Myth of a Gentile Galilee*.

suffered deportation, or descended from intermarriage with those the Assyrians sent to repopulate the area some 700+ years earlier. Rhetorical polemic toward those from the Northern tribal areas (or toward those who in various ways claimed to be the true Israelites or Judahides, depending upon the context) has a long history (see Ezra-Nehemiah). So too do appeals to legitimate ancestry for members of the "lost" tribes (Tobit). Intra-Jewish rhetoric even takes place between Judeans who accuse the other party of being like Ephraim (i.e., the "rebellious" Northern tribes). Apparently the Dead Sea Scrolls sectarians [471] referred to the Pharisees as Ephraim because of their "false teachings" (4QpNah. 3–4 ii 8).[51] These are just the kinds of tensions with which interpreters expect the authors of the Gospels to have been concerned in their post-temple context.

The Canaanite woman insists on Jesus' help, kneeling and pleading with him. Jesus responds (although it is not clear whether it is to her directly or to the disciples within her hearing) with a metaphor (unattested before this case):[52] "It is not fair to take the children's food and throw it to the dogs." Her rejoinder cleverly accepts the insult to being metaphorically categorized as a dog,[53] to make the point that "even dogs eat the crumbs that fall from their master's table," which gains Jesus' approval.[54]

Her reply accepts that she does not have equal status, but appeals for treatment as a welcome guest. Jesus' challenge appears to be based on a zero-sum game, that is, if the food is fed to the dogs, there will not be enough to feed the children (and likely, with echoes of giving set-apart [472] [priestly] food to those who are not priests; cf. Matt 7:6). If we stay

---

51. See Goranson, "Others and Intra-Jewish Polemic as Reflected in Qumran Texts," 542–43.

52. From Euripides, *Phoenician Women* (Euripides, *Phoenissae* [E. P. Coleridge (ed.)] line 1650): "*Creon:* Isn't it right for that other to be given to the dogs?" (3.10); note that the context concerns Phoenician women.

53. In the early twentieth century, Israel Abrahams, a Jewish interpreter, disputed the Gospel commentary tradition's continued assertion, when explaining this verse, "that the Jews habitually called the heathens 'dogs,'" and he discussed some of the texts to which an appeal has been made (*Studies in Pharisaism and the Gospels*, 2.195); cf. Luz, *Matthew: A Commentary: 8–20*, 341 n. 62.

54. Dogs eating from the table scraps is attested as a literary trope, although not the twist that she puts on it regarding children; see Luz, *Matthew 8–20*, 340 n. 59, and the references listed there, although above I take issue with his reading of the rabbinic examples he includes from Strack and Billerbeck, *Kommentar zum Neuen Testament* 1.724–26, which do not predate this case anyway. Philostratus, *Life of Apollonius* 1.19, scoffs at one who has gathered sayings from his teacher as reminding him "of dogs who pick up and eat the fragments which fall from a feast"; Athenaeus, *Deipnosophists* 3.96f–97a: "'it is the custom to throw the remnants [λείψαν] to the dogs [χυσίν {sic}],' as Euripides has said in *The Women of Crete*" (Loeb, transl. Gulick).

within the shepherd metaphor—since diminutive κυνάρια is used, implying pet dogs, rather than wild, threatening dogs—then perhaps the idea of the family's shepherd dogs is involved.[55] They are fed, but not the food intended for the family. Her rejoinder evokes the generous feeling the family would have nevertheless toward their dogs in the event that they hung around the table and scavenged some scraps. Might this imply that the woman counts herself (or Jesus or the Gospel writer see her) in some way to be within the orbit of Israel's (and thus Judah's) self-concern? The message Matthew seeks to communicate may be that the nations who turn to Israel's God are to recognize that they do so as those who are under the reign of Israel's king (or is it more salient that it is Judah's king?) as ruler of the world. Perhaps she is alluding to the Israelite concept of leaving a portion of the field available for the alien (Lev 19:9–10; Deut 24:19–22; Ruth 2). This non-Israelite woman could serve as a type: she is represented as specifically interrupting Jesus' ministry to the lost from among the Northern tribes, being one who lived in the area that should instead belong to these Israelites, nevertheless seeking mercy from one whom she recognized as the awaited king from the house of David, who should be expected to be concerned for others within Israel's social world.

By way of this metaphor the Canaanite woman accepts either the lower standing of being one of the "lost" children of the Northern tribes of Israel, albeit one without a provable claim to that identity, or perhaps even lower standing, that she is not of the house of Israel at all. Rather, she is a despised Canaanite to whom Jesus has not in any way sought to come, one who wrongfully lives in the land that is not rightfully hers, and thus depletes the resources that should belong to Israelites.[56] Might [473] she be appealing to a Judean manifest destiny in order to challenge Northern Israelite aspirations that confront her where she lives? Canaanites are in the land that Israel claims for herself (here as represented by the Jesus-believing author of the Gospel), perhaps in the context of a rivalry within the land of Northern Israel over who has the right to the blessings of the awaited Davidic king's rule.[57] In a different direction, might her reply be an appeal to be regarded as

---

55. Also in Mark 7:27, the diminutive κυνάρια is used. Luz, *Matthew 8–20*, 340, observes that this refers to household pet dogs, but some have disputed that this can be inferred from the usage of diminutives by this period. The idea of shepherd dogs, which D. Stramara, Jr., raised in conversation, is more in keeping with the metaphorical language. M. Ḥallah 1.8, indicates that there is a dough associated with shepherd-dogs.

56. Somewhat similarly, Downing, "The Woman from Syrophoenicia, and her Doggedness," 138, observes that this may be the connection between a request for exorcism and a reply about food.

57. Similarly, see chapter 8 in Willitts, "Matthew's Messianic Shepherd-King."

a *ger* or "stranger within the gates," thereby entitled to the blessings of being a part of the family of Israel in a kind of guest status?

What I hope to have demonstrated is that it is not clear that gentiles per se are analogized with dogs in this metaphor. She is a Canaanite, a perhaps affectionately appreciated, or alternatively, especially despised neighbor who looks to a future Davidic dynasty, and also one who is a woman.[58] The context of this language appears to be political and specific.[59] It does not likely represent a generalized degradation of gentiles per se as dogs,[60] which further undermines the commentary traditions' legitimation of Paul calling Jews dogs as a reversal of a common Jewish prejudice expressed toward gentiles by Jesus, by pointing to this text.

[474] If I am judged nevertheless to be mistaken and this text is determined to be a case in which the epithet dogs is used by a Jew (Jesus) to negatively value a non-Jew, it should be recognized that it is the first attested case, likely post-dates Paul's letter, and expresses the viewpoint of a writer from a specific Jewish group, the early Christ-believers.[61] And it should be observed that it is not on just any Jewish lips, but from Jesus alone (by way of the Gospel writers) that "dogs" is used in this derogatory manner toward this non-Jew or (perhaps better) non-Israelite, or potential descendant of the so-called lost Northern tribes.[62]

---

58. That the choice of metaphor depends instead on her being a woman cannot be dismissed either: Sir. 26:25 derisively states: "A headstrong wife is regarded as a dog, but one who has a sense of shame will fear the Lord."

59. In sympathy with the suggestion of Cynics for Paul's usage below, see the proposal for a Cynic *topos* here, in Downing, "The Woman from Syrophoenicia," 140-49, who suggests that she is acting the part of a Cynic, and that Chrysostom's comments indicate that he was aware of this at play (145-46; Chrysostom, *Homilies on Matthew* 52 [PG LVIII, 521-22]; 23 [PG LVII, 306-8]). The reputation of Cynics for hanging around the symposia for food is suggestive (see Athenaeus, *Deipnosophistae* 3.96-97; 6.246).

60. Interpreting this to indicate gentiles in general is attested since Tertullian, *Adversus Marcionem* 4.7.5; *De Fuga* 6.3; Pseudo-Clementine, *Homilies* 2.19-20 (PG XI, 87-88); *Recognitions* 7.32; Ibid., 144-46.

61. If this represents a later addition, as some exegetes argue it to be, then it may express the projection of a negative "Christian" caricature of Jewish views developed to demonstrate "Christian" superiority. It is notable that at the end of his essay on "dogs," Michel wants to clarify that Jesus and the NT authors' use of this kind of language for reproach "differs plainly from later Jewish usage" (*TDNT* 3.1104), although it is not clear to me on what basis he claims this, in view of the rabbinic material discussed above.

62. The Jewishness of Jesus' identity and its nationalism (particularism) is often clearly recognized for commentators in this case, while, in other cases, when Jesus is depicted as generous, his behavior is interpreted to be specifically representative of superior "Christian" values, such as universalism. Supposed universalism is even

ALTERNATIVE INTERPRETATIONS FOR PAUL'S EPITHET "DOGS"

[475] Efforts to offer alternatives for Paul's reference to dogs have not been made to date, since interpreters have universally understood Paul to have been engaged in a reversal of specifically Jewish rhetoric, combined with the prevailing idea that Paul denounced the value of Jewish identity and behavior in the verses that follow.[63] The extent of this tendency is witnessed by the fact that the *Hellenistic Commentary to the New Testament* does not list any suggestions for salient primary texts to consult for parallels to the language or message of 3:2, that is, for "dogs," "evil workers," or "the mutilation," or for the various referents that arise in vv. 18–19 either.[64] In this essay I can only point to some of the relevant options that are the subject of my current research.

The possibilities for the referents for Paul's epithet dogs (and the other referents throughout chapter 3) in Philippi are numerous. They include various cult figures such as Silvanus, Diana, Cerberus, Hekate, and Cybele, gods and goddesses associated with dogs, and variously with some of the other attributes that Paul negatively characterizes. For example, Silvanus and Diana were portrayed accompanied by dogs in the reliefs carved into the hills overlooking Philippi.[65] Hekate, a goddess involved in conduct-

---

imported here, by way of the exception Jesus is understood to make, adumbrating that gentiles will believe after the Jews reject him. This trend is evident from early commentators, e.g., in Epiphanius, *Interpretation of the Gospels* 58, when commenting on the Canaanite woman's reply: "you came to the Jews and manifested yourself to them, and they didn't want you to make exceptions. What they rejected, give to us who are asking for it" (from Simonetti [ed.], *Matthew 14–28*, 29. See also Burkill, "The Historical Development of the Story of the Syrophoenician Woman").

The way that this is often interpreted suggests that Jews (including Christ-believing Jews) operate from an exclusivistic framework that negatively values non-Jews metaphorically as dogs, while suggesting that Christian inclusiveness would not be guilty of this kind of prejudice, except to turn the rhetoric upside-down in self-defense, or by Jewish-Christians, who are regularly maligned for failing to dismiss the value of Jewishness, thus betraying such lingering negative characteristics in their portrayals of Jesus. For my discussion of the unintended failure of intra-Christian scenarios to avoid implicit negative valuations of Judaism in the way NT interpreters often suppose, see Nanos, "How Inter-Christian Approaches to Paul's Rhetoric," 255–69.

63. The few who take exception to the referent for dogs as Jews are listed above.

64. Boring et al. (eds.), *Hellenistic Commentary to the New Testament*, e.g., a useful volume, which "might be thought of as a 'Hellenistic Strack-Billerbeck'" (p. 12). For the mutilated as other than Jews, an alternative is offered by Ulonska, "Gesetz und Beschneidung." It is common for commentators to explore options for vv. 18–19, wherein libertines, gnostics, and others are the subject of various studies.

65. Abrahamsen, *Women and Worship at Philippi*, 25–26; Dorcey, *The Cult of*

ing the dead to Hades, in helping or alternately hindering successful child-bearing and rearing, and often invoked in the practice of magic, an "evil worker" par excellence, was often pictured not only accompanied by dogs, but she (or one of her three heads, or feet) was sometimes portrayed as a dog, and dog-meat was an important ingredient in the "Suppers" offered to her. The cult of Cybele was [476] notorious for its orgiastic rituals and the mutilation of its initiates, who castrated themselves, behaving shamefully like dogs, from Paul's cultural point of view, so that not only would reference to "evil workers" be salient, but especially so would be his negative reference to "the mutilation."

In a different direction, philosophical groups often call each other dogs. Most importantly, the Cynics were philosophers who were literally called "Dogs [κύων; ὁ Κυνικός]," and who aspired to the highest level of doggishness as a matter of honor![66] The connection was made explicit by Philo:

> For instance, the name of dog is beyond all question a homonymy, inasmuch as it comprehends many dissimilar things which are signified by that appellation. For there is a terrestrial barking animal called a dog; there is also a marine monster with the same name; there is also the star in heaven, which the poets call the autumnal star, because it rises at the beginning of autumn, for the sake of ripening the fruits and bringing them to perfection. *Moreover, there were the philosophers who came from the cynic school.* Aristippus and Diogenes; and other [sic] too who chose to practise the same mode of life, an incalculable number of men.[67]

In the second century CE, the church father Clement of Alexandria observed that when debating pagans it was necessary to define terms, for example, to clarify "Whether a dog were an animal? For I might have rightly said, Of what dog do you speak? For I shall speak of the land dog and the sea dog, and the constellation in heaven, and of Diogenes too, and all the other dogs in order."[68]

There are many relevant reasons to suppose that Paul has in view Cynics throughout chapter 3. Although we cannot explore the topic here in any detail, this would have implications for the entire letter, and for general

---

Silvanus, 67, 91.

66. Cf. Philo, *Planter* 151; Diogenes Laertius, *Lives* 6 (*passim*); Lucian, *Demonax* 21; Athenaeus, *Deipnosophistae* 3.96–99; Clement, *Strom.* 8.12.4–7.

67. *Planter* 151; trans. Yonge (emphasis added).

68. Clement, *Strom.* 8.4 (Roberts and Donaldson [trans. and eds.], *The Ante-Nicene Fathers*, vol. 2, 561).

studies of Paul as well. Just as the Cynics exemplified "boldness of speech [παρρησία]," that is, freedom to speak one's mind [477] (Diogenes Laertius, *Lives*, 6.69), exemplified by freedom to act accordingly,[69] Paul claims the same for his own choice to live and speak "with all boldness [παρρησία]" (Phil 1:20), and certainly exemplifies that style in his argument in chapter 3. Was Paul perhaps imitating the Cynics and their ideals in the harsh, abusive, and even crass street-language (note the use of "crap" in v. 8), when seeking to express prophetic critique of the cultural alternatives, and pressure to conform therewith? Paul's emphasis on endurance, including appeal to the athletic imagery of training to succeed in order to make the case (vv. 12-16), parallels the common Cynic emphasis on discipline or practice in training (ἄσκησις), which was often made in metaphorical athletic terms, encouraging persistence in the face of constant resistance and discouragement.[70] Likewise, Paul's emphasis on self-denial in order to succeed (vv. 7-21; 4:5-13), is similar to the concerns of the Cynics to gain self-mastery, the exercise of which will fly in the face of conventional measures of success.[71] And note that Paul's claim that "our citizenship is in heaven" rather than in this world (3:19-20) is intriguingly contextualized if juxtaposed with the Cynic's claim to be "citizen[s] of the world [κοσμοπολῖται]" (Diogenes Laertius, *Lives* 6.63).

Moreover, as we can see from the biblical examples as well as common usage in other Greek and Latin texts, references to dogs and dog-like behavior can be used in a general derogatory way. It need not denote a specific group per se, but the out-group, in order to make the point [478] that the author's own group's identity and behavior are different and superior.[72]

It should also be noted that Paul's language choices for name-calling here may be shaped more by intertextuality than has been realized.[73] In

---

69. Cf. Vaage, "Like Dogs Barking: Cynic Parrêsia and Shameless Asceticism."

70. Diogenes Laertius, *Lives* 6.49, 70-71; Crates, *Ep.* 16, 20, 21, 33; Diogenes, *Ep.* 31; Epictetus, *Discourses* 3.22.51-52.

71. Diogenes Laertius, *Lives* 6.27-30, 45, represent examples of the critique, e.g., of the need for one to be better trained than a Spartan warrior, to be master of one's self more than of another man, to do more to uphold the laws than do the rulers themselves; cf. *Lives* 6.23, 31-34, 59; Crates, *Ep.* 11, 12; Diogenes, *Ep.* 12; 14; Epictetus, *Discourses* 3.22.51-52; Dio Chrysostom, *Or.* 6.8-9; cf. Long, "The Socratic Tradition: Diogenes, Crates, and Hellenistic Ethics."

72. Similarly noted, but to different conclusions, see Garland, "The Composition and Unity of Philippians," 141-73; DeSilva, "No Confidence in the Flesh," 27-54.

73. Most commentators do not note this; one who does, Meyer, *Critical and Exegetical Handbook to the Epistles to the Philippians and Colossians, and to Philemon*, 122, is adamantly opposed to the idea: "A description of *idolatry* with allusion to Lev. xxi.5, 1 Kings xviii.28, *et al.* . . . is quite foreign to the context."

the Tanakh, references to "dogs" as well as to "mutilation" and to "evil workers" as prophets, all arise in 1 Kgs 18:1—22:40, in the story of Elijah and the rival prophets who advised Ahab to follow Baal. In Kings, "evil-working false prophets" (18:19—19:1) "mutilate themselves" (18:28: κατετέμνοντο: a verbal form of the word Paul uses in Phil 3:2 to refer to the "mutilation"), in order to evoke God's action—i.e., they put confidence in the flesh, but to no effect. Moreover, the house of Ahab and Jezebel was condemned to be devoured by "dogs" (21:22–29; cf. 2 Kgs 9:33–37; 10:11, 17). The parallels are tantalizing.

Acts 16:12–40, especially vv. 16–21, should also be probed for relevance to the situation in Philippi. This text purports to describe Paul's experiences in Philippi. Luke depicts a fortune-telling slave woman with a spirit of *python* (πύθωνα: divination, "belly-talking," speaking in a strange voice), a ventriloquist in the sense of having a demon in the stomach which speaks through the subject's mouth (cf. Phil 3:19: "whose God is the belly"). She follows Paul, crying out, "These men are servants of the Most High God, who proclaim to you the way of salvation." After several days of this, Paul was annoyed and exorcised the demon, provoking local opposition to his influence, for she had represented a profitable enterprise. In view of these inter-textual clues, a possible rivalry with prophets and competing truth claims could be profitably examined for the context of the rhetoric of Philippians.

Whatever the particular referent(s), Paul's language is probably intended to evoke a general negative stereotyping of options outside of [479] Judaism and outside of his Christ-believing coalition within Judaism in particular. In other words, Paul is expressing opposition to "pagan" alternatives and any associations that might be drawn by his audience or others seeking to understand them. They are not to be pursued by his addressees in their effort to not only understand who they are in the world, but to whom they should look for models and instruction going forward. Paul will have none of that. They are to look to Judaism in general ("we are the circumcision") as well as to Paul, and to Jesus Christ, to whom Paul himself looks, and, in his view, to whom all those who are set apart to God should look. Note that Paul does not write what commentators universally read, that is, he does not write that "we are the true circumcision," "the circumcision of the heart," "the spiritual circumcision," or some such thing. By writing "we are the circumcision," he emphasizes the contrast between circumcision identity and identity associated with other kinds of cuts in the flesh made by the uncircumcised.

The pun on the similarity of sounds for the Greek endings of mutilation/circumcision (*tomên/tomê*), along with the shared lexical element of being cut (τομή), are used to punctuate the fact that in spite of these common elements, which make for a dramatic turn of phrase, the two identities these words signify are anything but the same! Jewish identity and behavior are upheld as positive referents in v. 3: being the circumcision means being those who are "worshiping God in spirit, boasting in Christ Jesus, and not trusting in the flesh." That identity and lifestyle is contrasted to the negative "pagan" referents of v. 2, stereotyped as dogs, evil-workers, and the mutilation.[74] These two ways of being in the world are as different as day and night, (males) being cut around (περι-τομή) to be set apart to the God of Israel, as commanded in Scripture, versus being cut into (κατα-τομή) in order to invoke the gods, as was supposed to be effective by the rest of the nations. The contrast is with the uncircumcised, the "pagan" world of the addressees, about which Paul is expressing a specifically Jewish—i.e., circumcision-oriented—point of view.

[480] Rather than warning his audience to beware of Jews or the values of Judaism, the opposite is the case: Paul is warning his audience to eschew the "pagan" options to which they might be expected to be drawn, or from which they are encountering opposition.[75] He seeks to enculturate his audience into Judaism, but of a particular subgroup, one that believes the end of the ages has dawned in Jesus Christ. Even if many, if not most of them, are not themselves circumcised, being non-Jews, they are to understand themselves to be no longer members of the larger pagan world of their natural birth—"for *we* are the circumcision." The values of the circumcised, Jewish identity, are not portrayed as carnal, but quite the opposite; they are defined in terms of the ideals at the heart of Christ-faith, just as they are in Jewish groups generally, and must not be compromised by turning them into the seeking of rank as measured in Greco-Roman pagan cultural terms.[76]

---

74. Philo, *Cherubim* 91–100, offers many parallels, including a contrast of the pious soul with the festive assemblies of Greeks and barbarians, which are polemically portrayed to involve many of the same characteristics that Paul mentions in Phil 3:2, 18–19, including animal-like behavior, evil works, and mutilation.

75. It is unclear whether βλέπετε here means "to beware of," as in issuing a warning, meaning "watch out for," or alternatively "to behold," meaning "to consider" or "reflect upon." It is not of significance for this essay to decide. Kilpatrick, "ΒΛΕΠΕΤΕ, Philippians 3.2," makes the case that when followed by an accusative, as it is here, it always means "to look at, consider," rather than "to beware." To mean "to beware" in the sense of watch out for, this verb must be followed by μή and the aorist subjunctive, or by ἀπό, which is not the case here. Reed, *A Discourse Analysis of Philippians*, 244–46, makes the case that words must be defined semantically as well as syntactically, providing examples that undermine the universality of definition Kilpatrick claims. Thus, he concludes, the context of usage here "gives it a 'cautionary' tone." In either case, it probably means "to avoid," based on the negative characterizations posed in the epithets.

76. Gruen, *Diaspora: Jews Amidst Greeks and Romans*, 227, notes a similar way of portraying the Jewish values in contrast to those of others: "Philo refers frequently

At the same time, because they are now identified into Judaism, Paul apparently recognizes that in his absence the temptation for these former [481] pagans will be to seek to enhance their honor-rating among their new peers in Christ-faith-based Judaism by applying the norms of the pagan cultural heritage from which they have come, in the midst of which they still live, to their new communal situation within this Jewish subgroup (vv. 3, 17–20). Because it is Judaism to which they are called, it is only from mistakenly seeking advantage within Judaism from which they need to be specifically dissociated (to count to be loss). Thus, Paul communicates the relative devaluation of his own advantages specific to Jewish group identity because, although they are probably not Jews and thus cannot do so, Paul could boast as a natural born and accomplished Jew, if so inclined (3:4—4:1, in fact, his argument appeals to this implicit boast). But the reader risks missing the point of the relativizing of all things to Christ-faith within this Judaism, including any advantage such as Paul's claim to apostleship otherwise represents for him (vv. 13–16; cf. Gal 1:1; 1 Cor 9), if overlooking Paul's dissociation from "everything"—relativizing every claim to enhanced honor rating among one's peers in the present age as but dog waste—to the degree that anything compromises upholding Christ's honor alone (vv. 8, 20).

CONCLUSION

Interpreters of Philippians have been calling Jews "dogs" in Paul's name since at least Chrysostom, doggedly justifying this behavior based on reversing a supposed tradition of Jews calling gentiles dogs in spite of the fact that there is no such tradition evident in Jewish literature before Paul, or after him either. Jews do not call gentiles, or Christians, dogs. Unfortunately, that argument cannot be made in reverse. In addition, although there are a number of strong candidates for otherwise defining Paul's referents, alternative interpretations have not been explored.

On the one hand, it is notable that commentators to date who claim this is a reversal fail to observe that even so it does not make repeating this kind of malicious language toward Jews—or anyone else, for that matter—appropriate. Should not Christian interpreters instead express regret

---

to Greek and barbarians by contrast with Jews who fall under neither heading—and whose practices are decidedly preferable to both. Jews shun the love of luxury, the concern with physical beauty, the revelries, the imperialist ambitions and rivalries, the mutual distrusts, and the internecine warfare that mark the experience of Greeks and barbarians alike. The Jewish philosopher unhesitatingly employed Hellenic categories and endorsed the traditional differentiation dear to the Greeks. The advantage, however, went to his own nation."

at Paul's derogatory aims and language and suggest that the reader seek to distance themselves from repeating such invective toward those [482] who do not share the same viewpoint as the interpreter and his or her presumed reader? Should he or she not repudiate this dog-eat-dog based approach to legitimation; for if it was a reversal, is evil to be returned for evil, or suffered instead, *pace* Paul (Phil 4:5, *passim*!; cf. Rom 12:17–21, drawing on Prov 20:22; 25:21–22), not to mention Jesus (Matt 5:21–22, 38–48, drawing on Lev 19:18, 33–34; 7:1–5)?

On the other hand, if an interpreter accepts that this is not a reversal, but nevertheless maintains on other grounds that Paul referred to Jews as dogs (or "evil workers" or the "mutilation," for that matter)—and thereby degraded the continued practice of Jewish identity and behavior, or of any Jewish impulse to communicate their faith in positive terms to Christ-believers—would that justify perpetuating this rhetoric today? Should not interpreters who believe that is what Paul meant judge unacceptable this kind of assessment and language about "the other," and especially the Jewish other, who has suffered so much for centuries from just this kind of Christian polemic and associated policies? Should he or she not at least raise the awareness of their reader that it is not a viewpoint that should be internalized as appropriate, or shape Christian conceptions of, language about, or relationships with any other person or group? In addition, should he or she not point out that the tradition of a supposed reversal has been constructed on erroneous suppositions? Should it not also be explained that Paul apparently invented this essentializing, ethnically-oriented, polemical trope?

I trust that this study will serve as a reminder to all of us that we need to evaluate not only our interested points of view, especially when repeating a familiar refrain, but—"like a dog with a bone"—that we must persistently check our sources too. You might say, we should seek as far as possible to avoid allowing our ideological tales to wag our exegetical dogs.

BIBLIOGRAPHY

Abrahams, Israel. *Studies in Pharisaism and the Gospels. First and Second Series.* Library of Biblical Studies. New York: Ktav, 1967.

Abrahamsen, V. A. *Women and Worship at Philippi: Diana/Artemis and Other Cults in the Early Christian Era.* Portland, ME: Astarte Shell, 1995.

Ascough, R. S. *Paul's Macedonian Associations: The Social Context of Philippians and 1 Thessalonians.* WUNT 2.161. Tübingen: Mohr Siebeck, 2003.

Bateman, H. W. IV. "Were the Opponents at Philippi Necessarily Jewish?" *Bibliotheca Sacra* 155 (1998) 39–61.

Bockmuehl, M. N. A. *The Epistle to the Philippians.* Peabody: Hendrickson, 1998.

Boring, M. E., et al. eds. *Hellenistic Commentary to the New Testament*. Nashville: Abingdon, 1995.

Börner-Klein, D. *Pirke de-Rabbi Elieser: Nach der Edition Venedig 1544 unter Berücksichtigung der Edition Warschau 1852*. Berlin: de Gruyter, 2004.

Burkill, T. A. "The Historical Development of the Story of the Syrophoenician Woman (Mark vii: 24–31)." *Novum Testamentum* 9 (1967) 161–77.

Chancey, M. A. *The Myth of a Gentile Galilee: The Population of Galilee and New Testament Studies*. New York: Cambridge University Press, 2002.

Cohen, S. J. D. *The Beginnings of Jewishness: Boundaries, Varieties, Uncertainties*. HCS 31. Berkeley: University of California Press, 1999.

DeSilva, D. A. "No Confidence in the Flesh: The Meaning and Function of Philippians 3:2–21." *Trinity Journal* 15NS (1994) 27–54.

de Vos, C. S. *Church and Community Conflicts: The Relationships of the Thessalonian, Corinthian, and Philippian Churches with Their Wider Civic Communities*. SBLDS 168. Atlanta: Scholars, 1999.

Dorcey, Peter F. *The Cult of Silvanus: A Study in Roman Folk Religion*. Columbia Studies in the Classical Tradition 20. Leiden: Brill, 1992.

Downing, G. F. "The Woman from Syrophoenicia, and her Doggedness: Mark 7:24–31 (Matthew 15:21–28)." In *Women in the Biblical Tradition*, edited by G. J. Brooke, 129–49. Lampeter, UK: Mellen, 1992.

Friedlander, G. *Pirke de Rabbi Eliezer: (The chapters of Rabbi Eliezer the Great) According to the Text of the Manuscript Belonging to Abraham Epstein of Vienna*. 4th ed. New York: Sepher-Hermon, 1981.

Galán, J. M. "What is He, The Dog." *Ugarit-Forschungen* 25 (1993) 173–80.

Garland, D. E. "The Composition and Unity of Philippians: Some Neglected Literary Factors." *Novum Testamentum* 27.2 (1985) 141–73.

Ginzberg, L. ed. *The Legends of the Jews*. Translated by H. Szold. 7 vols. Philadelphia: Jewish Publication Society of America, 1946.

Ginsberg, M., ed. *Hebrew-English Edition of The Babylonian Talmud, Seder Mo'ed, Bezah*. Translated by M. Ginsberg; London: Soncino, 1990.

Goranson, S. "Others and Intra-Jewish Polemic as Reflected in Qumran Texts." In *The Dead Sea Scrolls After Fifty Years: A Comprehensive Assessment*, edited by P. W. Flint and J. C. VanderKam, 534–51. Leiden: Brill, 1999.

Götze, Albrecht, and Edgar H. Sturtevant. *The Hittite Ritual of Tunnawi*. American Oriental Series 14. New Haven, CT: American Oriental Society, 1938.

Grayston, K. "The Opponents in Philippians 3." *Expository Times* 97 (1986) 170–72.

Gruen, E. S. *Diaspora: Jews amidst Greeks and Romans*. Cambridge: Harvard University Press, 2002.

Hawthorne, G. F. *Philippians*. WBC 43. Waco, TX: Word, 1983.

Heen, E. M. "Phil 2:6–11 and Resistance to Local Timocratic Rule: *Isa theo* and the Cult of the Emperor in the East." In *Paul and the Roman Imperial Order*, edited by R. A. Horsley, 125–53. Harrisburg, PA: Trinity, 2004.

Hooker, M. D. "Philippians: Phantom Opponents and the Real Source of Conflict." In *Fair Play: Diversity and Conflicts in Early Christianity: Essays in Honour of Heikki Räisänen*, edited by Ismo DunderBerg et al., 377–95. Leiden: Brill, 2002.

Horsley, R. A. *Archaeology, History, and Society in Galilee: The Social Context of Jesus and the Rabbis*. Valley Forge, PA: Trinity, 1996.

Jewett, R. "Conflicting Movements in the Early Church as Reflected in Philippians." *Novum Testamentum* 12 (1970) 362–90.

Kilpatrick, G. D. "ΒΛΕΠΕΤΕ, Philippians 3.2." In *In Memorium Paul Kahle*, edited by M. Black and G. Fohrer, 146–48. Berlin: Alfred Töpelmann, 1968.

Koester, H. "The Purpose of the Polemic of a Pauline Fragment." *New Testament Studies* 8 (1961–62) 317–32.

Liddell, H. G., et al. *A Greek-English Lexicon*. 9th ed. Oxford: Clarendon, 1996.

Lightfoot, J. B. *St. Paul's Epistle to the Philippians: A Revised Test with Introduction, Notes and Dissertations*. J. B. Lightfoot's Commentary on the Epistles of St. Paul; 12th ed. Peabody, MA: Hendrickson, 1995.

Lohmeyer, Ernst. *Die Offenbarung des Johannes*. Handbuch zum Neuen Testament 16. Tübingen: Mohr, 1926.

Long, A. A. "The Socratic Tradition: Diogenes, Crates, and Hellenistic Ethics." In *The Cynics: The Cynic Movement in Antiquity and its Legacy*, edited by R. B. Branham and Marie-Odile Goulet-Cazé, 28–46. Hellenistic Culture and Society 23. Berkeley: University of California Press, 1996.

Luz, U. *Matthew: A Commentary: 8–20*. Translated by W. C. Linss. Hermeneia. Minneapolis: Fortress, 1989.

MacMullen, R. *Roman Social Relations, 50 B.C. to A.D. 284*. New Haven: Yale University Press, 1974.

Meeks, W. A., et al., eds. *The HarperCollins Study Bible: New Revised Standard Version, with the Apocryphal/Deuterocanonical Books*. 1st ed. New York: HarperCollins, 1993.

Meyer, Heinrich August Wilhelm. *Critical and Exegetical Handbook to the Epistles to the Philippians and Colossians, and to Philemon*. Translated by J. C. Moore and William P. Dickson. H. A. W. Meyer's Commentary on the New Testament. 6th ed. Peabody, MA: Hendrickson, 1983.

Nanos, Mark D. "How Inter-Christian Approaches to Paul's Rhetoric Can Perpetuate Negative Valuations of Jewishness—Although Proposing to Avoid that Outcome." *Biblical Interpretation* 13.3 (2005) 255–69. (Available in volume 1 of this essay collection.)

———. *The Irony of Galatians: Paul's Letter in First-Century Context*. Minneapolis: Fortress, 2002.

———. "What Was at Stake in Peter's 'Eating with Gentiles' at Antioch?" In *The Galatians Debate: Contemporary Issues in Rhetorical and Historical Interpretation*, edited by M. D. Nanos, 282–318. Peabody, MA: Hendrickson, 2002. (Available in volume 3 of this essay collection.)

Oakes, Peter. *Philippians: From People to Letter*. Cambridge: Cambridge University Press, 2001.

Phillips, A. A., and Malcolm M. Willcock, eds. *Xenophon & Arrian, On Hunting (ΚΥΝΗΓΕΤΙΚΟΣ)*. Warminster, UK: Aris & Phillips, 1999.

Reed, J. T. *A Discourse Analysis of Philippians: Method and Rhetoric in the Debate over Literary Integrity*. JSNT-Sup, 136. Sheffield, UK: Sheffield Academic Press, 1997.

Roberts, A., and J. Donaldson, trans. and eds. *The Ante-Nicene Fathers: Translations of the Writings of the Fathers Down to A.D. 325*. American reprint of the Edinburgh ed. 10 vols. Grand Rapids: Eerdmans, 1978.

Sandnes, Karl Olav. *Belly and Body in the Pauline Epistles*. Society for New Testament Studies Monograph Series 120. Cambridge: Cambridge University Press, 2002.

Schaff, P., ed. *A Select Library of the Nicene and Post-Nicene Fathers of the Christian Church. First Series*. 14 vols. Grand Rapids: Eerdmans, 1979.

Schmithals, W. *Paul & the Gnostics*. Translated by J. E. Steely. Nashville: Abingdon, 1972.

Scholz, Herbert. *Der Hund in der griechisch-römischen Magie und Religion*. Berlin: Druck, Trilitsch & Huther, 1937.

Simonetti, M., ed. *Matthew 14–28*. Ancient Christian Commentary on Scripture; New Testament 1b. Downers Grove, IL: IVP, 2002.

Stow, K. *Jewish Dogs: An Image and Its Interpreters: Continuity in the Catholic-Jewish Encounter*. Stanford Studies in Jewish History and Culture. Stanford: Stanford University Press, 2006.

Snyman, A. H. "A Rhetorical Analysis of Philippians 3:1–11." *Neotestamentica* 40.2 (2006) 259–83.

Strack, H. L., and P. Billerbeck. *Kommentar zum Neuen Testament aus Talmud und Midrasch*. 6 vols. Munich: Beck, 1922–61.

Tagawa, K. *Miracles et Évangile: la pensée personnelle de l'évangéliste Marc*. Études d'histoire et de philosophie religieuses. Paris: Presses universitaires de France, 1966.

Tellbe, M. *Paul between Synagogue and State: Christians, Jews, and Civic Authorities in 1 Thessalonians, Romans, and Philippians*. CBNTS 34. Stockholm: Almqvist & Wiksell, 2001.

Theological Dictionary of the New Testament. Edited by Gerhard Kittel and Gerhard Friedrich. 10 vols. Grand Rapids: Eerdmans, 1965.

Thomas, D. W. "Kelebh 'dog': Its Origin and Some Usages of It in the Old Testament." *Vetus Testamentum* 10.4 (1960) 410–27.

Tov, E., ed. *The Dead Sea Scrolls Electronic Reference Library 2*. Leiden: Brill, 1999.

Ulonska, H. "Gesetz und Beschneidung: Überlegungen zu einem paulinischen Ablösungskonflikt." In *Jesu Rede von Gott und ihre Nachgeschichte im frühen Christentum: Beiträge zur Verkündigung Jesu und zum Kerygma der Kirche: Festschrift für Willi Marxsen zum 70 Geburtstag*, edited by D. Koch et al., 314–31. Gütersloh: Guterloher Verlagshaus G. Mohn, 1989.

Vaage, L. E. "Like Dogs Barking: Cynic Parrêsia and Shameless Asceticism." *Semeia* 57 (1992) 25–39.

Willitts, Joel. "Matthew's Messianic Shepherd-King: In Search of 'The Lost Sheep of the House of Israel.'" Ph.D. diss., University of Cambridge, 2006.

Wright, D. P. *The Disposal of Impurity: Elimination Rites in the Bible and in Hittite and Mesopotamian Literature*. SBLDS 101. Atlanta: Scholars, 1986.

6

Paul's Polemic in Philippians 3 as Jewish-Subgroup Vilification of Local Non-Jewish Cultic and Philosophical Alternatives

[47] PAUL SHARPLY WARNS the Philippians in 3:2 to "Beware of the dogs... the evil workers... the mutilation." In v. 3 he offers a sharp contrast to "we" who "are the circumcision," and in vv. 18–19 he engages in vilification again by way of several similarly derogatory epithets.[1] His rhetoric suggests [48] specific referents would be immediately indicated for his audience, yet his polemical approach is too vague to provide clarity for the later reader. Nevertheless, the commentary tradition might lead one to suppose otherwise. It upholds relatively consistent identifications for the context of Paul's vituperation: Paul is opposing "Jews" who are (usually) also "Christians" (hence, Jewish Christians and "Judaizers" are common descriptions);[2] furthermore, they are "missionaries" who advocate circumcision

---

1. Translations are my own unless otherwise indicated.

2. Although the label *Christian* is usually employed in discussions of Philippians, it is avoided hereafter for describing the probable historical addressees because it is anachronistic and not helpful for trying to imagine the pre-Christianity setting of Paul's audiences; *Christ-followers* is adopted instead. Nevertheless, *Christian* is used sometimes herein to highlight the conceptual paradigms at work in the traditional interpretations being discussed, for which Christians and Christianity are what is indeed envisioned. The common trajectory of Pauline versus Jewish Christianity will be discussed below.

The term *Judaizers* is grammatically inaccurate to refer to those who seek to influence

and who have traveled to Philippi to do so in direct opposition to Paul and his mission (hence, "opponents" and "outsiders").[3] Their goal can almost always be summarized as being to influence Paul's addressees to undertake proselyte conversion and other elements of a Jewish way of life, behavior that Paul is understood to oppose adamantly as inappropriate if not entirely obsolete for those who believe in the gospel of Jesus Christ.[4] This paradigm (with [49] slight variations) has limited the interpretive options explored for constructing Paul's thought and behavior as well as that of his addressees in Philippi to conflicting views of the role of Judaism (that is, Jewish ways of life based on Torah-prescribed norms), and thus bears witness to a broad trajectory of Paulinism ("gentile Christianity") read in opposition to Judaism throughout his letters.

That traditional case is predicated on the following interpretive decisions:[5] Paul's warning in v. 2 to beware of "the dogs" is taken to be a reversal

---

non-Jews toward Judaism, although that is its common usage for discussions of Paul's "opponents." Instead, the term should be used (if at all) to refer to those who undertake becoming Jews, that is, proselytes have "judaized." It is problematic ideologically, because its usage carries a negative valence that has historically been used as though there is something self-evidently wrong with Jews who might seek to persuade non-Jews to become proselytes (note: -izers, versus Christian mission-aries, not mission-izers), and it has been often used in later inter-Christian rivalries as a negative label to denounce a rival Christian group for being heretical, even when the topic at issue may not be conversion to Judaism. See Cohen, *The Beginnings of Jewishness*, 175–97; Nanos, *The Irony of Galatians*, 115–19.

3. Although Paul's warning opposes the influence of some people or groups on those to whom he writes, the label *opponents* is avoided here unless it can be established from Paul's argument that he is being opposed.

4. In addition to the commentaries, specialized studies include Gunther, *St. Paul's Opponents and Their Background*, 2, for a list of seventeen options that are usually discussed for identifying those Paul opposes in Phil 3, all (but one: gnostics) of which focus on Jews or Jewish Christians, even when some other options are explored in addition (e.g., Jewish or Jewish-Christian gnostics, "Judaizers," libertines, pneumatics); and see variously Koester, "The Purpose of the Polemic of a Pauline Fragment"; Klijn, "Paul's Opponents in Philippians iii"; Holladay, "Paul's Opponents in Philippians 3"; Jewett, "Conflicting Movements in the Early Church as Reflected in Philippians"; Schmithals, *Paul & the Gnostics*, 65–122; Ellis, "Paul and His Opponents: Trends in Research"; Tyson, "Paul's Opponents at Philippi"; Garland, "The Composition and Unity of Philippians"; Grayston, "The Opponents in Philippians 3"; Sanders, "Paul on the Law, His Opponents, and the Jewish People in Philippians 3 and 2 Corinthians 11"; Bloomquist, *The Function of Suffering in Philippians*, 198–201; Sumney, '*Servants of Satan*', '*False Brothers*' *and Other Opponents of Paul*, 160–87 ("Opponents Everywhere—Philippians"); Oropeza, *Jews, Gentiles, and the Opponents of Paul*, 204–23. For good summaries in commentaries, see O'Brien, *The Epistle to the Philippians*, 26–35; Reumann, *Philippians*, 460–81.

5. The following details and conclusions are so widespread that there is little reason to refer the reader to any particular interpreter: they will be found, with little

of supposedly stereotypical Jewish slander of non-Jews as dogs; thus, Paul's denunciation of Jews and their influence is from a perspective calculated to appeal to his audiences' resentment toward Jewish ethnoreligious arrogance. The warning to beware of "the evil workers" ostensibly suggests Christ-following Jewish missionaries who have arrived or are anticipated to be on their way: Paul subverts their claim to bring *good* news or uphold the place of *good* works, combinations of faith and actions that interpreters have associated with gospel-based values for "Christian" *Jewish* groups in contrast to Paul's "Christian" universalist (read: *gentile*) value-based groups. The epithet "the mutilation" supposedly represents a negative reversal of the value of circumcision aimed at those who promote this rite, because Paul is understood to conflate the two in v. 3 to draw a supersessionistic "Christian" contrast, "we are the circumcision." Then Paul ostensibly denounces his (former) Jewish credentials in vv. 3–9 as meaningless, [50] amounting literally to "crap," or at least euphemistically to "rubbish" (NRSV), compared to his new identity in Christ (v. 8). Furthermore, in vv. 18–19, his specific invectives toward those accused of being "the enemies of the cross of Christ, whose end is destruction, whose god is the belly, who even glory in their shame, who are thinking earthly [thoughts]," are usually aligned with errors attributed to Judaism, including to Jews who have become Christ-followers but continue to practice and promote Judaism, which Paul is understood to oppose (unlike the case in v. 2, the commentary tradition does recognize several other possible referents for the invectives in vv. 18–19).[6]

These decisions are elements of a popular paradigm that often frames how the conflicts suggested by Paul's polemics have been interpreted since F. C. Baur: the Petrine/Jewish Christianity versus Pauline/gentile Christianity trajectory. According to this construction of Christian origins, Paul's mission is understood to be experiencing a challenge from a counter-missionary program under the leadership of James and Peter, and his letters reflect this more global dynamic. Thus, Paul's polemics in Philippians are expected to be expressing resistance to intruders, *opponents* from *outside* his communities who are Jewish Christ-followers (often, they are proposed to be associated with the ostensible Galatian opponents).[7] In addition to

---

variation, in every commentary and specific discussion of the situation in Philippi, such as those listed above.

6. Hawthorne, *Philippians*, 163. These include various kinds of antinomian Christ-followers, gnostic Christ-followers, and "pagans."

7. My challenge to the basis of such identifications is a central topic in *Irony of Galatians*, including why there is no evidence that Paul was being opposed or that the influencers have come from outside Galatia; rather, the evidence suggests that Paul is opposing the influence of local groups and social-identity norms. They appear to

the influence of this historical paradigm, it has become commonplace to uphold the idea that reading Paul in opposition to fellow Christ-followers is attractive because it focuses on Paul's criticism of fellow "Christians," thus making it an expression of inter-Christian polemic, rather than an attack on Jews or Judaism; would that it were so.[8]

[51] Recent efforts to revisit the interpretation of Philippians or to pursue a people's history approach, such as those that focus on the political (that is, Roman imperial) as well as Greco-Roman polytheistic "pagan"[9] social context of the letter overall, retain the consensus interpretation for identifying the targets of Paul's oppositional polemic in these verses. They also perpetuate, intentionally or not, the traditional view that Paul negatively values the continuation of Jewish identity and Judaism (or Christian Judaism) in his communities as well as in his own life, and make this issue an element in their constructions of the situation in Philippi, although it seems to arise more from the framework imposed on the letter (from prevailing constructions of Paul as well as of his communities as Christian in sharp contrast to Jewish/Judaism) than from the information derived from within it.[10]

These interpretive decisions have been repeated with little discussion of the indirect nature of the evidence on which they depend or exploration of alternatives, although they have enormous impact on how the letter is interpreted, as well as for constructions of Paul and Christian origins in

---

maintain the need for proselyte conversion apart from raising concern that it is oppositional to Paul's addressees' convictions about Christ and apart from attacking their patron, Paul; more likely, the influencers argue that these non-Jews have misunderstood their patron but are not outright opposing Paul; if they were, then it seems probable that Paul's addressees would not be so naively, from his point of view, considering this step complimentary to, rather than subversive of, their standing in Christ according to Paul's gospel.

8. Because it remains the practice of Judaism that Paul supposedly attacks, I find neither the benefits asserted as benign as they have been proposed to be nor the paradigm itself very convincing; see my "How Inter-Christian Approaches to Paul's Rhetoric Can Perpetuate Negative Valuations of Jewishness—Although Proposing to Avoid that Outcome."

9. Admittedly anachronistic, the term is employed herein to refer to those who are neither Jewish nor Christ-followers, with no negative judgment intended.

10. See, e.g., Oakes, *Philippians*, 105, 111–12, 117–18; Ascough, *Paul's Macedonian Associations*, 203–5; Heen, "Phil 2:6–11 and Resistance to Local Timocratic Rule"; de Vos, *Church and Community Conflicts*, 263–75, which challenges the prevailing views in a manner closest to what is proposed here. Also critical of the prevailing view in several ways and to various degrees, although often still conceptualizing Paul's opposition as to Jewish or Jewish Christian missionaries, see Sandnes, *Belly and Body in the Pauline Epistles*. Some note that the conflict in Philippi was probably precipitated by the Christ-followers' withdrawal from traditional cults, especially imperial cult.

general, and specifically for decisions about Paul's identity, teaching, and behavior relative to Judaism. Similarly, they influence decisions about the other Christ-following Jewish groups, including the other apostles and Paul's relationship to them. And they shape constructions of the identity and concerns of Paul's audience, including what kinds of options they are understood to be exploring, or at least what Paul (and his interpreter) supposes them to be exploring, which figure into explanations about what prompted him to write this letter, and what he meant to communicate therein.

[52] Anyone entering into research on Philippians, even someone focused on a people's history approach, is naturally influenced by such conclusions, beginning with the framing of the options to explore. However, because Paul nowhere explicitly identifies those he denounces as Jews or Christ-followers (or "Christians"), or missionaries, outsiders, or opponents of Paul for that matter, is it not time to revisit the evidence, for both constructions of Paul and of his Philippian audience?

RECONCEPTUALIZING THE PHILIPPIAN CONTEXT

In my view, the evidence available from Paul's rhetoric should lead to reconceptualizing hypotheses to test for identifying "the Philippians" addressed in several new directions. The concerns of the Philippians and Paul can be interpreted within a Greco-Roman cultural and politico-religious context apart from imagining it revolves around the introduction of, and Paul's resistance to, people or matters identified with jewishness. This rereading begins from the introduction of a simple but important hypothesis: that Paul writes *from within Judaism*, not Christianity, from and to those who understand themselves (non-Jews as well as Jews) to practice Judaism within (sub)groups that are distinguished by their convictions about Jesus, but otherwise still members of the larger Jewish communities (which are themselves minority communities, and in the case of Philippi, probably very small in number).

When Paul's polemics as well as the rest of his message are read from this perspective, his concerns can be understood to express *his Jewish sensibilities* and *his commitment to the practice of (Jesus-as-Messiah-based) Judaism within his communities—even by those non-Jews whom he insists remain non-Jews.*[11] Instead of warning against the practice of Judaism, as

---

11. Cf. my "Paul and Judaism: Why Not Paul's Judaism?" Reference herein is made to Jews and Jewish and jewishness or Judaism, unless the geo-ethnic element of judeanness is perceived to be specifically more salient (note: non-Jews could also be Judeans, just as today non-Jews can be Israelis). That there was a religious dimension to Judean/

usually [53] understood, Paul wants his audience to be fully enculturated into Judaism (that is, into a Jewish cultural and social way of thinking and living), and thus into assessing the groups he decries and their norms as competitors whose influence on them should be resisted. In other words, if the idea of "Judaizers" as the opposition in Philippi is questionable (in addition to being grammatically inaccurate); rather, in a very different direction, Paul may seek to influence his audience to be completely "judaized," albeit within the terms developed around his Jewish subgroup's propositional claims about the significance of Jesus.[12]

In this alternative approach to Paul's interests, and those of his audience, the issue revolves around how to live within Judaism, within Paul's new Jewish subgroups, where identity and concomitant behavior involved in living jewishly creates conflicts (especially for the members who remain non-Jews) with the cultural values and behavior of the larger (non-Jewish and non-jewishly oriented lifestyles of the) Greco-Roman population. For non-Jews, that includes new tensions with their families and friends, neighbors, and the civic leaders who populate the cultural context in which

---

Jewish ethnicity properly named Judaism seems to me evident from relevant sources for discussing Paul's period; it arises in Paul's language in Gal 1:13–14; 2:14–16; and in the Maccabean literature Judeans can either leave or return or observe in different ways and to different degrees the traditional religious practices of this people. It seems likely that those in Judea who are described in 2 Macc 6:1–11 as prohibited "even from confessing themselves to be *Ioudaioi*," are still Judeans, but they cannot confess to being Jews, to being those who practice Judaism, the way of life for Jews regardless of where they live, *mutatis mutandis*. Note also that Antiochus IV Epiphanes is described as willing to become a *Ioudaios*, which most likely means becoming a Jew, not a Judean, by adopting the identity of and thus the way of life of Jews, however that would be negotiated for him while remaining a Seleucid king and reigning from Syria, not by moving to Judea (9:13–17). Philo (*Spec.* 1.186) notes the range of observance among Jews. Josephus, *Ant.* 20.34–48, relates that Izates, the king of Adiabene, seeks to live a Jewish lifestyle guided by Scripture, apparently independent of participation in a Jewish community or role in ruling Judea or a Judean satellite nation. His interests and practices make more sense to classify as Judaism, even after his circumcision, although the geo-ethnic element is relevant, as witnessed by the concern about how his subjects will react. Moreover, note that the teacher advocating circumcision (Eleazar) is described as coming from Galilee, not Judea, so he is not arguably a Judean, although described as a *Ioudaios* (20.43), while the other one (Ananias) is described not in terms of coming from somewhere, but as a *Ioudaios* merchant. See Schwartz, "'Judaean' or 'Jew'? How Should We translate *ioudaios* in Josephus?"; Williams, "The Meaning and Function of *Ioudaios* in Graeco-Roman Inscriptions"; S. Cohen, *The Beginnings of Jewishness*, 69–139; Goodblatt, *Elements of Ancient Jewish Nationalism*; Jones and Pearce, eds., *Jewish Local Patriotism and Self-Identification in the Graeco-Roman Period*; Runesson, "Inventing Christian Identity: Paul, Ignatius, and Theodosius I." *Contra* Mason, "Jews, Judaeans, Judaizing, Judaism."

12. See also Fredriksen, "Judaizing the Nations."

they live and move, the social world in which they are identified, carry on relationships, and access goods. These forces present challenges to the Jewish [54] ideals Paul upholds for how non-Jews turning to God through Jesus as Christ should now think and live, including how they should remain faithful and suffer as required by the marginalized state this creates for them. To put this another way, a Torah-centered communal way of life (that is, based on God's "instructions" for how to live rightly, which is the general meaning of *nomos* when used by Jews to translate from the Hebrew, rather than "law" per se) is by definition countercultural in terms of the dominant social values, politics, and practices of cult in Philippi. The addressees are learning an alternative *Jewish* way of life from Paul's teaching, from Scripture, from the Jewish subgroup members (if there are any), and from the larger Jewish community. (However large or small it is in Philippi, it would represent a minority group and culture, but one in which their own groups function as subgroups.)

This way of framing Paul and his probable concerns and those of his audience in Philippi, as well as of those of whom Paul warns them to beware, offers several new avenues for interpreters to explore by way of the evidence provided by Paul's rhetoric. There is not space to develop the alternatives in full here, so I will focus on the language of vv. 2–3 and vv. 18–19, accompanied with sideward glances at other language in the chapter and in the letter.[13] My research leads me to believe that the most likely referents of his vilification are neither Jews nor Judaism, nor Christ-followers (or from so-called Jewish Christianity), nor outsiders to Philippi on a mission to counter Paul's influence, but possibly opponents of Paul and his influence on these non-Jews. I think it probable that the influences Paul addresses in Philippi arise from local Greco-Roman "idolatrous" cults and or philosophical groups and their various behavioral norms, which are, from Paul's perspective, in conflict with the values that these non-Jews should now subscribe to in their new identification within Jewish communal sub-groups, within Judaism, albeit remaining non-Jews. That is why he appeals to himself and others (including, most importantly, Jesus himself), whom he represents as models for them throughout ch. 3 and the rest of the letter—which he sets in contrast to the conflicting models they observe and encounter in their current circumstances from those who do not share Paul's views (3:2–9, 15–17; 3:20—4:2; cf. 1:9–11; 1:27—2:18; 4:8–9; *passim*). There are a number of suggestive candidates to explore for identifying the influences and influencers he opposes for the Philippians.

13. There is also not space to discuss the various partition theories for the letter or letters, but it is relevant that the various positions depend on how they read 3:2 as a break from the concerns raised earlier in the letter.

After discussing [55] several of them, more attention will be given to the promising topic of the Cynics, which offers interesting new dynamics to consider for constructing the identity, circumstances, and concerns of these Philippians, as well as new implications for the study of Paul.

PHILIPPI AND PHILIPPIANS

Paul's letter was sent to a Romanized city, populated by many Romans, with special colony status, highly stratified according to Roman elites' standards (inescapable maintenance of status and distinctions), agriculturally oriented (and thus highly interdependent), and with Romanized Greek, Macedonian, Thracian, and other peoples.[14] Many gods were worshipped, and many cults are attested from the material remains. Roman religious practice was characterized by civic ideology, which incorporated the local gods and cults.[15] Inscriptions indicate that Romanized foreign cults such as the Egyptian gods and Cybele were linked to the practice of imperial cult.[16]

This milieu should, on its own merits, warrant an investigation of Philippians based on the supposition that Paul's negative references signal a call for resistance to the influence of "non-Jewish" or "pagan" factors on the addressees. When combined with my working hypothesis that Paul continued to practice Judaism and establish groups practicing Judaism (albeit having a significant proportion of non-Jews), this naturally suggests that his teaching challenges how they negotiate their new social identity within the larger non-Jewish world, in addition to how they do so within the larger (non-Jesus-oriented) Jewish community (however small it may be).[17] Thus, [56] I expect his letters to express Jewish sensibilities (including specifically Christ-based Jewish subgroup sensibilities) that he believed would shape his audiences' worldviews in directions new to them. Given this perspective, it seems to me that Paul is in this letter expressing a general revulsion

---

14. Bormann, *Philippi*, 11–84; Pilhofer, *Philippi*, vol. 1; Koukouli-Chrysantaki, "Colonia Iulia Augusta Philippensis"; Bakirtzis, "Paul and Philippi: The Archaeological Evidence"; de Vos, *Community Conflicts*, 234–50; Oakes, *Philippians*, 1–76; Hellerman, *Reconstructing Honor in Roman Philippi*.

15. Beard, North, and Price, *Religions of Rome*, 167–363; Scheid and Lloyd, *An Introduction to Roman Religion*.

16. Bormann, *Philippi*, 54–60; Hawthorne, *Philippians*, xxxiv. On the Thracian, Greek, and other indigenous practices, see especially Pilhofer, *Philippi*, 49–113; Hellerman, *Reconstructing Honor*, 100–109.

17. See www.marknanos.com for a detailed list of research projects and published work that examines the bases of these claims, including downloadable papers and essays.

toward the practices of some of the idolatrous cults and/or philosophical and other cultural norms that conspire to shape the thinking and behavior of his disciples in direct contrast to the (Christ-oriented Jewish sub-group) values to which he wants them to now subscribe.

Although there is little evidence of Jewish communities in Philippi at the time,[18] the absence of any Jews during Paul's period would be remarkable. The author of Acts 16:11–40 imagined that discussing a Jewish community there would be believable for his audience, even if this constitutes questionable evidence, because Paul wrote years earlier. In that report, there is communal opposition from crowds and magistrates in response to the particular kind of Jewish influence on their Romanized cult that the stranger Paul was perceived to represent.

Of particular interest for this inquiry, that account does seem to reflect some of the tensions that arise in Philippians. Paul's call to suffer for the message of good in Jesus Christ in Phil 1:27–30 and 2:12–18, following discussion of his own faithful persistence in the face of suffering imprisonment by Roman authorities (1:12–26)—albeit not in Philippi, but from where he writes this letter—has led commentators to recognize that the threat to the addressees involves at least in part opposition to changes in their behavior that run afoul of their local "pagan" civic context. This is also supported by Paul's comments to the Thessalonians about his previous experience in Philippi (1 Thess 2:1–2). He explains that he suffered there, being insulted with insolence (with *hubris*). He feels that he was treated shamefully for behavior considered unbecoming according to Roman customs of religious expression, which pitted Paul's confession of a Jewish figure (Christ/Messiah) against the idolatrous orientation of the Philippian cults toward many gods, including Caesar as lord and savior of humankind. These various accounts agree that Paul's proclamation of Jesus Christ as Lord is opposed because it does not conform to the city's expression of Roman cultural values.

If Paul was engaged in calling the Philippians, although non-Jews, away from compromising accommodation to their Roman social world, he would be seeking to persuade them to think and behave differently, to resist being [57] shaped by the worldview that has fashioned their self- and group-identity since birth. That world was the one in which status and access to goods had been gained, and could still be gained. It was thus in continued competition with their new marginalizing social reality as Christ-following non-Jews within this (newly emerging on the scene)

18. Ascough, *Paul's Macedonian Associations*, 191–212, traces the evidence. There are no material remains for our period and, besides the generalization in Philo, *Embassy* 281–82, making reference to Macedonia among the many provinces of Rome with Jewish populations, no literary evidence except in Paul and Acts.

Jewish coalition. If taken in this direction, the construction of those Paul opposes in Phil 3 need not be approached as though it is so different from the dynamics of the oppositional context suggested in ch. 1, where "pagan" elements are often recognized.

Let us consider several groups and cults that seem to be the most likely candidates for reconsidering the referents in Paul's negative epithets. But first, a discussion of the epithets will help clarify the issues.

PAUL'S POLEMICAL WARNINGS IN VERSE 2

"Beware the Dogs"

In a recent publication, I explained many problems with the traditional view that Paul intended to signal Jews of any kind when referring to dogs in 3:2. I will only repeat a few salient points here.[19]

The common refrain that Paul is engaged in reversing toward Jews a traditional Jewish invective aimed at non-Jews cannot be substantiated: there is no literary evidence from Paul's time, or before (and virtually none afterwards), that Jews referred to non-Jews as dogs to express ethnic prejudice.[20] There are a number of alternative referents to consider; some offer [58] little clarity for the specific situation in Philippi, and others are very suggestive—they all indicate the probability of non-Jews as the referents.

In a general sense, it is possible that Paul refers to dogs, often females ("bitches"), in the usual derogatory way that it was employed then and since, so that it holds no clues to the identity of the referents.[21] It is also possible

---

19. "Paul's Reversal of Jews Calling Gentiles 'Dogs' (Philippians 3:2)."

"*Beware*": It is unclear whether βλέπετε here signifies "to beware of," as in issuing a warning, meaning "watch out for," or alternatively "to behold," meaning "to consider" or "reflect on." It is not of significance for this essay to decide; based on the negative characterizations posed in the epithets, it probably communicates that the referents are to be avoided. For opposite conclusions, see Kilpatrick, "ΒΛΕΠΕΤΕ, Philippians 3.2"; Reed, *A Discourse Analysis of Philippians*, 244–46.

20. The possible exception (I am aware of) is in *Pirke de Rabbi Eliezer* 29, where eating with the uncircumcised slave in the house of Israel is likened in theory to eating with a dog that has also not had the foreskin circumcised (a comparison that raises its own questions), although this language is not present in all editions. This edition dates to hundreds of years after Christians began calling Jews dogs and developed social policies to ensure that Jews did not defile the body of Christ (Stow, *Jewish Dogs*), so that it is probably a response to Christian invective, however ironic that suggestion might be. Moreover, it is specifically a slave to which reference is made, which may be the basis for the comparison with dogs.

21. Grayston, "Opponents in Philippians," 3, 171, similarly notes that Paul's usage here may be likened to the general statement today: "Look out for those rats," and he

that, for this referent as well as evil workers and mutilation, Paul is drawing on an intertextual echo from 1 Kgs 18:1—22:40, in order to evoke God's action by way of the flesh, with which Paul contrasts his and his audience's behavior in v. 3. In this story, in contrast to Elijah (with whose experiences Paul in Rom 11:1–5 explicitly compares himself), *"evil-working false prophets"* (18:19—19:1) *"mutilate themselves"* in order to *"persuade"* the gods (18:28, which uses a verbal form of the same word used by Paul), and the house of Ahab and Jezebel is condemned to be eaten by *dogs* (21:22–29; cf. 2 Kgs 9:33–37; 10:11, 17). One may wonder if Paul had been reflecting on this text when he composed his thoughts for this letter. If so, perhaps Paul introduces polemic here that has little to do with contemporary details about the identity of those he opposes in Philippi, his language reflecting his negative characterization of any influence or influencers who might be on the scene in terms that reflect scriptural polemics, often against idolatry and those who seek to invoke other gods to action.

The possible specific referents that are called to mind by the epithet "dogs" are very interesting. They include several deities, magic, prostitution, and several philosophical groups, especially the Cynics. To avoid repetition, these will be considered in more detail after the other two epithets in v. 2 have been briefly discussed.

"Beware the Evil Workers"

The designation "evil workers" provides little basis from which to construct any specific identity.[22] Contrary to the traditional interpretations, there is no philological reason to understand workers to signify either travelers or missionaries, that they have arrived from outside Philippi or are anticipated to do so, or that the referents are either Jewish or Christ-followers. [59] Likewise, there is no signal that Paul is reversing their self-labeling as workers of good or proponents of the role of good works alongside faith, as some suggest. For the most part, the identity signified by this phrase is filled out on the basis of decisions made about Paul's use of dogs and mutilation, or from other factors. There is, however, one element of information in Acts that is worth considering—regardless of how anachronistic appeal to Acts might be, which I am not seeking to dispute—because it involves Paul interacting with one who, from his perspective, is most certainly an *evil worker*.

---

also similarly argues that the insult is most logically focused on non-Jews. See Cadwallader, *Beyond the Word of a Woman*, for full discussion of gender issues raised by this epithet.

22. *Pace* Haraguchi, "Das Unterhaltsrecht des frühchristlichen Verkündigers."

Acts 16:12–40 discuss Paul's time in Philippi, and vv. 16–21 introduce a slave woman who is accused of making money for her owners by engaging in divination, prophecy, or fortune telling (μαντευομένη).[23] The author of Acts describes this woman having the "spirit of python [πνεῦμα πύθωνα]," that is, she was able to speak in an alternate voice; this is called "belly-talking."[24] It is possible that the woman represented the cult of Apollo (the special god for Augustus, who won the battle for him at Philippi!), or Cybele, or some other kind of "belly-talker" uttering strange voices.[25]

[60] Certainly, her association with the belly is suggestive, because Paul later polemicizes against those whose "god is their belly" in Phil 3:19. In a similar vein, Plutarch writes of soothsayers of Cybele and Serapis whom he calls "false prophets [*pseudomantesin*]" who sell their prophecies (*Pyth. orac.* 407c).[26] In any case, Paul's contrasting claim in Phil 3:3 to "serve God by spirit" instead of "trusting in" or "persuading by flesh" could certainly signify opposition to just these alternative ways of serving or invoking gods, including by way of claims to be possessed by a spirit.

When Paul is represented to have exorcised the spirit from her, he and Silas are dragged before the magistrates in the marketplace and accused of engaging in *Jewish* activities that were unlawful according to *Roman* customs. This implies that their fortune-telling business operated within the confines of Roman policy, expressing civic cult that could be linked with honoring Caesar as lord, in contrast to the lord whom Paul promotes. The tension runs along a Jewish/non-Jewish institutional line, and the specific

23. It is interesting to note that the Septuagint always refers to μαντεύομαι in pejorative terms connected with the practices of non-Israelites: those who speak falsely, evil workers whose influence should be resisted by the people of God: Deut 18:10 (note, a passage cited in Acts 3:22 and 7:37); 1 Sam 28:8; 2 Kgs 17:17; Mic 3:11; Jer 34:9; Ezek 12:24; 13:6, 23; 21:21, 23, 29; 22:28; see Klutz, *The Exorcism Stories in Luke–Acts*, 216, 225, and his larger discussion of this incident in Acts 16 (207–64).

24. Aune, *Prophecy in Early Christianity and the Ancient Mediterranean World*, 40–41, 268–69.

25. Plutarch, *Def. orac.* 9.414E, calls these soothsayers ventriloquists [note: *engastrimy-thoi* "belly-talkers"] who uttered words beyond their control. See Menander, *Theophoroumenē* (Act 2, Scene 1), for similar possession by Cybele. Bruce, *The Acts of the Apostles*, 360–62; Maurizio, "Anthropology and Spirit Possession"; Brenk, "The Exorcism at Philippi in Acts 16.11–40." See also Klutz, *Exorcism Stories*, 243–47, and 217 n. 37, where Klutz observes that her pronouncement of Paul and Silas as "slaves of the Most High God" "could be associated with any deity one might imagine at the top of the cosmic hierarchy." It can refer to the Jewish deity as well as various pagan deities, as can the phrase "slaves of God," which is associated with Apollo as well. See also Trebilco, "Paul and Silas: 'Servants of the Most High God' (Acts 16.16–18)"; Rapske, *The Book of Acts and Paul in Roman Custody*, 116–19; Reimer, *Women in the Acts of the Apostles*, 160–67; Levinskaya, *The Book of Acts in Its Diaspora Setting*, 83–103.

26. Aune, *Prophecy in Early Christianity*, 42.

matter is whether this group's expression of Judaism conforms to the prevailing non-Jewish legal-cultural norms to which every Jewish group is expected to subscribe in the colony of Philippi.

The point is that, independent of larger constructions of Paul's opponents, "evil workers" would not likely denote Jewish missionaries of any sort, but would probably be aimed at Greco-Roman religious or philosophical rivals who challenge the practices of Paul's addressees for not meeting community standards for Jewish practice. For Paul, it would not be hard to imagine that he would regard such activity to represent "enemies of the cross of Christ," to which he refers later in Phil 3:18; moreover, all of his language in ch. 3 could apply to this sort of behavior from his perspective. The referents for this epithet must be decided on other evidence.

"Beware the Mutilation"

This is the warning most central to the traditional identification of Jews, and specifically of Jews who supposedly promote proselyte conversion (circumcision). The "mutilated ones," or "mutilation [κατατομήν]," is interpreted to be an allusion to a stereotypical Greek and Roman derogatory description of Jewish circumcision, often as though Paul had written "the mutilators" instead. That interpretation is in keeping with the assumption that Paul is engaged in opposing those promoting circumcision, combined [61] with the idea that Paul was opposed to circumcision itself, maintaining that all such ritual or outward or simply Torah-defined identity behavior was no longer appropriate for Christ-followers. The prior decision that Paul was reversing the negative epithet *dogs*, supposedly used by Jews toward non-Jews, but now ostensibly reversed by Paul to describe Jews, leads interpreters to suppose that Paul is also playing the same game with mutilation, and vice versa. Having already found such claims for Paul's use of dogs without merit, one of the strengths of the traditional approach to mutilation as a continuation of that line of argument for Paul is suspect, at the very least; if it too is found to be unlikely, then this further undermines the traditional argument about the referents for dogs, because each of these two epithets has been approached as confirming Jewish identity for the other one. I suggest they instead work together to confirm the likely identification of the referents for all the warnings aimed specifically toward *non-Jewish* influences to be avoided by Christ-followers, non-Jews as well as Jews.

The prevailing interpretation logically involves the decision that Paul actually decried this marker of Jewish identity, which Jews carried out in obedience not only to the Mosaic Covenant with Israel but also to the

Abrahamic Covenant made with him and all of his sons into perpetuity. Obviously, deciding that Paul opposed circumcision of the sons of Jews who turned to Christ in addition to non-Jews completing the rite of proselyte conversion is of enormous significance for constructions of Paul and his communities. If mutilation is the way that Paul values circumcision, then the traditional conclusion that Paul no longer practices Judaism and opposes continuation of Jewish identity and behavior for all Christ-followers gains significant support here.

Grammatically, however, this epithet does not indicate opposition to those who promote mutilation; rather, it denotes those who are mutilated, being a comment on those in that state. Moreover, Torah refers to mutilation in very different terms from circumcision. Torah makes plain the Jewish aversion to "mutilation" as practiced by the idolatrous nations (Lev 19:28; 21:5 [LXX uses the verbal form of the same Greek word for mutilation as does Paul]; 1 Kgs 18:28; Hos 7:14). But interpreters of Paul fail to contemplate that this negative valuation of the practices of the non-Jewish world from the perspective of one still shaped by and practicing Judaism might be guiding Paul's view of the situation of his non-Jewish addressees.[27]

[62] Interpreters maintain that "circumcision" is in view when Paul contrasts it with "mutilation" in part because of the influence of prevailing constructions that understand Paul to be against the practice of Torah, thus Paul's language in the following verses ostensibly conflates together rather than contrasts between mutilation and circumcision: "for we are the circumcision, who serve God in/by spirit (or: who serve [enabled] by God's Spirit) and boast [revel/glory] in Christ Jesus and do not trust in [or: persuade by] flesh" (v. 3). This conflation is further supported by the way that Paul's dissociating argument about his own Jewish credentials in vv. 4–9 is interpreted to indicate that he no longer values or practices the Torah-oriented norms he details, which include his circumcision as an infant. Note, however, that in v. 3 Paul does not write of being "the *true* circumcision," "the *spiritual* circumcision," or of "the circumcision *of the heart*," although interpreters proceed as though he had done so, and often translations explicitly add these qualifiers.[28] At least if he had qualified the kind of circum-

---

27. Meyer, *Critical and Exegetical Handbook to the Epistles to the Philippians and Colossians, and to Philemon*, 122, is adamantly opposed to the idea: "A description of idolatry with allusion to Lev. xxi.5, 1 Kings xviii.28, et al. . . . is quite foreign to the context."

28. E.g., NASB: "for we are the 'true' circumcision," which is notably preceded by translating "mutilation" as "beware of the false circumcision"; Lightfoot, *St. Paul's Epistle to the Philippians*, 144–45: "we are the 'true' circumcision," and Lightfoot understands the contrast to be between "the material and the spiritual circumcision"; Hawthorne, *Philippians*, 126: "The church of Jesus Christ, however . . . is the true Israel (Gal 6:16),

cision in the way interpreters have, it might suggest that the comparison is with others [63] who claim to be the circumcision, while for his own group he makes a superior claim. But Paul does not seem to be troubled that trust in the flesh would be conflated with circumcision, a God-commanded cut made around the flesh. He does not write that "we are not the mutilation" either. And most notably, Paul did not write, "we are the Christians," or "the Christ-followers," or even "the church!"[29]

The traditional interpretation, moreover, fails to answer a number of questions, including the following: Why would he identify himself and his audience as "the circumcision" without qualifying the term if he meant to degrade this specifically Jewish rite as merely "mutilation" in the preceding statement? And when he does qualify it in the following explanation, why does he do so in positive terms, as representative of marking those who live unto the Lord as the circumcised ones? Moreover, in v. 5, why does he choose to include his own circumcision at eight days old in his catalog of honored identity alongside righteousness according to Torah, perpetuating the historical Jewish perspective on this particular cut as something wholly different from mutilation, but also not as though he has changed its usage to signify something spiritual or broadly applied to all Christ-followers?

Paul claims "we are the circumcision" without the qualifiers that translators and commentators find necessary to add when writing to a presumably largely, if not entirely, uncircumcised audience, which profoundly affects the interpretation of the name-calling in v. 2. Paul appears to play on the similarities of sound in Greek between "mutilation" and "circumcision"

---

heir of all the rights and privileges belonging to it (Rom 9:24–26; 1 Pet 2:9–10), including the right to the title, περιτομή ('circumcision'). 'We,' says Paul emphatically, 'are the circumcision,' and not they'"; Bruce, *Philippians*, 80, "It is we, not they, says Paul, who have received the true circumcision.... Those who have received this circumcision render to God true heart devotion"; Donfried and Marshall (*The Theology of the Shorter Pauline Letters*, 152) interpret it to be "a contrasting description of the church. Basically, it is 'the [true] circumcision'"; Fee (*Paul's Letter to the Philippians*, 298–99) translates as "the circumcision," but discusses how "Paul first describes the true circumcision as 'we who "minister" by the Spirit of God'"; although Bockmuehl (*The Epistle to the Philippians*, 191) says that it should not be "true," he nevertheless explains what Paul means in these terms: "it is those who have faith, the circumcised in heart, who are the real 'circumcision'" [Note: on the same page], and "the contrast is between the true circumcision whose service is empowered by and directed towards the Spirit of God, and those whose service is narrow-mindedly focused on their 'works of the Law' as defining their service and status before God"; Fowl (*Philippians*, 147–48) states that it should not be read as true circumcision, but argues that it refers to circumcision of the heart, and "Paul's assertion seeks to locate the worship of the Christian community in Philippi already within the *true* worship of the God of Israel apart from circumcision and taking on the yoke of Torah" (emphasis added).

29. *Contra* Reumann, *Philippians*, 472–78.

(*kata-tomé / peri-tomé*), that is, paronomasia, similar sound for effect, a point that is all the more significant to the degree that Paul's letters are understood to be designed for oral presentation. Although a play on sounds can be made in order to equate two different things, which is what the interpretive tradition requires here,[30] it can also emphasize just how different the two elements are.[31] This pun communicates to the hearer that these two items, ending in roughly similar sounds and sharing reference in that syllable to cutting, should *not* be in any sense naively understood as *comparable*! They are as *different* as cutting *around* and cutting *into*, as *different* [64] as making a covenant with Israel's God *or* with other gods, with serving by spirit *or* serving by flesh.

When the contrastive element is recognized, it suggests that Paul's polemic is not aimed at Jewish people or groups, Christ-boasters or not. In the balance of v. 3, he does not differentiate in strictly Christ-oriented based terms; rather, glorying in Christ is one of three elements. The other two are declarations that any Jewish group would be expected to make ("serving God in/by spirit" and "not trusting in [or: persuading by] flesh"). If we allow that other Jewish groups could also claim a messianic element if not also orientation, which the proper name *Christ* in our translations tends to obscure, then even this element need not suggest anything other than a particular Jewish group's emphasis on a specific messianic figure, Jesus. It is thus unlikely that Paul is setting out circumcision as a metonym for Christ-following identity in contrast to Jewish identity, or in contrast to other Christ-following groups (who would also claim to glory in Christ Jesus), whether Jewish or not, or even other Jewish messianic groups.[32] Instead, he is claiming Jewish-group-based identity and ways of living combined with subgroup Jesus-Christ-following-based identity and ways of living in contrast to non-Jewish, non-Jesus-Christ-following-based identities and ways of living.

---

30. Köster, "κατατομή," *TDNT* 8:109–11; Sumney, "Servants of Satan," 166.

31. As defined in the Poetry Glossary: "A play on words in which the same word is used in different senses or words similar in sound are used in opposition to each other for a rhetorical contrast."

32. *Contra* Wright ("Paul's Gospel and Caesar's Empire," 174–77), who interprets Paul here (in reference to the mutilated if not also in the first two names, which he admits could refer to pagan groups) to be communicating that Jews (Jewish groups) who do not believe in Christ participate "in a form of paganism" and are "subject to the same critique as paganism" (176), and that Paul "has Judaism and paganism . . . simultaneously in mind, and is here using warnings against the former as a code for warnings against the latter" (174). Although I disagree with this analysis, which is based on a decision for "mutilation" that I am challenging herein, the admission of "pagan" referents for the first two epithets is to be noted.

I propose that Paul does not reject circumcision identity for himself or his audience: he claims this rite to be "ours." He also does not claim to be "the non-mutilation" or "non-circumcision" group either, which should give pause to interpreters who believe Paul is using these terms synonymously. That is not to deny the aural pun between mutilation and circumcision in Greek, but to challenge the direction in which it has been interpreted. The pun is based on contrasting—not comparing—circumcision to mutilation as its mirror opposite. Paul's language here echoes the Maccabean slogan, "we are the circumcised" (1 Macc 1:15, 48, 60–61; 2:44–46; 2 Macc 6:10). In [65] other words, circumcision functions as a metonym for the ethno-religious identity of Judaism in contrast to all other ethno-religious identities.[33]

Paul's slogan is based on internalizing circumcised identity as exceptional, as identifying a group that is set apart to God in a way that is to be both celebrated as superior to the practices of other nations and that carries within itself a responsibility to uphold superior, spiritual values in the midst of them, which Paul enumerates in the balance of v. 3, and thereafter in vv. 4–6! Paul is drawing a communal boundary around the addressees as members of the circumcised, that is, of Judaism, and thus different from the foreskinned in the ways that characterize Judaism as practiced by the subgroups of Christ-followers, whether they are circumcised (Jews) or foreskinned (non-Jews). That this metonymical identity excludes non-circumcised males in the community in literal terms is notable, but what has been apparently overlooked for interpreting its meaning here is *that it is no less problematic at the literal level for excluding any women in the community*! Yet interpreters do not thereby conclude from this text that there are no women in the community (the letter makes plain that there are), or that female identity and ways of life are replaced or eliminated or spiritualized by "Christianity," unlike the way that circumcision is interpreted here. Although we may find the metonymic choice of *circumcision* to signify *Judaism* insufficient due to its noninclusiveness, Paul appears to proceed as though this metonym communicates the inclusion of the males who are not circumcised as well as the females in these groups of Christ-followers, and he uses this language to communicate that this identity obliges them to identify themselves *within Judaism* (that is, "Jewish ways of living," albeit as interpreted by a specific subgroup) in contrast to the "pagan" alternative, non-Jewish ways of living available to them. "The

---

33. Livesey, *Circumcision as a Malleable Symbol*, for a recent discussion of various ways of construing the meaning of circumcision by Paul and his contemporaries, although she does not come to the same conclusion I am suggesting for Paul's contrast here.

circumcision" represents their group identity within Judaism, not their individual physical or spiritual state.[34]

Reading Paul's denunciation of mutilation apart from signifying circumcision, but rather in terms of non-Jewish groups and behavior from the majority culture opens several interesting pathways to explore. In the context of the city of Philippi, one might expect (from the point of view of a Jewish [66] writer) that mutilation would be a term of reference to signify those castrated, such as the *galli* of the Cybele cult, or some other kind of mutilation associated with similar religious observances (cf. 1 Kgs 18:28, mentioned above).[35] Self-mutilation is widely associated with "pagan" groups and the way that they seek to provoke God to action (to persuade by or trust in flesh), including by those who employ magic. As will be discussed, a Jew such as Paul might also associate such behavior with Cynics.

ALTERNATIVE INTERPRETATIONS TO EXPLORE

There are several alternatives that immediately come to mind for constructing the situation of Paul's audience in Philippi. Some of the possible referents represent one of the epithets and one or more of the values that Paul decries in vv. 18–19 better than the others; however, there is no reason to assume that Paul has in view only one kind of influence or group, so that each of the alternatives warrants consideration. Nevertheless, some referents can be associated with all three of the epithets in v. 2 and many if not all of the negative comments in vv. 18–19, as well as in terms of the argument of the chapter, and in the case of the Cynics in particular, of the letter overall.

Cults to Gods and Goddesses

Paul could have had a specific cult or deity in view, or made a general reference to these kinds of groups and influences. A number of gods and goddesses were closely associated with dogs, which, from Paul's point of view, would be considered evil workers, and some can also be associated with mutilation. Moreover, images of goddesses (and gods) with dogs were "cut" into the rock

---

34. Cf. Hogg and Abrams, *Social Identifications*.
35. Beard et al., *Religions of Rome*, 218–19, discuss Augustine's use of Seneca, *On Superstition*, frr. 34–37 (Haase), to attack aspects of paganism incorporated into Roman cult, such as self-mutilation, which may well refer to Magna Mater or Cybele (*City of God* VI.9–10). For more on the *galli*, including discussion of their self-mutilation by laceration during traveling blood-letting rituals, see Elliott, *Cutting Too Close for Comfort*, 158–229, esp. 189–93.

hill from which Philippi was built, and under which it stood! They also make relevant referents for the terms expressed in vv. 18–19. In addition, as already noted, the practice of cult involved an integration of local and imperial gods and goddesses with the recognition of the rulers of the empire: it may be that Paul is using veiled language to critique not only the goddess suggestively associated with dogs, but the imperial rulers [67] and their culture. A coin struck in Philippi under Claudius appears to show Augustus on a pedestal alongside a Philippian goddess, or the *Genius* of the city, who is crowning him, with the inscription *DIVVS AVG*, an image that is suggestive of the kind of local, imperial, cultural setting in which Paul's language might have suggested a very different referent from what has usually been considered.[36]

Diana/Artemis/Bendis

To this day, one can see many carved reliefs on the quarried hillside overlooking Philippi. Some of these "incisions" date to the quarrying undertaken during construction in second century C.E.; however, some experts maintain that they were a feature of the area in Paul's period also, for the same hillside was quarried to build the city he visited. Intriguingly, the reliefs are often of Silvanus and Diana (for Greeks, Artemis; for Thracians, Bendis), who are accompanied by dogs in the simple carvings.[37] Diana is associated with fertility, safe delivery of and protection for the newborn, and healing. Some of the rock reliefs depict her killing an animal with a spear or bow and arrow, which bespeaks also of her role as one who wields death.[38]

An interesting twist to consider regarding these inscriptions is that the word we translate "mutilation" (κατατομή) is lexically most commonly used not for "mutilation" at all but to denote an "inscription," "carving," "incision," "notch," or "groove," including specifically the cutting of a rock face or quarry[39]—which is precisely where these reliefs are found! In addition to bearing testimony to continued cult activity, they may also represent [68] gratitude to

---

36. I am grateful to Robert L. Brawley ("From Reflex to Reflection? Identity in Philippians 2.6–11 and Its Context," esp. 128–46) for bringing to my attention this coin (which is pictured in Brawley's essay, 143) and its relevance for the exploration of the goddesses of Philippi, which Brawley finds more salient than the Cynic alternative, in reaction to my survey of these possibilities in "Paul's Reversal." For discussion of the coin's imagery and its significance, see "Philippi, Macedonia."

37. Abrahamsen, *Women and Worship at Philippi*, 25–26; Dorcey, *The Cult of Silvanus*, 67, 91.

38. Abrahamsen, "Evidence for a Christian Goddess: The Bendis-Zodiac Relief at Philippi," esp. 99.

39. *LSJ* 917.

the gods for the rock hill from which the city was hewn.[40] Might Paul's threefold warning seek to alert his audience to beware of cults whose evil-working divinities and their companion iconic dogs were cut into the hillside? Combined with the implications of the above-mentioned "incision" depicting the emperor on local coins, might not allusions to imperial culture be expected to be drawn in Philippi? Does Paul's exclamation later in the chapter of not seeking identity in any earthly colony (v. 20), following the invectives of vv. 18–19, perhaps fashion a contrast with just this sort of commemorative iconography standing over the colony of Philippi? A contrast is drawn between those to whom his addressees are to be grateful and loyal; in other words, they owe their allegiance as citizens to the God of the circumcised, not to the gods celebrated by the imperial rulers and their subjects.

Diana/Artemis carved in Philippian hillside quarry; photo by Mark D. Nanos

Quarried hillside overlooking Philippi; photo by Mark D. Nanos

Cybele

During Claudius' reign (presumably before Philippians, if written under Nero), the Cybele cult was popularized for Romans.[41] A newly developed

---

40. I owe the latter explanation to Alex Lamprianidis, who generously guided my wife and me to the hillside to see these carvings.

41. However, it is not clear whether Romans during Paul's time could participate directly in the processions or join the ranks of the castrated priests (*galli*); see Bormann, *Philippi*, 55–60; Tripolitis, *Religions of the Hellenistic-Roman Age*, 33–34. Also, such "savage" behavior, especially involving human victims, was not generally well received by emperors and officials of our period and was sometimes officially suppressed: Garnsey and Saller, *The Roman Empire: Economy, Society and Culture*, 168–74, explains how, although, e.g., Cybele (Magna Mater) was officially summoned to cope with national

festival introduced Attis—Cybele's consort, who bled to death after castrating himself for Cybele—into the Roman cult. On the "day of blood" the *galli* flagellated themselves while engaged in frenzied, ecstatic dancing, while the initiates castrated themselves with a shard. Castration of *galli* would represent a clear case of "mutilation" and of figures whom Paul would likely regard as "evil workers," perhaps even as behaving like dogs in a general derogatory sense, if not also specifically involving dogs or dog imagery. Many of the comments he makes in vv. 18-19 fit as well.[42]

Cybele (seated) with Hekate; photo by Mark D. Nanos

[69] Divine possession for the Cybele priests was made manifest during ecstatic dancing through prophetic speaking with strange voices

---

emergency such as the invasion by Hannibal, the Senate purged the cult of some extreme features and made it illegal for Roman citizens, and that during the Principate until the early third century C.E. no more exotic cults became part of the official religion, being considered more a threat to ancestral religion than a supplement.

42. Cf. Ulonska, "Gesetz und Beschneidung," 320-21; *contra* Sumney, "*Servants of Satan*," 165.

emanating from their bellies ("belly-talker" or "belly-prophet" [*engastrimantis*], or "ventriloquists" who speak or prophesy from a demon inside of themselves [*engastrimythos*]). This is considered synonymous with "Pythones," and as discussed, the divining woman in Acts 16:16 is described as *pneuma pythōna*, and the witch of Endor in 1 Sam 28:3–25, of whom Saul enquires, is called an *engastrimythos*.[43] Paul's accusation that their god is the belly could be so described.

The Cybele cult provides plenty to regard as "glorying in their shame." The Cybele priests were ridiculed for shameless sexual behavior, including the exchanging of the male active role for that of the female (penetrated) passive role (cf. Rom 1:27).[44]

If the two clauses "whose god is the belly" and "who glory in their shame" are linked, as Hawthorne advocates on grammatical grounds ("they have made their stomach *and* their glory in their shame their god"),[45] then the various links to the Cybele cults and the other options discussed apply all the more. Perhaps most relevant is the observation that in the Septuagint (Hos 9:10; Jer 3:24–25) "shame" is a euphemism for "idols"!

Hekate

Hekate was a ubiquitous goddess often accompanied by dogs, portrayed as a dog, and dogs (puppies) were sacrificed to her. She was a goddess especially associated with passageways and crossroads, that is, with places of liminal danger. She was also involved in conducting the dead safely to Hades, or not doing so, and she was the goddess of magicians.[46] Her cult is ancient, popular with Thracians as well as Greeks, and known as Trivia by [70] the Romans (lit., "three ways"), for statues of her were erected where three roads met, and votive offerings were made for guidance and safety. She is

---

43. Ogden, *Magic, Witchcraft, and Ghosts in the Greek and Roman Worlds*, 30–32; Aune, *Prophecy in Early Christianity*, 40–41; Elliott, *Cutting Too Close*, 190–92, for discussion of Apuleius's account, and 205–7.

44. Elliott, *Cutting Too Close*, 174–82.

45. Hawthorne, *Philippians*, 166, although he understands the implications very differently from how I am arguing the case to be!

46. Ogden, *Magic, Witchcraft*, 4–7, 91–93, 108, 254–56, 272–73; Dickie, *Magic and Magicians in the Greco-Roman World*, 35. The image of dogs is quite common in the world of magic, however defined, including various religious practices and so-called mystery religions. It is common to find the sacrifice of puppies in magical papyri and curse tablets, and described in various ways in incantations, erotic attraction spells, and initiations: see Ogden, *Magic, Witchcraft*, 91–93, 108, 177–78, 233–34, 254–56, 258–59.

sometimes depicted with three faces or heads, looking each of three directions. Is the threefold repetition of *blepete* playing to such imagery?

Hekate can be associated with many of Paul's derogatory terms. In Chaldean literature, dated slightly later than Paul, Hekate is called a "work-woman," and one who bestows life from her "belly" (womb).[47] As a chthonic deity who communicated with those below the ground and was involved in transporting the deceased, Hekate and her cult could also account for Paul's denunciation of those who "think about terrestrial things."[48] Puppies were sacrificed to her and prepared in cakes presented at her shrines, a practice that may be viewed as mutilation (more on this below in discussion of the Cynics).

Dionysus

The cult of Dionysus was popular in Philippi, and apparently associated with Artemis/Diana. Thracian women were supposedly tattooed as punishment for killing Orpheus (Plutarch, *Moralia* 557D), which could be viewed as mutilation by Paul. Dionysus's birth is connected to nearby Mount Pangaion, where Thracians celebrated an oracle belonging to Dionysus and had an ecstatic priestess as well as priests (Herodotus, 5.7; 7.111).[49] In their rituals, apparently the maenads danced ecstatically, and perhaps ate raw meat along with wine in a ritual in which women reversed roles and behaved like men, that is, glorying in their shame. In terms that might be maligned as mutilation, a phallus inside a sacred wicker basket was carried in their processions.[50] There is some indication that Iamblichus, a second-century C.E. novelist, associated belly talkers and other sorcerer figures with initiation into the mysteries such as are associated with this cult.[51]

---

47. Johnston, *Hekate Soteira*, 64ff.

48. Artemidorus, *The Interpretation of Dreams [Oneirocritica]* 2.34; in Hesiod, *Theogony* 411–15, she is said to "have a share of the earth and the unfruitful sea" as well as to be "honoured exceedingly by the deathless gods." Portefaix, *Sisters Rejoice: Paul's Letter to the Philippians and Luke–Acts as Seen by First-Century Philippian Women*, 80–81, and n. 41. See Johnston, *Hekate Soteira*, 32–33, for interesting connection of Hekate with earthly realm and demons.

49. Portefaix, *Sisters Rejoice*, 98–114.

50. Abrahamsen, "Artemis and Dionysos Worshippers at Philippi in the First Century."

51. *Babyloniaka* at Photius *Bibliotheca* 75b; from Ogden, *Magic, Witchcraft*, 32.

Magic, Prostitution

[71] The topic of magic and related terms such as *sorcery, witchcraft,* and *divination* as well as the mystery cults provides a natural avenue to account for Paul's language. Mutilation is commonly associated with magic and divination,[52] which were referred to as arts (ἐργάτας). From Paul's point of view, these would constitute evil "works," malevolent forces against which one should be on watch. From the viewpoint of the author of Rev 22:15, "Outside are the dogs and sorcerers and fornicators and murderers and idolaters [ἔξω οἱ κύνες καὶ οἱ φάρμακοι καὶ οἱ πόρνοι καὶ οἱ φονεῖς καὶ οἱ εἰδωλολάτραι]." Here, dogs are aligned with magicians and immoral people as well as murderers and idolaters.

There is a history of punning on dogs to indicate temple prostitutes, or the penis that has been dogged, that is, suffered a flesh wound from sexual activity.[53] In Deut 23:19, the "wages of a dog" that are not to be brought as offerings in the temple apparently refers to funds derived from male prostitution.[54] If taken in this direction, then evil workers might be a euphemism for prostitutes, those who work in this malicious enterprise, and mutilation might connote eunuchs or some other self-mutilating group, including the *galli* of Cybele.

Philosophical Groups

A number of Paul's epithets in v. 2 and vv. 18–19 are commonly associated with denunciations of philosophical groups by their rivals. As Julian puts the case, philosophical groups would denounce the others as "sorcerers and sophists and conceited and quacks" (*Orations* 6.197; Loeb, trans. W. Wright). The satirist Timon denounced Epicurus as "the lowest *dog* among the physicists."[55] Although later than Paul, Lucian refers to the philosophers whom he is about to encounter as "beasts" who "act like *dogs* that bite and devour one another" (*The Fisherman* 36; cf. *Philosophies for*

---

52. Grayston ("Opponents," 171) suggests the promotion of circumcision as a "semi-magical belief in ritual blood-shedding" arising from "Jewish fantasies of Gentile propagandists."

53. *LSJ*, 1015.7, *frenum praeputii*; cf. Grewel, "The Frenum Praeputii and the Defloration of the Human Male." I am grateful to Daniel Stramara for bringing to my attention the option of sexual activity such as temple prostitution as a possibility for the referent.

54. LEH Lexicon.

55. DeWitt, *St. Paul and Epicurus*, 24; Malherbe, *Paul and the Popular Philosophers*, 84.

Sale 10; [72] cf. Gal 5:15).⁵⁶ In a similar way, Philo depicts the virtues of the Therapeutae in contrast to

> the banquets of others, for others, when they drink strong wine, as if they had been drinking not wine but some agitating and maddening kind of liquor, or even the most formidable thing which can be imagined for driving a man out of his natural reason, rage about and tear things to pieces like so many ferocious dogs, and rise up and attack one another. (*Contemplative Life* 40)

In general terms that apply to some of the language in vv. 18–19 as well, Philo states:

> When it [covetous desire] affects the parts about the belly it makes men gluttonous, insatiable, intemperate, debauched, admirers of a profligate life, delighting in drunkenness, and epicurism, slaves to strong wine, and fish, and meat, pursuers of feasts and tables, wallowing like greedy dogs; owing to all which things their lives are rendered miserable and accursed, and they are reduced to an existence more grievous than any death. (*Laws* 4.91)

The epithet *dogs* especially calls to mind the Cynics. For the sake of space, we will forgo investigation of several other alternatives (Epicureans especially are interesting), as well as the general category of rival religio-philosophical groups.

Cynics

The philosophical group known in English as Cynics is based on the Greek word for "dogs" (κύων; ὁ κυνικός).⁵⁷ They aspired to outdo all others in "doggish" behavior! Yet this option has been rarely noted, and not pursued even then. It is more commonly noted that the language in vv. 18–19 could express negative views of Cynics as well as Epicureans and other philosophical groups. These have probably not been developed for v. 2 because of the force of the traditional interpretation for controlling the options to explore

---

56. Malherbe, *Paul and the Popular Philosophers*, 84.

57. Philo, *Planter* 151; Epictetus 3.22; Diogenes Laertius, *Lives* 6 (*passim*); Lucian, *Demonax* 21; Athenaeus, *Deipnosophistae* 3.96–99; Clement, *Strom.* 8.12.4–7; Malherbe, ed., *The Cynic Epistles*, 99; Vaage, "Like Dogs Barking"; Downing, *Cynics, Paul, and the Pauline Churches*, 35, 40.

here, and because mutilation is not usually associated with such groups,[58] although certainly a case can be made for Paul seeing these philosophers [73] as evil workers. As will be discussed, it is also possible to propose Cynics for mutilation and many of the other invectives in vv. 18–19.

Cynics as Dogs

During Paul's time, anyone warning to beware of the dogs, if not imagined to be taken to refer literally to the animal, might be expected to first of all suppose that the referent was the Cynics. They were a common presence in towns and cities during Paul's time, including in the public squares, where they lived and carried on their lives in squalor calculated to offend. Cynics were famously characterized as harassing those passing their way by "barking" insults at them for living according to the norms of "civilized" behavior. As a result of their lifestyle and tactics, Cynics were regularly accused of shamelessness. It was common for Cynics to be called "mad" (as in "mad dogs") because of their ascetic lifestyle (Ps.-Socrates, *Ep.* 6.1; 9.3; Dio Chrysostom, *Discourses* 34.2–4; 45.1; 66.25; 77/78.41–42; Ps.-Lucian, *Cynic Ep.* 5) and unconventional, vulgar behavior (Dio Chrysostom, *Discourses* 8.36; 9.8).[59] They sought to provoke the realization that civilization masks the way in which humans exploit each other under the cover of civility, in effect exemplifying the worst of behavior associated with the uncontrolled passion of dogs. By eschewing the trappings of society and behaving like dogs, the Cynics ostensibly avoided that hypocrisy and exemplified instead the philosophical ideals that should be the central purpose of human life (ironically, a lie exposed by their own dependence upon those who participated in society to gain the goods on which Cynics relied, however meager, through begging).

The various epithets and invectives Paul employs in 3:2 and vv. 18–19 can be aligned with his probable view of Cynics. "Evil workers" in the general sense of his estimation of their influence is not hard to imagine, although "mutilation" seems to present a challenge. We will return to the topics in v. 2 after a brief survey of the invectives arising in vv. 18–19: "the enemies of the

---

58. Downing (*Cynics, Paul*) does not understand Paul to be referring to Cynics here because he is convinced that this language is "so clearly directed against 'Judaisers'"; he understands Paul in Philippians to be moving away from earlier expressions of Cynicism, and he observes that if taken to refer to Cynics here, vv. 2 and 19 "would have afforded a still clearer sign of a break with Cynics!" (35, 40, 272 n. 5). On mutilation not associated with such groups, see Reumann, *Philippians*, 471–72.

59. Malherbe, *Paul and the Popular Philosophers*, 159–60.

cross of Christ, whose end is destruction, whose god is the belly, who even glory in their shame, who are thinking earthly [thoughts]."

It seems highly unlikely that Paul would refer so vaguely to those who are Christ-followers as *"enemies of the cross of Christ,"* for example, as often maintained, as a denouncement of Christ-followers because they still [74] upheld Jewish values. Be that as it may, anyone challenging Paul and his groups for allegiance to Christ could be accused of being an enemy of the cross of Christ.[60] This invective could be a response to anyone upholding that those aligned with someone who was executed as a feared terrorist is an enemy of the empire.[61] There is no special indication of Cynics, but it is not hard to imagine that Cynics, who were also often maligned as enemies of the empire, could be in view either because they sought to declaim the Christ-followers as more threatening than themselves to the interests of the Philippians, or alternatively, that the Christ-followers were being compared to the Cynics as enemies of Rome, and Paul was seeking to dissociate them from comparisons based on such ideals and norms (they had their own Christ-based Jewish associations, not those of the Cynics).

The accusation that someone's or a group's *"end is destruction"* is also quite vague. In 1:28, Paul uses the same language about opponents of the addressees, or perhaps in a more general sense, of opponents of the message of Christ: "For them this is evidence of their destruction, but of your salvation. And this is God's doing." Here too, the story of Elijah and the prophets of Baal may be at work in Paul's choice of language. Nevertheless, Paul's phrase could easily be taken as ironic criticism of the ultimate ends of several philosophical groups. Stoics upheld that the goal (τέλος) of life was happiness, accomplished by living in accordance with nature, by practical wisdom expressed in moral purpose, but not striving to control what is not under one's control, such as health or death (Cicero, *Fin.* 3.26; Epictetus, *Diss.* 2.19.24), which compares interestingly with Phil 4:11–13, where these are attributed to divine provision. Josephus describes how the Epicureans suppose that "the world runs by its own movement without knowing a guide or another's care," a view of Providence that he considers a mistaken notion of how the world operates that would lead to its being "shattered through taking a blind course and so end in destruction [ἀπωλώλει], just as we see ships go down when they lose their helmsmen or chariots overturn when they have no drivers" (*Ant.* 10.276–81, citation from p. 279; LCL, trans. Marcus).

---

60. Cf. Sumney, "Servants of Satan," 171.

61. Horsley and Silberman (*The Message and the Kingdom*, 202) suggest that vv. 18–19 refer to Nero.

Paul may hold a similar view of the Cynics, who were regarded as actively seeking self-destructive courses of behavior as part of their mission, which Paul may well have in mind when referring to those whose "end [75] is destruction."[62] Cynics could be regarded a positive example for their lack of concern for gaining honor according to the Roman cultural status norms, calling for a return to natural living before civilization's so-called civilizing norms cloaked the legitimation of moral, political, and economic exploitation of the many by the few, for which they were sometimes severely punished in the Roman period[63]—although employing immodest and immoral behavior by prevailing Jewish communal standards (such as the kind listed in vv. 18–19).[64] Would Paul not have found Cynic agnosticism (Lucian, *Zeus Refutatus* 15; Tertullian, *Ad Nationes* 2.2)[65] a sign of their ultimate end, that is, destruction?

The polemical charge that someone or group's *"god is the belly"* is relatively common among philosophers. Among ancient moral philosophers, accusations of serving the belly for pleasure and to avoid responsibility to one's fellow citizens were often contrasted with the self-discipline required of athletes or soldiers, not unlike what we find in Paul's language in this chapter.[66] In general, the Cynics attacked the indulgence of human appetite as misguided. However, this critique was not one-dimensional, because dogs by nature are stereotypically maligned for overeating. Diogenes speaks against indulging appetites (Diogenes Laertius, *Lives* 6.60), [76] but Cynics cleverly expressed preference for eating during *symposia* (suggesting the

---

62. Cf. Downing, *Cynics, Paul*, 143–50.

63. Dio Cassius, *Historia Romanorum* 56, for insulting magistrates publicly, that is, *parrēsia*; Seneca, *Ep.* 20; introduction to Branham and Goulet-Cazé (eds.), *The Cynics*, 12–18; Griffin, "Cynicism and the Romans"; Navia, *Diogenes of Sinope*, 146.

64. And according to the standards of some others who otherwise admire the Cynic tradition, such as Lucian in *Demon.*, *Peregr.*, and *Fug.*; Branham and Goulet-Cazé (eds.), *The Cynics*, introduction, 17.

65. Goulet-Cazé, "Religion and the Early Cynics."

66. Sandnes, *Belly and Body*, 35–60. Bloomquist (*Suffering in Philippians*, 131–33, 178–81, 197–201; also 90), drawing on Neyrey ("The Form and Background of the Polemic in 2 Peter"), observes the possibility that Paul might be engaging in the kind of polemical stereotyping of those considered a threat to piety in Judaism, especially because of their rejection of providence, such as Epicureans, as found in Josephus's depiction of the Sadducees as Epicureans (*War* 2.164–65), in 2 Peter, and in rabbinical texts (cf. Urbach, *The Sages*, 29); cf. Plutarch on Middle Platonism. In this sense, their construction here by Paul may be more a foil than a description of real opponents per se, in order to set out Paul's own position clearly, in this case, against the this-worldly hope of those Paul opposes. Although with some equivocation, Bloomquist regards the likely real historical opponents to be Jewish-Christian pneumatics (*Suffering in Philippians*, 131–33, 198–201).

vice of gluttony) in order to seek to subvert the conventional attention to word games at the meals. Cynics thus sought to attack civilized *talk about* morality instead of undertaking to *practice* actual moral behavior—because those enjoying the symposia gained the wealth that made such civilized dinner entertainment possible through the immoral exploitation of the poor, at least from the perspective of Cynic guests. For this insulting behavior the Cynics were maligned as dogs whose god is the belly (*Lives* 6.61, 270c–d). This topic warrants a bit more discussion.

In a story by Athenaeus (written in the late second century C.E.), the Cynic Cynulcus ("leader of dogs"; 1.1d) traded barbs during a banquet with other guests over the delay of the meal for the sake of continued philosophical discourse. The guest named Ulpian insulted Cynulcus for gluttony, asking if he will gnaw to pieces even the bones, being a dog, to which Cynulcus responded in kind: "You glutton, whose god is your belly [κοιλιόδαιμον], and with no wit for anything else!" (Athenaeus, *Deipnosophistae* ["The Sophists at Dinner"], 3.96f–97). The context involves a Cynic, but it seems that the accusation can be hurled at a Cynic opponent as an insult focused on elevating carnal pleasures above philosophical pursuits; in this case, it appears to imply a preemptive strike by a Cynic turning on his accuser a slam he anticipates. And indeed, the rejoinder flies: "You are another!"

Ulpian not only analogizes the madness of the Cynics with that of dogs, but he also threatens Cynulcus that he will strike him, turning the day into a slaughter like the one in which dogs are slaughtered at Argos, if he will not stop his barking at them instead of at least behaving grateful for the meal, in contrast to the grateful response one gets from a real dog, shown by a wagging tail (3.99e-f). He also informs Cynulcus that his use of "belly-god [κοιλιοδαίμων]" derives from Eupolis having used this language to denote "flatterers [κόλακας] by that name in the play of that name," i.e., "Flatterers" (3.100b). It appears to be the case that flattery was associated with dogs and their bellies in the sense that they flatter their masters, symbolized by having their bellies rubbed in mutual appreciation of each other, but a dog's real motive is self-seeking: it wants to be fed.[67] Ulpian, by articulating this definition of the epithet Cynulcus had used with the intention of insulting [77] Ulpian, is turning it around on Cynulcus, insulting him in stereotypi-

---

67. Interestingly, Athenaeus, *Deipnosophistae*, 6.236e, relates the story of Eupolis's play, "Flatterers," to explain that parasites were called flatterers by earlier poets. Many examples of parasitic or flattering activity (concise definition in 6.255) follow throughout book 6 (234c–262a), many stories involving banquet behavior, continually making the point that flattery is cousin to gluttony, for its purpose is to gain access to food provided by another, with several clever remarks about those who get a "bellyful" as the reward for their fawning lifestyles (e.g., 6.246a–c). Note that Macedonians frequently serve as examples of this flattering behavior (6.255c–257c; 259f–261b).

cal terms as the one whose behavior is recognized to be dog-like, that is, gluttonous (belly-oriented). Cynulcus failed to live up to the conventions of the *symposia* because he sought to undermine its concern for philosophical discussion for discussion's sake by focusing attention on the food itself as the way to express his exasperation with their lack of concern with that to which philosophy should point, moral values as witnessed by concern to feed the poor. In any case, the point is simply that Paul's language may readily call to mind the kind of invectives associated with declamations of Cynics and other philosophical groups.

When Paul writes of those *"who glory in their shame,"* this language can naturally refer to any behavior that is contrary to what Paul believes honorable behavior should be. The phrase can refer euphemistically to the Cynic's strategic public demonstration of animal-like behavior, including stereotypical provocative acts such as farting and defecating, masturbating, and the like, in order to expose that conventions of human social behavior are human constructions: the Cynic thus glories in his shame (Diogenes Laertius, *Lives* 6.69; Diogenes, *Ep.* 44). This language is close to that used by Lucian when specifically writing of a Cynic who practiced erections in public, euphemistically referring to the penis as the "shameful thing [αιδοιον]" (*Peregrinus* 17). Hesychius included reference to "the shameless one" in his lexicon entry for κυών: "the male member, and the barking animal, *and the shameless one*, and the star, and the sea animal."[68] Later lexicons continue to equate Cynics and shamelessness.[69]

Paul's criticism of those who *"think earthly"* or *"terrestrially"* could be aimed at the Cynic philosophical stance that upholds the function of language is to identify the objects of the physical world, not to play linguistic games, as is the case in the discourse of philosophy and science. Even ordinary speech acts are misguided, and reading and writing maligned: "nothing can be either defined or explained, except by pointing to the object."[70] This observation can be combined with the Cynic's general disdain for religious beliefs and practices, for concern with those things about which we [78] cannot know.[71] The idea of living according to "nature" is at work here, that the processes of the physical world occur according to their nature, their essence, the logical laws that govern them,

---

68. Hesychius of Alexandria, *Lexicon*, 555, entry Kappa 1763; cf. Ulonska, "Gesetz und Beschneidung," 327.

69. *Etymologicum magnum*, col. 498: "Dog for the philosopher who does the same as dogs do." "Shameless ones" is also offered as a definition here. Cf. the *kuōn* entry of the Hellenistic *Homer Lexicon* of Apollonius Sophista (*Lexicon Homericum*, 510).

70. Navia, *Diogenese of Sinope*, 94.

71. Ibid., 113–14.

and not outside sources such as divine figures.[72] This means not that a human should behave like a dog per se, but that one should live like a human being naturally, apart from invented conventions such as religion and state (with its wars, slavery, unequal distribution of goods, unequal dispensation of justice) and many other social conventions by which taking advantage of other human beings is legitimated.

Cynics were not necessarily opposed to religion as much as to public expressions of religion, and different Cynics expressed different sensibilities, from opposition to the gods to belief in the gods but not in the human conventions for defining and worshiping, especially images and temples and ritual practices such as sacrifices. Heraclitus defended himself against accusations of impiety and attacked his accusers in Ephesus for their idolatry and temples instead of true piety (*Ep.* 4.10–13),[73] and he mocked ritual castration (*Ep.* 9.15–19). Instead, he recognized the cosmos is god's temple (*Ep.* 4.17), and heavenly creations are to be enjoyed (*Ep.* 4.20–26; 5.14).[74] Demonax notes that if prayer must take place in temples, then this suggests that the god is deaf and cannot hear prayers said away from the temple (Lucian, *Demonax* 27).[75] However, Dio Chrysostom (*Or.* 12) and Maximus of Tyre (*Or.* 2) justify cult images and respect popular piety.

From the perspective of common social conventions, including Jewish conventions, Cynics can easily be associated with the derisive language Paul employs in vv. 18–19, whose "god is their belly," who "glory in their shame," and who actively seek self-destructive courses of behavior as part of their [79] mission: whose "end is destruction," as Paul might put the case.[76] Let us return to the other two epithets in 3:2 in view of this survey.

---

72. Ibid., 116.

73. Attridge, *First-century Cynicism in the Epistles of Heraclitus*.

74. See Attridge, "The Philosophical Critique of Religion under the Early Empire," 64–66; Goulet-Cazé, "Religion," 47–80; Navia, *Classical Cynicism*, 27–31, on 28, observes that while mounting an attack on traditional beliefs and practices, Cynics believed in a spiritual dimension in a way similar to Socrates' ostensible distance from politics, although being himself the quintessential political man (*Apology* 32b; *Gorgias* 521d; *Meno* 100a).

75. See also *Demonax* 11, 32, and 27, for additional criticisms of offerings, the idea of immortality, and prophecy. For a discussion of Oenomaus' criticism of oracles, see Attridge, "Philosophical Critique of Religion," 45–78, 56–60.

76. Cf. Downing, *Cynics, Paul*, 143–50.

Cynics as the Evil Workers

As already mentioned, this vague label could be used for just about anyone or group whose influence Paul opposed. There are, nevertheless, specific associations with Cynics that can be drawn. Just as the belly-talking woman with the spirit of Pythos described in Philippi in Acts 16 can be associated with Apollo, so too the Cynics can be associated with Apollo, the Pythos, and the Delphic precept to "Know Thyself," which is a central theme in Julian's discussion of the Cynics (*Orations* ["To the Uneducated Cynics"] 6.183-89; cf. Diogenes Laertius, *Lives* 6.21). Epictetus notes the commissioning of Cynics by Zeus to reach humankind (*Discourses* 3.22.81-82, 95-96), and he observes that Cynics "enjoyed the privilege of 'dreams and omens, and converse with the gods.'"[77] Dio Chrysostom (*Orations* 32.12) appeals to his work deriving not from his own choice, but by the will of the divine, who provides the appropriate and profitable words to communicate to the listener.

There are many parallels in Philippians with Cynic discourses, although only a few can be discussed here. It seems that Paul is engaged in challenging Cynics over who has the rightful claim to be upholding such ideals. In a sense, Paul may be seeking to out-Cynic the Cynics, to be claiming to have the right to be called the good worker and accuse the other of being the bad one.

Like Paul, the Cynics sought disciples,[78] or in their terms, like physicians, they sought to bring healing to those willing to listen by way of challenging the status quo that sickened the minds of the people, from which they needed to recover by seeing through the conventions to their true nature.[79] Like a surgeon, the Cynic must cut first with bold speech (παρρησία) before healing can begin (Diogenes Laertius, *Lives*, 6.69; Ps. Diogenes, *Ep.* 27-29), [80] which parallels Paul's appeal to using bold speech (παρρησία) for the benefit of the Philippians and others whom he seeks to persuade (1:20). Epictetus describes Cynics as scouts bringing back the truth to humankind so that instead of wandering around in darkness they can return to the "true path" (*Discourses* 3.22.23-26, 69), and he analogizes them to a

---

77. Dudley, *History of Cynicism*, 170.

78. Epictetus, *Discourses* 3.22.23-26; Moles, "'Honestius Quam Ambitiosius'? An Exploration of the Cynic's Attitude to Moral Corruption in His Fellow Men," 112.

79. Cf. Diogenes Laertius, *Lives* 6.4, 6; Dio Chrysostom, *Discourses* 8.5-7; 32.17; 33.6-8, 44; Ps.-Diogenes, *Ep.* 28; 29; Ps.-Socrates, *Ep.* 24; Epictetus, *Discourses* 3.22.72-74; and see Plutarch, *How to Tell a Flatterer from a Friend* 59C-60B, 61D-62C, 73D-74DE; *Progress in Virtue* 80B-C; Malherbe, *Paul and the Popular Philosophers*, 131-35; Navia, *Diogenes of Sinope*, 136; on *typhos*, see 141.

father who has "made all mankind his children; the men among them he has as sons, the women as daughters; in that spirit he approaches them all and cares for them all. Or do you fancy that it is in the spirit of idle impertinence he reviles those he meets? It is as a father he does it, as a brother, and as a servant of Zeus, who is Father of us all" (*Discourses* 3.22.81–82). Lucian portrays Diogenes as "a liberator of men and healer of their passions" (*Philosophies for Sale* 8; cf. *Demonax* 7; *The Fisherman* 46, 52; *Apology* 2; *Downward Journey* 7).[80] Diogenes claims that his dog-like style is undertaken on behalf of others: "Other dogs bite their enemies, but I my friends, to save them."[81] The true Cynic even practices the art of confronting others, understanding the ridicule of themselves that results to be for the ultimate benefit of their victim/accuser as well as for their own training in endurance (Diogenes Laertius, *Lives* 6.64), a feature that is interesting to compare with how Paul defines his own evaluation of the negative response that his activity, and that of his addressees, elicits. Diogenes is the example of how to live well with nothing, including in suffering (Epictetus, *Discourses* 3.22.45–61). Compare Paul's telling the Philippians that his wrongful suffering was gain to him and that similarly their suffering is a privilege:

> Only, live your life in a manner worthy of the gospel of Christ . . . in no way intimidated by your opponents. For them this is evidence of their destruction, but of your salvation. And this is God's doing. For he has graciously granted you the privilege not only of believing in Christ, but of suffering for him as well—since you are having the same struggle that you saw I had and now hear that I still have. (Phil 1:27–30 NRSV; see also 1:16–26; 4:10–14)[82]

If those who argue that Philippians represents a Greco-Roman letter of friendship are correct,[83] then the parallels Paul draws between his service [81] to the addressees at enormous personal cost, like that of Christ toward them (emphasized in ch. 2), is delivered in a way arguably calculated to draw comparisons to the style of delivery that Cynics championed, albeit in person, rather than in letter form.

The parallels between Paul's approach to the Philippians and Cynic discourses are intriguing, and several more fall into this general category

---

80. Baldry, *The Unity of Mankind in Greek Thought*, 111.

81. Attributed to Diogenes by John Stobaeus, *Anthology* 3.13.44, among examples of *parrēsia*.

82. Cf. Stowers, "Friends and Enemies in the Politics of Heaven," 118.

83. White, "Morality between Two Worlds: A Paradigm of Friendship in Philippians"; Stowers, "Friends and Enemies," 105–21.

around what kind of worker Paul is when compared to the Cynics, especially in his approach in ch. 3. Paul's emphasis on endurance, including appeal to the athletic imagery of training for success (vv. 12-16), parallels the common Cynic topos on discipline or practice in training (ἄσκησις), often made in similar athletic terms, in order to be able to persist in the face of constant resistance and discouragement from all other sources.[84] Paul's emphasis on self-denial in order to succeed (vv. 7-21; 4:5-13) is similar to the concerns of the Cynics to gain self-mastery (εγκρατὴς εαυτοῦ), the exercise of which will fly in the face of conventional measures of success.[85] Paul's use of harsh, abusive, and even crass street language throughout ch. 3 (especially the use of "crap" in v. 8), in order to express prophetic critique of the cultural alternatives and any pressure to conform therewith, is similar to the kind of startlingly bold speech (παρρησία) characteristic of Cynics.[86] Finally, in sharp contrast to Paul's claim that "our citizenship is in heaven" [82] rather than in this world (3:19-20), Cynics claim to be "citizens of the world [κοσμοπολίται]." That is, they claim not to be constrained by conformity to the conventions of the citizens of any particular city, but true only to their own self-judgment about what is virtuous in universal terms.[87] Cynics could be regarded as a positive example for their lack of concern for gaining honor on the Roman cultural status norms, although a quite-negative example for immodest and immoral behavior by Jewish communal standards.

84. Diogenes Laertius, *Lives* 6.49, 70-71; Ps.-Crates, *Ep.* 16, 20, 21, 33; Ps.-Diogenes, *Ep.* 31; Epictetus, *Discourses* 3.22.51-52; introduction in Branham and Goulet-Cazé (eds.), *The Cynics*, 26-27.

85. Diogenes Laertius, *Lives* 6.27-30, 45, represent examples of the critique, e.g., of the need for one to be better trained than a Spartan warrior, to be master of one's self more than of another man, to do more to uphold the laws than do the rulers themselves; cf. *Lives* 6.23, 31-34, 59; 7.172; Ps.-Crates, *Ep.* 11, 12; Ps.-Diogenes, *Ep.* 12; 14; Epictetus, *Discourses* 3.22.51-52; Dio Chrysostom, *Or.* 6.8-9; Long, "The Socratic Tradition: Diogenes, Crates, and Hellenistic Ethics," 28-46. That self-mastery was also a Roman value and also espoused by the Stoics (Epictetus, *Discourses* 3.12 [about Cynics]; 3:13.2; Seneca, *Ep.* 18.5-13; 108.15-16, 23) should not be overlooked; Griffin, "Cynicism and the Romans," 201-2.

86. Perhaps there is a parallel concern in Paul's mention of receipt of funds from the Philippians in 4:10-19, wanting to make sure that they understood it was not required, and the implicit contradiction Cynics created with their eschewing of work for pay in order to remain free (the highest value: Diogenes Laertius, *Lives* 6.69-71; Lucian, *Demonax* 21), yet at the same time begging. In other words, they are complicit in the non-freedom of those from whom they receive support, although their philosophy claims to uphold practicing it without harming the other (i.e., that they are friends of humankind [φιλανθρωπία]: Diogenes, *Ep.* 28.3; Heraclitus, *Ep.* 7.2; Dio Chrysostom, *Orr.* 4.24; Epictetus, *Discourses* 3.22.81; 3.24.64; Lucian, *Demonax* 11, 21; Julian, *Orations* 6.201; cf. Moles, "Exploration of the Cynic's Attitude," 112-16.

87. Diogenes Laertius, *Lives* 6.63; Rist, *Stoic Philosophy*, 58-59.

Cynics as the Mutilation

The Cynic option can also be explored in terms of the epithet *mutilation*, as surprising as this might seem.[88] There are both specific and general elements that can be construed as mutilation from the point of view of rivals, especially if the rival is shaped by and communicating based on Jewish sensibilities. The accusation of mutilation might be another way of saying what is reported negatively of a virtuous Cynic according to Julian:

> with his hair unkempt and his clothes in tatters on his chest and wearing a wretched cloak in severe winter weather: "What evil genius can have plunged him into this sad state which makes not only him pitiable.... [N]eglecting everything and no better than a beggar!" (*Orations* 6.198; LCL, trans. Wright)

In a more graphic direction, Diogenes is reported to have endorsed cannibalism, as a "natural," ideal way of eating in some cultures (*Lives* 6.73). In his polemic against Cynics, Philodemus (first century B.C.E.) proclaims that Cynics usually "kill dying members of their family with their own hands and eat them."[89] In a Cynic Epistle addressed to "the so-called Greeks," the corpses of executed criminals (on the cross and on the rack) are derided for having no good use "except to eat as the flesh of sacrificial victims" (εἰ μὴ ὥσπερ ἱερείων σάρκας ἐσθίειν), a paraenetic harangue on the immorality of non-Cynics, who ignore what nature teaches.[90] The topos of cannibalism [83] invoked the barbarian wildness of the Scythians, a famous Cynic icon. The relevance for defining those who might be regarded by Christ-followers as "enemies of the cross of Christ" involved in "mutilation" is intriguing.

The Cynics turned the normally negative connotations of cannibalism into a positive icon of their movement's *autarkeia* ("self-sufficiency"), *parrēsia* ("bold speech"), and freedom from cultural conventions.[91] Al-

---

88. Reumann (*Philippians*, 472), who is otherwise one of the few to consider Cynics the possible referent for "dogs," omits this option because he finds the other two warnings to be "specifically Jewish—one would not call wandering Cynic freeloaders 'workers,' and 'incision/circumcision.'"

89. Höistad, *Cynic Hero and Cynic King*, 147–48.

90. Diogenes, *Ep.* 28 (Malherbe, *Cynic Epistles*, 121). This Cynic topos may inform Trimalchio's satire of cannibalism in Petronius, *Sat.* 141; see Henrichs, *Die Phoinikika des Lollianos*, 70 n. 78.

91. Moles, "Cynic Cosmopolitanism," 112, 117; Romm, "Dog Heads and Noble Savages: Cynicism before the Cynics?," 122–23; Krueger, "The Bawdy and Society: The Shamelessness of Diogenes in Roman Imperial Culture," 226–27; Rappe, "Father of the Dogs? Tracking the Cynics in Plato's Euthydemus," 291–93; Onfray, *Cynismes*, 99–114; Höistad, *Cynic Hero and Cynic King*, 145–46. The Cynic ideal of ἀνθρωποφαγία entered Stoic traditions about the wise; see Bett, *Sextus Empiricus, Against the Ethicists*,

Paul's Polemic in Philippians 3 as Jewish-Subgroup Vilification

though later, Stobaeus claims that Diogenes allegorized the story of Medea to exemplify the virtues of toil because she made those who had grown flabby through luxurious living take up exercise and sweat-baths, and the legend arose that she boiled their flesh to make them into young men (*Flor.* 29.92).[92] Perhaps relevant, traditions circulated that Diogenes made a habit out of eating meat raw in public, which ultimately led to his end when he gnawed into raw but tainted Octopus (*Lives* 6.34, 76), and he was said to have left instructions on his death that his body remain unburied so it could be devoured by wild beasts (*Lives* 6.79).

Painting by Jean-Léon Gérôme, 1860; Walters Art Museum

In yet another direction, Diogenes was said to live in an urn in Athens within the *Metroön* (Mother's Building),[93] which was the location of the cult of the Mother of the Gods, Cybele, with obvious associations to mutilation arising in that cult.[94] Also, Cynics were accused of eating the food left at crossroads in the "Suppers of Hekate," an association that also arises in Talmudic literature and thus, although depicting a later time, nevertheless

---

32, 207–9, 265; and Vander Waerdt, "Zeno's Republic and the Origins of Natural Law," 300–301; cf. Downing, *Cynics and Christian Origins*, 50, 173–74; and the response by McGowan, *Ascetic Eucharists*, 73–75.

92. Dudley, *A History of Cynicism*, 33.

93. Diogenes Laertius, *Lives*, 6.23; Diogenes, *Ep.* 16.

94. On the other hand, the Cynic Heraclitus of Ephesus criticized the castration of priests in the cult of the Mother Goddess, likening it to men enslaving men and impious behavior toward nature, wherein dogs do not castrate other dogs (Attridge, *Heraclitus*, 85).

reflects Jewish stereotypical notions about and polemic concerning Cynics. This brings up a specific "Jewish" context to consider in more detail.

[84] M. Luz argues that third-century rabbis discuss Cynics when defining madmen in the Talmud, where they are called *kynukos*, versus the madman, who is called *kurdyakos*.[95] The *kynukos*, that is, the dog/Cynic, is one who is characterized by four things: he "sleeps in the graveyard, burns incense to the demons, rends his clothing, and destroys what people give him."[96] Here is the case that Luz lays out:[97]

1. Lucian mocks a Cynic for living in "a tomb,"[98] and it is in sepulchers also where the Gospels' report that mad demoniacs live,[99] in the area of Gadara/Gerasa, from where several prominent Cynics came, near Tiberias, and thus within the orbit of the rabbis.[100]

2. Lucian also mocks Menippus, the Cynic from Gedara,[101] for eating Hecate's suppers at the crossroads with the poor and eggs discarded there after purification rites.[102] If the Cynics were seen eating the offerings to Hekate, including some people cooking the largely uncooked meat left for her at these altars and crossroad posts, or toasting the cheese cakes (flame-cakes; an option for the smoke apparently unrealized by Luz), this activity might well be misconstrued (or misrepresented) by the rabbis to be the burning of incense to demons.

3. That the mad who were suffering demon possession mutilated their clothes and their bodies is referred to commonly, including in the Gospel accounts (Matt 5:1ff.; Luke 8:27) and could easily be

---

95. y. Giṭ. 7.1; y. Ter. 1.1; and b. Ḥag. 3b–4a; Luz, "A Description of the Greek Cynic in the Jerusalem Talmud."

96. y. Giṭ. 7.1 (trans. Luz).

97. The following comparison draws from Luz, "Description of the Greek Cynic," 55–60.

98. Lucian, *Philosophies for Sale* 9.

99. Matt 8:28; Mark 5:1; Luke 8:26.

100. Strabo 25.759.29. Luz argues that the rabbis involved had witnessed the behavior of Cynics in Gadara, near Tiberias. Gadara was the birthplace of the Cynics Menippus (third century B.C.E.), Meleager (first century bce?), and Oenomaos (second or third century ce?); Navia, *Classical Cynicism*, 166–74.

101. Diogenes Laertius, *Lives* 6.99; Dudley, *History of Cynicism*, 69–74, for discussion of the life of Menippus.

102. Lucian, *Philosophies for Sale* 8; Lucian, *Downward Journey* 7; Lucian, *Dialogues of the Dead* 1.331; 2.425.

dismissively applied to the tattered *tribon* (cloak) worn by the Cynic with great pride.[103]

4. [85] Especially telling for the comparison by the rabbis of the *kynukos* and *kurdyakos* was the destroying of what one receives, which applies well to the Cynics, who celebrated the dispossession of their property: stereotypically, their famed defacing of the currency.[104] I would add that this could also be categorized as mutilation, for which the defacing of the currency by chisel stands for the mutilation of prevailing social convention by their development of frank speech and provocative lifestyle (Julian, *Orations* 7.211), as well as being a play on what "incision" of the coin signifies, namely, "mutilation." The Cynics celebrate *katatomē*!

Luz demonstrates that the rabbis were describing Cynics in general terms that included exaggerated misunderstandings of certain traits; these can be summarized as follows: the Cynic "wears torn clothes, destroys/throws away his property, sleeps in the graveyard, and handles offerings left to netherworld demons."[105] The case can be considered all the stronger if we take into consideration Hekate's association with dogs in her persona and as her companions depicted in iconography, as well as in the puppy meat of which offerings to her consisted. Then the rabbis were involved in punning on *kynukos* all the more, involving double entendre, as was Lucian when speaking of Cynics' eating the suppers of Hekate, that is, the dogs eating dog food. For our purpose, these associations might also help explain why Paul includes evil workers and the mutilated along with reference to the dogs: Paul's polemic builds on stereotypical associations one might expect from the perspective of his Jewish sensibilities where these "pagan" groups are concerned.

Cynics as the Target of Paul's Invectives?

It is not clear that Paul had in view Cynics in ch. 3 in every case, or even in any case, but it is a tantalizing idea to pursue. There are a number of parallels that I have not undertaken to discuss in this essay, but the value of exploring this identification is further heightened when we take into account 1 Thess

---

103. Diogenes Laertius, *Lives* 6.22; 7.87; Lucian, *Dialogues of the Dead* 1.332; Ps.-Lucian, *Cynic Ep.* 1.
104. Diogenes Laertius, *Lives* 6.37, 87; Lucian, *Philosophies for Sale* 9.
105. Luz, "Description of the Greek Cynic," 59.

2:1-2, where Paul indicates that he had suffered shameful treatment in Philippi before his arrival in Thessalonica.

Paul's language in 1 Thess 2:1–8 has been compared by Abraham Malherbe to Dio Chrysostom's polemical descriptions of Cynics who do not [86] represent the Cynic ideals to which Dio subscribed.[106] Malherbe notes that Paul's description of his willingness to suffer for speaking boldly in spite of the negative reaction of the crowd exemplifies Chrysostom's portrait of the true Cynic philosopher's bold struggle against social pressure (vv. 1–2).[107] Paul claims to preach unlike the charlatans who deceive and lead their hearers into error (v. 3).[108] This might suggest that the Thessalonians know Paul to have been mistaken for a Cynic in Philippi (perhaps also by those who responded positively to his message?) or to express himself in contrast to certain stereotypical Cynic qualities that could be easily polemicized, or even to be exemplifying popular philosophical ideals to which he believes his audience subscribes.[109]

What might an identification of Cynics suggest about the identity of the audience in Philippi and their concerns? Several options readily come to mind.

1. Paul's addressees might be maligned by their non-Jewish families and neighbors as Cynics or Cynic-like for failing to uphold the norms of social life to which they had formerly subscribed—including family and civic cult as well as the pursuit of honor and success on Roman society's prevailing terms. This would be perhaps a natural way for their families and neighbors to classify their newly adopted countercultural lifestyles,[110] albeit in terms that Paul regards to be inappropriate comparisons for them to internalize for themselves.

2. Cynics might be attacking his addressees. They may be perceived to be Cynic-like in many ways, but the Philippians' commitment to Christ and the norms of the Jewish groups to which they have become members could bring criticism on them from Cynics, or from those

---

106. Malherbe, *Paul and the Popular Philosophers*, 35–48. It should also be noted that Ignatius, in his *Letter to the Ephesians* 7.1-2, refers to "mad dogs, biting in secret," who are to be avoided, which may refer to docetic teachers or Cynics: see Schoedel and Koester (eds.), *Ignatius of Antioch*, 59–60.

107. Malherbe, *Paul and the Popular Philosophers*, 47.

108. Ibid.

109. Cf. Theissen, *The Social Setting of Pauline Christianity*, 39.

110. This is a central idea for how Paul would have been perceived among non-Jews for Downing, *Cynics, Paul,* however, interestingly, not with respect to Philippians.

who appreciate Cynic values, for having failed to exemplify Cynicism because of these conventions and beliefs.

3. [87] It is within the scope of either of these options that his Christ-following non-Jews may be looking to Cynics as role models in view of the alienation they were suffering since becoming followers of this Jewish subgroup loyal to Christ. They might even be considering themselves Cynics, or on their way to becoming Cynics ideally. (This is a kind of loose rather than formal affiliation with initiation rites, and *Cynic* was a rather loosely used term, along the lines of defining a "hippie" in more recent years; it was not unusual for Cynics to consider others claiming this identity or adopting certain behavior to be imposters by their own standards).

It is intriguing to wonder whether this was indeed the option that his addressees were exploring if not also adopting in order to make sense of the implications of the message of Christ as they interpreted it after Paul departed. The one to whom they claimed loyalty was executed by the Romans as a threat to society, not unlike how the Cynics considered themselves, and were considered by many to be, which may have suggested a positive affiliation to pursue. His message led them into a marginalized identity and threatened their access to honor and goods: how were they to negotiate living "in the present age," although claiming to be living according to the chronometrical proposition that "the end of the ages had dawned" and was to be exemplified in their communal and personal lives? Had they become aware of their group as a subgroup of Jewish communal ways of living that was itself countercultural, not only in terms of the Roman city in which they lived and into which they had been enculturated, but also in terms of the larger Jewish community and its other, various (rival?) subgroups in Philippi or elsewhere throughout the empire? In such a place, without Paul to guide them into his own particular Jewish Christ-based subgroup's way of interpreting the options for how they should now live, did they suppose that the Cynic culture offered them the best alternative to explore to make sense of their new identity, for how to be non-Jews in a new, unconventional Jewish subgroup?

If so, then Paul's presentation of his message to them in very Cynic-like terms may have been constructed with the expectation they would recognize that, for all of its similarities to Cynic values and the marginalization they suffered, their new identity was also very different from that of the Cynics, or should be. In this direction, it may be that Paul wants them to "consider"—as in "reflect on"—the Cynics (and or other groups), which, as noted earlier, is the way that some have argued that the repetition of βλέπετε in 3:2 should be interpreted, rather than "beware" or "watch out" for them.

[88] Paul may be, as it were, seeking to out-Cynic the Cynics, as well perhaps to demonstrate the failure of any criticism of his addressees based on comparisons to Cynics. For Paul argues that they are to value identity and lifestyle norms in Christ above the status and access to goods that might be available to them through compliance with the majority cultural values, including the (non-Christ-following) Jewish majority cultural values, but also with any countercultural groups and values that may seem to provide available models or to be attractive options. Although Cynics may vie for the right to be the *top dog* among themselves, Paul denies that this should be so for himself (3:4–14, even if his argumentative strategy betrays his dependence on being able to make just that claim!) or anyone else who shares his loyalty to Christ; even Christ himself did not do so (2:5–8)!

If Cynics were in view, Paul would presumably want to clarify the differences between his addressees as members of the Jewish community ("we are the circumcision") and Cynics or other similar representatives of "non-Jewish" cultural values (the "dogs," "evil workers," "mutilation," and so on of vv. 2, 18–19). If so, then Paul dissociates them from Cynics in polemical style, making plain the ethos of Christ-followers within this Jewish subgroup. They are those who worship God by spirit, boast in Jesus Christ, and do not seek honor-ranking in normal social terms (or perhaps, who do not seek to persuade by παρρησία according to the flesh; vv. 3ff.). All this sort of ranking, however desirable, as birth and fidelity obviously remain for Paul himself in order to make his point—a valuation that he apparently believes his audience shares with him to expect it to carry the rhetorical weight his argument depends on—is mere "crap" *if* it would threaten to come between him and his standing in Christ above *all other honors*.[111] Paul calls his audience to share this comparative point of view toward any "pagan" rank and privilege that might lead to discrimination among themselves.

CONCLUSION

Although recent interpreters of Philippians observe that a tension between honoring Christ versus honoring Caesar appears to be a major concern of this letter—for example, in 1:27–30 (that their suffering is like Paul's, who is in prison for anti-imperial activity); 2:5–15 (the elevation of Jesus to lord of all, rather than Caesar's claim to that role); and 3:20 (their [89] citizenship

---

111. Similarly, see Campbell, "'I Rate All Things as Loss': Paul's Puzzling Accounting System."

in the colony of heaven, rather than Philippi)—they have not focused on a clash of values with "pagan" culture in 3:2–19, because they continue to draw on the traditional interpretation of these verses, wherein Paul's opposition is supposedly from Jewish or Jewish Christian missionaries.[112] In view of the many options discussed, however, it is unlikely that Paul's argument and the specific phrases he employed in Phil 3 suggest that he was opposing Jews or problems arising from rivalry with Jews (Christ-following or not) or Jewish ways of life (Judaism). Quite the opposite, Paul appears to oppose local "pagan" influences and influencers and to promote Jewish values and ways of life. In the face of competing non-Jewish "pagan" communal alternatives on offer in Philippi with which his (primarily if not exclusively) non-Jewish addressees are tempted to identify (seeking status and goods), Paul aims to persuade them to instead identify with Paul's Jewish norms because they are followers of Christ.

I thus suggest that Paul's appeal to his own Jewish identity and behavioral credentials in 3:4–6 was not presented to oppose alternative Jewish groups or individuals appealing to their superior Jewish identity and behavioral credentials but to qualify his authority to instruct them to adopt a path that will not resolve their marginalization on any other community's, subgroup community's, or even countercultural community's terms. He did not want to give the impression that they were to compete for honor or rank on Jewish or non-Jewish terms, or that he did so either, and thus he qualified the advantages of his own ranking—although at the same time implicitly (that is, rhetorically) appealing to his advantaged identity in order to make his point.[113] In other words, interpreters miss the rhetorical force of his point when suggesting that Paul here denounces his "past" identity as a Jew who practiced Judaism: his argument is predicated on his audience knowing him to be a Jew who "still" practices Judaism in exemplary fashion. Thus, [90] he wants to communicate that he does not let the social advantage normally accompanying Jewish identity to come before his shared identity with them "in Christ"; nor should they seek social advantage among themselves by the various "pagan" communal terms available to them. The qualification

---

112. There is a growing consensus on the imperial context of Paul's rhetoric in certain texts: see, e.g., Brewer, "The Meaning of πολιτεύεσθε in Phil 1:27"; Miller, "πολιτεύεσθε in Phil. 1.27"; Seeley, "The Background of the Philippians Hymn (2:6–11)"; Fee, *Philippians*, 29–33; Bockmuehl, *Philippians*, 234–35; Oakes, *Philippians*, 129–74; Wright, "Paul's Gospel," esp. 173–81; de Vos, *Community Conflicts*, 263–75.

113. Marchal, *The Politics of Heaven*, discusses many factors to consider for undertaking a people's history approach to Philippians, including a sustained analysis of Paul's reinscription of various cultural values he ostensibly opposes in the actions of others, a dynamic that interpreters often fail to recognize in their advancement of Paul as role model.

is based on a comparative identity he shares with them, that of knowing, or seeking to know and be known by God in Christ—"everything" else pales *in comparison*.

For Paul's addressees, the "pagan" identity and behavioral alternatives were not brand new. They had guided their self- and group-identity until they became followers of Christ, and they still appear to offer desirable advantages. It is not easy for them to abandon the status and access to goods that affiliation with these "pagan" groups can offer, especially when they cannot claim access to status and goods as though they had become Jews, because unlike Paul, they have been and remain non-Jews. But Paul has brought them into Judaism, with the result that they are confused and seeking relief from the consequences that have developed from their ambiguous new identity in Christ-following Jewish (sub)groups. Even though Paul could easily seek honor in Jewish community terms, as the addressees are tempted to seek to be able to do in "pagan" community terms, he calls them to resist that temptation (even if we witness him doing just that to make this point). Together they must suffer communal disapproval for their identification with the marginalized community of believers in Jesus Christ, whom they believe to be the true "lord" of all.

Paul's call to suffering for faithfulness to the example of Christ (and of Paul himself) echoes Elijah's pointed language, which, as noted earlier, seems to be a salient passage for Paul when he composed Philippians, especially ch. 3. Paul's approach bespeaks a conflict between the Christ-following Judaism into which these non-Jews have now been, or should be, enculturated and the alternatives outside this Judaism to which they may be attracted, or by which they may be threatened: "How long will you keep hopping between two opinions? If the Lord is God, follow Him; and if Baal, follow him!" (1 Kgs 18:21, NJPSV).

If ch. 3 is interpreted around a conflict between Jewish and "pagan" values and groups, perhaps Cynics, or various cults and other possibilities in some combination, including in terms of conflicting imperial allegiances (citizenship), then this language can be integrated into the overall focus of the letter. That appears to revolve around the choice that Paul calls his audience in Philippi to make between the "pagan" cultural alternatives that remain attractive or otherwise constrain the options available to themselves if they wish to avoid suffering, and the Jewish cultural values that their commitment [91] to Jesus as Christ should compel them, from Paul's point of view, to undertake instead.

This alternative at least raises the prospect of considering new ways to understand how these conflicting cultural norms might be shaping the lives of the audience and the choices they are making before the arrival of Paul's letter, as well as how they might react to it. I hope that sufficient questions have been raised to encourage interpreters to reconsider perpetuating the prevailing paradigm when sketching out the options to consider for the identity and concerns of Paul's audience, as well as Paul's communication goals.

BIBLIOGRAPHY

Abrahamsen, Valerie A. "Artemis and Dionysos Worshippers at Philippi in the First Century." Paper presented at the Philippians People's History Working Group, annual meeting of the Society of Biblical Literature, Boston, 2008.
———. "Evidence for a Christian Goddess: The Bendis-Zodiac Relief at Philippi." *Forum* 3rd series 1/1 (2007) 97–112.
———. *Women and Worship at Philippi: Diana/Artemis and Other Cults in the Early Christian Era*. Portland, ME: Astarte Shell, 1995.
Ascough, Richard S. *Paul's Macedonian Associations: The Social Context of Philippians and 1 Thessalonians*. WUNT 2/161. Tübingen: Mohr Siebeck, 2003.
Attridge, Harold W. *First-century Cynicism in the Epistles of Heraclitus*. Harvard Theological Studies 29. Missoula, MT: Scholars, 1976.
———. "The Philosophical Critique of Religion under the Early Empire." In *Aufstieg und Niedergang der römischen Welt: Geschichte und Kultur Roms im Spiegel der neueren Forschung*, edited by Wolfgang Haase, 45–78. Berlin: de Gruyter, 1978.
Aune, David Edward. *Prophecy in Early Christianity and the Ancient Mediterranean World*. Grand Rapids: Eerdmans, 1983.
Bakirtzis, Charalambos. "Paul and Philippi: The Archaeological Evidence." In *Philippi at the Time of Paul and After His Death*, edited by C. Bakirtzis and H. Koester, 37–48. Harrisburg, PA: Trinity, 1998.
Baldry, H. C. *The Unity of Mankind in Greek Thought*. Cambridge: Cambridge University Press, 1965.
Beard, Mary, John A. North, and S. R. F. Price. *Religions of Rome*. 2 vols. Cambridge: Cambridge University Press, 1998.
Bett, Richard. *Sextus Empiricus, Against the Ethicists (Adversus Mathematicos XI)*. Oxford: Clarendon, 1997.
Bloomquist, L. Gregory. *The Function of Suffering in Philippians*. JSNTSup 78. Sheffield, UK: JSOT Press, 1993.
Bockmuehl, Markus N. A. *The Epistle to the Philippians*. Peabody, MA: Hendrickson, 1998.
Bormann, Lukas. *Philippi: Stadt und Christengemeinde zur Zeit des Paulus*. SNT 78. Leiden: Brill, 1995.
Branham, Robert Bracht, and Marie-Odile Goulet-Cazé, eds. *The Cynics: The Cynic Movement in Antiquity and Its Legacy*. Berkeley: University of California Press, 1996.
Brawley, Robert L. "From Reflex to Reflection? Identity in Philippians 2.6–11 and Its Context." In *Reading Paul in Context: Explorations in Identity Formation*, edited by Kathy Ehrensperger and J. Brian Tucker, 128–46. London: T. & T. Clark, 2010.

Brenk, Frederick E. "The Exorcism at Philippi in Acts 16.11–40: Divine Possession or Diabolic Inspiration?" In *With Unperfumed Voice: Studies in Plutarch, in Greek Literature, Religion and Philosophy, and in the New Testament Background*, edited by Frederick E. Brenk, 495–513. Stuttgart: Steiner, 2007.

Brewer, R. R. "The Meaning of πολιτεύεσθε in Phil 1:27." *Journal of Biblical Literature* 73 (1954) 76–83.

Bruce, F. F. *The Acts of the Apostles: The Greek Text with Introduction and Commentary*. 3rd ed. Grand Rapids: Eerdmans, 1990.

———. *Philippians*. A Good News Commentary. San Francisco: Harper & Row, 1983.

Cadwallader, Alan H. *Beyond the Word of a Woman: Recovering the Bodies of the Syrophaenician Women*. ATF Biblical Series 1. Adelaide, Australia: ATF, 2008.

Campbell, William S. "'I Rate All Things as Loss': Paul's Puzzling Accounting System. Judaism as Loss or the Re-evaluation of All Things in Christ?" In *Celebrating Paul: Festschrift in Honor of Jerome Murphy-O'Connor, O.P., and Joseph A. Fitzmyer, S.J.*, edited by Peter Spitaler, 39–61. CBQMS 48. Washington, DC: Catholic Biblical Association of America, 2011.

Cohen, Shaye J. D. *The Beginnings of Jewishness: Boundaries, Varieties, Uncertainties*. HCS 31. Berkeley: University of California Press, 1999.

de Vos, Craig Steven. *Church and Community Conflicts: The Relationships of the Thessalonian, Corinthian, and Philippian Churches with Their Wider Civic Communities*. SBLDS 168. Atlanta: Scholars, 1999.

DeWitt, Norman Wentworth. *St. Paul and Epicurus*. Minneapolis: University of Minnesota Press, 1954.

Dickie, Matthew. *Magic and Magicians in the Greco-Roman World*. London: Routledge, 2001.

Donfried, Karl P., and I. Howard Marshall. *The Theology of the Shorter Pauline Letters*. New Testament Theology. Cambridge: Cambridge University Press, 1993.

Dorcey, Peter F. *The Cult of Silvanus: A Study in Roman Folk Religion*. Columbia Studies in the Classical Tradition 20. Leiden: Brill, 1992.

Downing, F. Gerald. *Cynics and Christian Origins*. Edinburgh: T. & T. Clark, 1992.

———. *Cynics, Paul, and the Pauline Churches*. London: Routledge, 1998.

Dudley, Donald Reynolds. *A History of Cynicism: From Diogenes to the 6th Century A.D.* Hildesheim, Germany: Olms, 1967.

Elliott, Susan M. *Cutting Too Close for Comfort: Paul's Letter to the Galatians in Its Anatolian Cultic Context*. JSNTSup 248. London: T. & T. Clark, 2003.

Ellis, E. Earle. "Paul and His Opponents: Trends in Research." In *Christianity, Judaism and Other Greco-Roman Cults: Studies for Morton Smith at Sixty*, edited by Jacob Neusner, 264–98. Leiden: Brill, 1975.

Etymologicum magnum. Edited by Frederic Sylburg. Leipzig: Wiegel, 1816.

Fee, Gordon D. *Paul's Letter to the Philippians*. NICNT. Grand Rapids: Eerdmans, 1995.

———. *Philippians*. IVP New Testament Commentary 11. Downers Grove, IL: IVP, 1999.

Fowl, Stephen E. *Philippians*. Two Horizons New Testament Commentary. Grand Rapids: Eerdmans, 2005.

Fredriksen, Paula. "Judaizing the Nations: The Ritual Demands of Paul's Gospel." *New Testament Studies* 56 (2010) 232–52.

Garland, David E. "The Composition and Unity of Philippians." *Novum Testamentum* 27 (1985) 141–73.

Garnsey, Peter, and Richard Saller. *The Roman Empire: Economy, Society and Culture.* Berkeley: University of California Press, 1987.

Goodblatt, David. *Elements of Ancient Jewish Nationalism.* Cambridge: Cambridge University Press, 2006.

Goulet-Cazé, Marie-Odile. "Religion and the Early Cynics." In *The Cynics: The Cynic Movement in Antiquity and Its Legacy,* edited by Robert Bracht Branham and Marie-Odile Goulet-Cazé, 47–80. Berkeley: University of California Press, 1996.

Grayston, Kenneth. "The Opponents in Philippians 3." *Expository Times* 97.6 (1986) 170–72.

Grewel, F. "The Frenum Praeputii and the Defloration of the Human Male." *Folia Psychiatrica, Neurologica et Neurochirurgica Neerlandica* 61.2 (1958) 123–26.

Griffin, Miriam. "Cynicism and the Romans: Attraction and Repulsion." In *The Cynics: The Cynic Movement in Antiquity and Its Legacy,* edited by Robert Bracht Branham and Marie-Odile Goulet-Cazé, 190–204. Berkeley: University of California Press, 1996.

Gunther, John J. *St. Paul's Opponents and Their Background: A Study of Apocalyptic and Jewish Sectarian Teachings.* NovTSup 35. Leiden: Brill, 1973.

Haraguchi, Takaaki. "Das Unterhaltsrecht des frühchristlichen Verkündigers: Eine Untersuchung zur Bezeichnung ἐργάτης im Neuen Testament." *Zeitschrift für die neutestamentliche Wissenschaft und die Kunde der älteren Kirche* 84 (1993) 178–95.

Hawthorne, Gerald F. *Philippians.* WBC 43. Waco, TX: Word, 1983.

Heen, Erik M. "Phil 2:6–11 and Resistance to Local Timocratic Rule: *Isa theo* and the Cult of the Emperor in the East." In *Paul and the Roman Imperial Order,* edited by Richard A. Horsley, 125–53. Harrisburg, PA: Trinity, 2004.

Hellerman, Joseph H. *Reconstructing Honor in Roman Philippi: Carmen Christi as Cursus Pudorum.* SNTSMS 132. New York: Cambridge University Press, 2005.

Henrichs, Albert. *Die Phoinikika des Lollianos: Fragmente eines neuen griechischen Romans.* Papyrologische Texte und Abhand-lungen 14. Bonn: Habelt, 1972.

Hesychius of Alexandria. *Lexicon.* Vol. 2. Edited by Kurt Latte. Copenhagen: Munksgaard, 1953.

Hogg, Michael A., and Dominic Abrams. *Social Identifications: A Social Psychology of Intergroup Relations and Group Processes.* London: Routledge, 1988.

Höistad, Ragnar. "Cynic Hero and Cynic King: Studies in the Cynic Conception of Man." PhD diss., University of Uppsala, 1948.

Holladay, Carl R. "Paul's Opponents in Philippians 3." *Restoration Quarterly* 12 (1969) 77–90.

Horsley, Richard A., and Neil Asher Silberman. *The Message and the Kingdom: How Jesus and Paul Ignited a Revolution and Transformed the Ancient World.* New York: Grossett and Putnam, 1997.

Jewett, Robert. "Conflicting Movements in the Early Church as Reflected in Philippians." *Novum Testamentum* 12 (1970) 362–90.

Johnston, Sarah. *Hekate Soteira: A Study of Hekate's Role in the Chaldean Oracles and Related Literature.* American Classical Studies 21. Atlanta: Scholars, 1990.

Jones, Siân, and Sarah Pearce, eds. *Jewish Local Patriotism and Self-Identification in the Graeco-Roman Period.* JSPSup 31. Sheffield, UK: Sheffield Academic Press, 1998.

Kilpatrick, George D. "ΒΛΕΠΕΤΕ, Philippians 3.2." In *In Memorium Paul Kahle,* edited by M. Black and G. Fohrer, 146–48. Berlin: Töpelmann, 1968.

Klijn, A. F. J. "Paul's Opponents in Philippians iii." *Novum Testamentum* 7 (1964) 278–84.

Klutz, Todd. *The Exorcism Stories in Luke-Acts: A Sociostylistic Reading*. SNTSMS 129. Cambridge: Cambridge University Press, 2004.

Koester, Helmut. "The Purpose of the Polemic of a Pauline Fragment." *New Testament Studies* 8 (1961–62) 317–32.

Koukouli-Chrysantaki, Chaido. "Colonia Iulia Augusta Philippensis." In *Philippi at the Time of Paul and After His Death*, edited by Charalambos Bakirtzis and Helmut Koester, 5–35. Harrisburg, PA: Trinity, 1998.

Krueger, Derek. "The Bawdy and Society: The Shamelessness of Diogenes in Roman Imperial Culture." In *The Cynics: The Cynic Movement in Antiquity and Its Legacy*, edited by Robert Bracht Branham and Marie-Odile Goulet-Cazé, 226–27. Berkeley: University of California Press, 1996.

Levinskaya, Irina. *The Book of Acts in Its Diaspora Setting*. The Book of Acts in Its First Century Setting. Grand Rapids: Eerdmans, 1996.

Lexicon Homericum. Vol. 2. Edited by J. C. Molini. Paris: 1773.

Lightfoot, J. B. *St. Paul's Epistle to the Philippians: A Revised Text with Introduction, Notes and Dissertations*. J. B. Lightfoot's Commentary on the Epistles of St. Paul. 12th ed. Peabody, MA: Hendrickson, 1995.

Livesey, Nina. *Circumcision as a Malleable Symbol*. WUNT 2/295. Tübingen: Mohr Siebeck, 2010.

Long, A. A. "The Socratic Tradition: Diogenes, Crates, and Hellenistic Ethics." In *The Cynics: The Cynic Movement in Antiquity and Its Legacy*, edited by Robert Bracht Branham and Marie-Odile Goulet-Cazé, 28–46. Berkeley: University of California Press, 1996.

Luz, M. "A Description of the Greek Cynic in the Jerusalem Talmud." *Journal for the Study of Judaism in the Persian, Hellenistic, and Roman Periods* 20.1 (1989) 49–60.

Malherbe, Abraham J. ed., *The Cynic Epistles*. Missoula, MT: Scholars, 1977.

———. *Paul and the Popular Philosophers*. Minneapolis: Fortress, 1989.

Marchal, Joseph A. *The Politics of Heaven: Women, Gender, and Empire in the Study of Paul*. Paul in Critical Contexts; Minneapolis: Fortress, 2008.

Mason, Steve. "Jews, Judaeans, Judaizing, Judaism: Problems of Categorization in Ancient History." *Journal for the Study of Judaism in the Persian, Hellenistic, and Roman Periods* 38 (2007) 457–512.

Maurizio, L. "Anthropology and Spirit Possession: A Reconsideration of the Pythia's Role at Delphi." *Journal of Hellenic Studies* 115 (1995) 69–86.

McGowan, Andrew. *Ascetic Eucharists: Food and Drink in Early Christian Ritual Meals*. Oxford Early Christian Studies. Oxford: Clarendon, 1999.

Meyer, Heinrich August Wilhelm. *Critical and Exegetical Handbook to the Epistles to the Philippians and Colossians, and to Philemon*. Translated by J. C. Moore and William P. Dickson. H. A. W. Meyer's Commentary on the New Testament. 6th ed. Peabody, MA: Hendrickson, 1983.

Miller, E. C. "πολιτεύεσθε in Phil. 1.27: Some Philological and Thematic Observations." *Journal for the Study of the New Testament* 15 (1982) 86–96.

Moles, John L. "Cynic Cosmopolitanism." In *The Cynics: The Cynic Movement in Antiquity and Its Legacy*, edited by Robert Bracht Branham and Marie-Odile Goulet-Cazé, 105–20. Berkeley: University of California Press, 1996.

———. "'Honestius Quam Ambitiosius'? An Exploration of the Cynic's Attitude to Moral Corruption in His Fellow Men." *Journal of Hellenic Studies* 103 (1983) 103–23.

Navia, Luis E. *Classical Cynicism: A Critical Study*. Contributions in Philosophy 58. Westport, CT: Greenwood, 1996.

———. *Diogenes of Sinope: The Man in the Tub*. Contributions in Philosophy. Westport, CT: Greenwood, 1998.

Nanos, Mark D. "How Inter-Christian Approaches to Paul's Rhetoric Can Perpetuate Negative Valuations of Jewishness—Although Proposing to Avoid that Outcome." *Biblical Interpretation* 13.3 (2005) 255–69. (Available in volume 1 of this essay collection.)

———. *The Irony of Galatians: Paul's Letter in First-Century Context*. Minneapolis: Fortress, 2002.

———. "Paul and Judaism: Why Not Paul's Judaism?" In *Paul Unbound: Other Perspectives on the Apostle*, edited by Mark D. Given, 117–60. Peabody, MA: Hendrickson, 2010. (Available in volume 1 of this essay collection.)

———. "Paul's Reversal of Jews Calling Gentiles 'Dogs' (Philippians 3:2): 1600 Years of an Ideological Tale Wagging an Exegetical Dog?" *Biblical Interpretation* 17 (2009) 448–82. (Available in this volume.)

Neyrey, Jerome H. "The Form and Background of the Polemic in 2 Peter." *Journal of Biblical Literature* 99 (1980) 407–31.

Oakes, Peter. *Philippians: From People to Letter*. Cambridge: Cambridge University Press, 2001.

O'Brien, Peter Thomas. *The Epistle to the Philippians: A Commentary on the Greek Text*. NICC. Grand Rapids: Eerdmans, 1991.

Ogden, Daniel. *Magic, Witchcraft, and Ghosts in the Greek and Roman Worlds: A Sourcebook*. Oxford: Oxford University Press, 2002.

Onfray, Michel. *Cynismes: Portrait du philosophe en chien*. Paris: Bernard Grassett, 1990.

Oropeza, B. J. *Jews, Gentiles, and the Opponents of Paul: The Pauline Letters*. Apostasy in the New Testament Communities 2. Eugene, OR: Cascade, 2011.

"Philippi, Macedonia." *Numiswiki: The Collaborative Numismatics Project*. Online: http://www.forumancientcoins.com/NumisWiki/view.asp?key=Philippi.

Pilhofer, Peter. *Philippi*, vol. 1: *Die erste christliche Gemeinde Europas*. WUNT 87. Tübingen: Mohr Seibeck, 1995.

Portefaix, Lilian. *Sisters Rejoice: Paul's Letter to the Philippians and Luke-Acts as Seen by First-Century Philippian Women*. ConBNT 20. Stockholm: Almqvist & Wiksell, 1988.

Rappe, Sarah. "Father of the Dogs? Tracking the Cynics in Plato's Euthydemus." *Classical Philology* 95 (2000) 291–93.

Rapske, Brian. *The Book of Acts and Paul in Roman Custody*. The Book of Acts in Its First-century Setting. Grand Rapids: Eerdmans, 1994.

Reed, Jeffrey T. *A Discourse Analysis of Philippians: Method and Rhetoric in the Debate over Literary Integrity*. JSNTSup 136. Sheffield, UK: Sheffield Academic Press, 1997.

Reimer, Ivoni Richter. *Women in the Acts of the Apostles: A Feminist Liberation Perspective*. Translated by Linda M. Maloney. Minneapolis: Fortress, 1995.

Reumann, John. *Philippians: A New Translation with Introduction and Commentary*. AB 33B. New Haven, CT: Yale University Press, 2008.
Rist, J. M. *Stoic Philosophy*. Cambridge: Cambridge University Press, 1969.
Romm, James. "Dog Heads and Noble Savages: Cynicism before the Cynics?" In *The Cynics: The Cynic Movement in Antiquity and Its Legacy*, edited by Robert Bracht Branham and Marie-Odile Goulet-Cazé, 121–35. Berkeley: University of California Press, 1996.
Runesson, Anders. "Inventing Christian Identity: Paul, Ignatius, and Theodosius I." In *Exploring Early Christian Identity*, edited by Bengt Holmberg, 59–92. WUNT 226. Tübingen: Mohr Siebeck, 2008.
Sanders, E. P. "Paul on the Law, His Opponents, and the Jewish People in Philippians 3 and 2 Corinthians 11." In *Anti-Judaism in Early Christianity: Paul and the Gospels*, edited by Peter Richardson and David M. Granskou, 75–90. Waterloo, ON: Wilfrid Laurier University Press, 1986.
Sandnes, Karl Olav. *Belly and Body in the Pauline Epistles*. SNTSMS 120. Cambridge: Cambridge University Press, 2002.
Scheid, John, and Janet Lloyd. *An Introduction to Roman Religion*. Bloomington, IN: Indiana University Press, 2003.
Schmithals, Walther. *Paul & the Gnostics*. Translated by John E. Steely. Nashville: Abingdon, 1972.
Schoedel, William R., and Helmut Koester, eds. *Ignatius of Antioch: A Commentary on the Letters of Ignatius of Antioch*. Hermeneia; Philadelphia: Fortress, 1985.
Schwartz, Daniel R. "'Judaean' or 'Jew'? How Should We translate *ioudaios* in Josephus?" In *Jewish Identity in the Greco-Roman World*, edited by J. Frey et al., 3–27. Ancient Judaism and Early Christianity 71. Leiden: Brill, 2007.
Seeley, David. "The Background of the Philippians Hymn (2:6–11)." *Journal of Higher Criticism* 1 (1994) 49–72.
Stow, Kenneth. *Jewish Dogs: An Image and Its Interpreters: Continuity in the Catholic-Jewish Encounter*. Stanford Studies in Jewish History and Culture. Stanford: Stanford University Press, 2006.
Stowers, Stanley K. "Friends and Enemies in the Politics of Heaven: Reading Theology in Philippians." In *Pauline Theology, vol. 1: Thessalonians, Philippians, Galatians, Philemon*, edited by Jouette M. Bassler, 105–21. Minneapolis: Fortress, 1991.
Sumney, Jerry L. *"Servants of Satan," "False Brothers" and Other Opponents of Paul*. JSNTSup 188. Sheffield, UK: Sheffield Academic Press, 1999.
Theological Dictionary of the New Testament. Edited by Gerhard Kittel and Gerhard Friedrich. 10 vols. Grand Rapids: Eerdmans, 1965.
Theissen, Gerd. *The Social Setting of Pauline Christianity: Essays on Corinth*. Translated by John H. Schütz. Philadelphia: Fortress, 1982.
Trebilco, Paul R. "Paul and Silas: 'Servants of the Most High God' (Acts 16.16–18)." *Journal for the Study of the New Testament* 36 (1989) 51–73.
Tripolitis, Antonia. *Religions of the Hellenistic-Roman Age*. Grand Rapids: Eerdmans, 2002.
Tyson, Joseph B. "Paul's Opponents at Philippi." *Perspectives in Religious Studies* 3 (1976) 82–95.
Ulonska, Herbert. "Gesetz und Beschneidung: Überlegungen zu einem paulinischen Ablösungskonflikt." In *Jesu Rede von Gott und ihre Nachgeschichte im frühen Christentum: Beiträge zur Verkündigung Jesu und zum Kerygma der Kirche:*

Festschrift für Willi Marxsen zum 70. Geburtstag, edited by Dietrich-Alex Koch, Gerhard Sellin, and Andreas Lindemann, 314–31. Gütersloh: Guterloher Verlagshaus, 1989.

Urbach, Efraim Elimelech. *The Sages: Their Concepts and Beliefs.* Vol. 1. Jerusalem: Magnes, 1975.

Vaage, Leif E. "Like Dogs Barking: Cynic Parrêsia and Shameless Asceticism." *Semeia* 57 (1992) 25–39.

Vander Waerdt, Paul A. "Zeno's Republic and the Origins of Natural Law." In *The Socratic Movement,* edited by Paul A. Vander Waerdt, 272–308. Ithaca, NY: Cornell University Press, 1994.

White, L. Michael. "Morality between Two Worlds: A Paradigm of Friendship in Philippians." In *Greeks, Romans, and Christians: Essays in Honor of Abraham J. Malherbe,* edited by David L. Balch, Everett Ferguson, and Wayne A. Meeks, 201–15. Minneapolis: Fortress, 1990.

Williams, Margaret H. "The Meaning and Function of *Ioudaios* in Graeco-Roman Inscriptions." *Zeitschrift für Papyrologie und Epigraphik* 116 (1997) 249–62.

Wright, N. T. "Paul's Gospel and Caesar's Empire." In *Paul and Politics: Ekklesia, Israel, Imperium, Interpretation,* edited by Richard A. Horsley, 160–83. Harrisburg, PA: Trinity, 2000.

Index of Ancient Sources

TANAKH/HEBREW BIBLE

Genesis

34:15	68

Exodus

2:11	25
15:11	7, 37
20:2–6	7, 37
22:28	7, 37
23:24	7, 37
24:11	7, 42
32	7, 42
32:27	25

Leviticus

7:1–5	138
19:9–10	130
19:17	25
19:18	138
19:28	155
19:33–34	138
21:5	134, 155

Numbers

23:10	68
25	7, 19, 42

Deuteronomy

3:28	25
4:6–7	15
4:19	7, 37
7:1	127
7:5	7, 37
14:22–26	7, 42
15:2–3	25
15:11–12	25
18:10	153
23:19	25, 121, 165
24:7	25
24:19–22	130
29:26	7, 37
32:8–9	7, 37
32:16–17	7, 37
32:17	75, 101
32:21	7, 37

Judges

7:5	121
16:11	68
17:11	68
20:13	25
21:6	25

Ruth

2	130
4:12	68
9:13	7
17:43	121
24:15	121
28:3–25	163
28:8	153

2 Samuel

3:8	121
9:8	121

2 Samuel (continued)

16:9	121–22
18:32	68

1 Kings

1:25	7, 42
14:10–11	118
16:4	118
18:1—22:40	135, 152
18:19—19:1	135, 152
18:28	135, 152, 155, 159
18:21	184
21:19	118
21:22–29	135, 152
21:24	118
22:38	118
28:28	134, 155

2 Kings

8:7–13	121
8:13	121
9:33–37	135, 152
9:35–37	118
10:11	135, 152
10:17	135, 152
17:17	153

2 Chronicles

19:10	25

Ezra-Nehemiah

	129

Nehemiah

5:1	25

Job

30:29	25

Psalms

21:17 LXX	120, 122
22:16	121–22
22:22	25
31:9 LXX	68
59	122
59:6	121
59:14	121
77:8 LXX	68
82:1	7, 37
87:5 LXX	68
Ps 95:5 LXX	75, 101
106:28	7, 37, 42
106:36–39	7
106:37	75, 101
108:19 LXX	68
118:83 LXX	68
125:1 LXX	68
128:6 LXX	68

Proverbs

18:24	25
25:21–22	138
20:22	138
26:11	119, 121

Ecclesiastes

3:4–5	67

Isaiah

1:9	68
8:19	7, 37
19:3	7, 37
37:27	68
40	7, 37
44	7, 37
48:18–19	68
56:10–11	121
63:19	68
64:6	68
64:10	68
65:3	75, 101
65:11	75, 101
66:20	25

Jeremiah

3:24–25	163
4:17	68
12:8	68
14:8	68
15:3	118

15:18	68	**Zechariah**	
20:9	68	11:14	25
22:18	25		
23:9	68		
23:14	68		
31:28	68	**APOCRYPHA**	
34:9	153	*Tobit*	

Lamentations

			129
1:1	68	1:3	26
1:6	68	1:10	26
2:5	68	1:16	26
		5:10–14	26
		7:1–12	26

Ezekiel

3:3	68	10:6	26
12:24	153	14:4	26
13:6	153		
13:23	153	*Judith*	
16:31	68	7:30	26
21:21	153	8:14	26
21:23	153	12:13	68
21:29	153		
22:28	153		
36:35	68	*Wisdom of Solomon*	
		13–16	7, 37

Daniel

4:33	68	*Sirach*	
		4:10	68
		13:18	121

Hosea

		18:23	68
5:10	68	26:25	131
7:14	155	31.1–2	67
7:16	68	32:1–2	69, 99
8:8	68	32:8	68
8:13	7, 42		
9:10	68, 163	*1 Maccabees*	

Amos

		1:15	158
4:11	68	1:48	158
		1:60–61	158
		2:44–46	158

Micah

		5:16	26
3:11	153	11:30	26
4:5	7, 37	12:10	26
7:1	68	12:17	26

2 Maccabees

1:1	26
6:1–11	147
6:10	158
9:13–17	147

1 Esdras

1:5–9	26
4:61	26
8:77	26

4 Maccabees

5:1–4	7, 42

PSEUDEPIGRAPHA

1 Enoch

19	7, 37
89.42–49	122
90.4	122

Letter of Aristeas

16	81
121–22	81
257, 267	67

Jubilees

11.4–6	7, 37

NEW TESTAMENT

Matthew

5:1ff.	178
5:21–22	138
5:38–48	138
7:6	116, 127, 129
8:28	178
10:25	68, 75
15:21–28	114, 120, 127–28
15:22	127
15:26	115
15:27	115
15:28	68
17:2	68
18:3	68
27:39–44	122

Mark

5:1	178
7:24–30	120, 127–28
7:26	127
7:27	130
15:29–32	122

Luke

8:26	178
8:27	178
10:7–8	67
22:26	68
23:35–37	122

Acts

2:5	31
2:29	25
3:17	25
3:22	153
7:2	25
7:37	153
10:35	31
11:14	25
11:26	25
11:38	25
13:15	25
15	10, 49
15:20	12
15:29	12
16	153, 173
16:3	56, 79
16:11–40	150
16:12–40	135, 153
16:16–21	135, 153
16:16	163
17	62, 78, 100
17:1–3	80, 102
17:10–12	80
17:16–31	31, 47
17:17–31	78, 101
17:17	80

Index of Ancient Sources

17:18	31, 47	4:6	25
17:23	31, 47, 78–79, 102	4:8-17	72
17:28	79, 102	4:10-16	105
17:29	31, 47	5	13, 17, 29–30, 45–46
17:26-31	31, 47	5:1—11:1	21
17:30-31	31, 47	5:1-8	29, 45
17:30	78, 102	5:1	19
18	80	5:9-13	21, 38, 49
18:4-5	80	5:9-12	28, 44
21	63, 79	5:9-11	19
21:25	12	5:9	28, 44
22:1	25	5:10	28, 45
23:1	25	5:11	25, 29, 44–45
28:17	25	5:12-13	29
		5:12	71

Romans

		5:13	29, 45
1:1-5	53	6:1-11	21, 38
1:27	163	6:5-8	25
1:33	53	6:6-8	19, 38
2	53	6:7	105
3	53	6:12-20	105
5:6-10	21, 44	7—11	21
5:12-19	31	7:1-6	73
7	53	7:1	19, 49, 71
8:38-39	15, 42	7:6	79
9:1	56, 96	7:8	71
9:3	24–25, 44	7:10-16	29, 46
9:24-26	156	7:12-16	21, 38
9:32—11:36	53	7:12-15	25
11:1-5	152	7:16	73
12:9-18	67	7:17-24	49, 55
12:17-21	138	7:18	60
14-15	xiv, 104	7:19	58, 97
14	24, 44	7:24	25
15:8-9	53	7:26	71
16:20	15, 42	7:29	25
		7:35	71

1 Corinthians

		7:37	71
		7:38	71
1:1	25	8—10	vii, xiv-xvi, 12, 19, 21,
1:10	25		23–24, 27, 29, 40, 45–46, 71–73, 76,
1:11-12	19, 38		100
1:11	19, 25	8	3, 13, 23, 25, 29–30, 36, 39,
1:26	25		42, 45–46, 48, 71
2:1	25	8:1—11:1	19, 22, 24, 38, 49–50
2:8	15, 42	8:1-3	22, 38
3:1	25, 71	8:1ff.	62
3:3-4	19, 38	8:1	4, 11, 19, 43, 49, 73

1 Corinthians (continued)

8:4-6	11, 74, 100
8:4	4, 14, 20, 37, 42, 73
8:5	74, 101
8:5a	15, 42
8:5b	15, 42
8:6	4, 14, 20, 42
8:7-13	10, 22, 38, 74, 101, 105
8:7ff.	73
8:7	xv. 4-6, 9, 11, 13, 20, 37, 40, 43-44
8:8	58, 74, 97, 100
8:9-13	15
8:10	4, 6, 8-9, 14, 18, 41
8:11-12	9
8:11	4, 9-10, 15, 20, 25, 44
8:12	4, 20
8:13	8, 18
9	62, 71, 73, 137
9:1-27	105
9:5	25
9:16-23	74
9:16-19	71
9:18	53
9:19-23	vii, xiv-xvi, xviii, 11-12, 18, 21, 28, 30-31, 38, 44, 47-48, 52-55, 58, 60, 64, 71, 73, 76, 79, 86-87, 96, 100
9:19	56
9:20-23	71
9:20-21	64
9:20	55
9:21	60, 79
9:22	12
9:22b-23	93
9:23	53
9:24-27	85
10	7, 42, 48
10:1-23	74, 101
10:1-22	14-15, 42-43
10:1	25
10:5-22	19, 43
10:14-33	74, 101
10:16-22	19, 43
10:19-22	74, 101
10:19	101
10:22	75, 101
10:23-31	24, 40
10:23-30	22, 38
10:23	71, 101
10:24	28, 44, 73
10:25-31	7, 42
10:25-26	101
10:25	5, 12, 39
10:27—11:1	22, 38
10:27-30	73
10:27	22-23
10:28-29	23, 39
10:28	22, 24, 39
10:31—11:1	73
10:32-33	28, 44
10:32	21, 38
10:33	40
11:1	28, 44
11:2-16	21
11:18-19	19, 38
11:27-34	106
11:27-32	21, 38
11:29-30	23
11:33	25
12—14	21
12:1	25
12:2	21
12:7	71
14	21
14:6	25
14:16-17	21, 38
14:20	25
14:22-25	15, 21-22, 38, 73
14:26	25
14:39	25
15:1	25
15:1-28	53
15:3	20
15:6	25
15:24-27	15, 42
15:30-34	106
15:31	25
15:45-49	31
15:50	25
15:58	25
16:11-12	25
16:13-14	106
16:15	25
16:20	25

2 Corinthians

4:4	15, 42
5:14–15	20
11:22	53

Galatians

1:1	137
1:6–10	106
1:13–14	147
2	106
2:4	24, 44
2:10–21	106
2:11–21	54
2:11–14	64
2:14–16	147
3	53
3:19	53
4	53
4:12	68
4:17–18	106
5:7–12	106
5:12	113
5:14	53
5:15	166
5:16–22	99
6:12–13	106
6:16	155

Philippians

	138
1	151
1:9–11	148
1:12–26	150
1:16–26	174
1:20	134
1:27—2:18	148
1:27–30	150, 174, 182
1:28	168
2	174
2:5–15	182
2:5–8	182
2:10	15, 42
2:12–18	150
3	xvi, 53, 114, 133–34, 143, 151, 175, 183–84
3:2–19	183
3:2–9	148
3:2–3	148
3:2–3a	111
3:2	xvi, 56, 114–15, 120, 126, 128, 132, 135–36, 142–43, 148, 151–52, 159, 165–67, 172, 182
3:3–9	143
3:3ff.	182
3:3	136–37, 142, 152–53, 155, 157–58
3:4—4:1	137
3:4–14	182
3:4–9	155
3:4–6	158, 183
3:5–6	53
3:7–21	134, 175
3:8	134, 137, 143, 175
3:12–16	134, 175
3:13–16	137
3:15–17	148
3:17–20	137
3:18–20	117
3:18–19	xvi, 132, 142–43, 148, 159–62, 165–69, 172, 182
3:19–20	134, 175
3:19	135, 153
3:20—4:2	148
3:20	137, 161
4:5–13	134, 175
4:5	138
4:8–9	148
4:10–19	175
4:10–14	174
4:11–13	168

Ephesians

5:1	68

1 Thessalonians

1:9–10	13, 40
2:1–8	180
2:1–2	150, 179–80
2:3	180
2:7	68

1 Peter

2:9–10	156

2 Peter

169

James

| 2:19 | 7 |

Revelation

2:14	12
2:19–20	12
6:12	68
22:15	165

DEAD SEA SCROLLS

1 QS

1.9	26
2.24–25	26
5.25	26
6.10	26
6:22	26

1 QSa

| 1.18 | 26 |

CD

| 6.20 | 26 |
| 7.1 | 26 |

4QpNah

| 3–4 ii 8 | 129 |

RABBINIC LITERATURE

Mishnah

m. ʿAbodah Zarah

1.4–5	7, 42, 73
2.3	7, 42, 73
3.4	7, 42, 73
4.3–6	7, 42, 73
5.1	7, 42, 73

m. Bekorot

| 5.6 | 124 |

m. Soṭah

| 7.8 | 26 |

Tosefta

t. ʿAbodah Zarah

3.6	124
6.4–6	17, 41
6.4	124

t. Berakot

| 2.21 | 67 |

Talmuds

b. Beṣah

| 25b | 125 |

y. Giṭṭim

| 7.1 | 178 |

b. Ḥagiga

| 3b–4a | 178 |

y. Šabbat

9	124
11d	124
23	124

y. Terumot

| 1.1 | 178 |

Other

Exodus Rabbah

31.9	124
34.38	67
42.5	67

Genesis Rabbah

| 81.3 | 126 |

18.8	67	**ANCIENT JEWISH**	
48.14	67	**WRITERS**	
Leviticus Rabbah		***Philo***	
33.6	126	*Allegorical Interpretation*	
Mekilta Mishpatim		1.8	27
20		*On the Cherubim*	
98a	124	91–100	136
Mekilta de R. Ishmael			
Exod. 22:30–31 (Kaspa 2)	124	*On the Posterity of Cain*	
Midrash on Psalms		100	27
Psalm 4 (comment 11)	125	*That the Worse Attacks the Better*	
Ps 22:17	122		
Pirqe Rabbi Eliezer		40	27
29	126, 151	66	27
		140	26
Shemoth [Exodus] Rabbah			
31.9	124	*That God is Unchangeable*	
Tanḥuma Temurah		65–67	57
6	124	*On Planting*	
		151	133, 166
Tanḥuma Terumah		*On Drunkenness*	
3, on Exodus 25.2	125	70–71	27
Targum Neofiti 1:		*On Flight and Finding*	
Exod. 22:30	124	90–91	27
Targum Onqelos		*On Dreams*	
Exod. 11:7	124	1.49	118
Targum Pseudo-Jonathan		1.109	27
Exod. 11:7	124	*On the Life of Joseph*	
Exod. 22:30	124	32–34	57
		74–79	57
Targum Yerushalmi		*On the Life of Moses*	
Exod. 22.30	124	1.130–31	120
Deut. 14:21	124		

Philo (continued)

On the Special Laws

1.186	147
4.91	123, 166

On the Virtues

82	26

That Every Good Person is Free

89–91	123

On the Contemplative Life

7	27
40	123, 166

On the Embassy to Gaius

139	123

Questions and Answers on Genesis

1.65–77	26
2.12	27
2.60	26–27
3.43	27
3.56	27
4.69	69, 99

Josephus

Against Apion

2.85	123

Antiquities of the Jews

7.207–10	122
7.284	66
10.276–81	168
16.301–4	69
20.34–48	147
20.43	147

Jewish War

2.122	26

2.164–65	169

GRECO-ROMAN WRITINGS

Antisthenis Fragmenta

51	83

Apollonius Sophista

Lexicon Homericum

510	171

Artemidorus

The Interpretation of Dreams [Oneirocritica]

2.34	164

Athenaeus

Deipnosophists

3.96–97	131
3.96–99	133, 166
3.96f–97	170
3.96f–97a	129
3.99e–f	170
3.100b	170
6.234c–262a	170
6.236e	170
6.246	131
6.246a–c	170
6.255	170
6.255c–257c	170
6.259f–261b	170

Crates (Pseudo-Crates)

Epistles

11	134, 175
12	134, 175
16	134, 175
20	134, 175
21	134, 175

Cicero

De finibus

3.26	168

De officiis

1.113–14	85

Dio Cassius

Historia Romanorum

56	169

Dio Chrysostom

Orations

4.24	175
6.8–9	134, 175
8.5–7	173
8.36	167
9.8	167
12	172
12.52	78
31.15	78
32.12	173
32.17	173
33.6–8	173
33.44	173
34.2–4	167
45.1	167
66.25	167
77	85, 167
78.35–38	85
78.41–42	167

Diogenes Laertius

Lives

6	133, 166
6.4	173
6.6	173
6.14	85
6.21	173
6.22	179
6.23	134, 175, 177
33	134, 175
6.27–30	134, 175
6.31–34	134, 175
6.34	177
6.37	179
6.45	134, 175
6.49	134, 175
6.59	134, 175
6.60	169
6.61	170
6.70–71	134
6.63	134, 175
6.64	174
6.69	134, 170, 173
6.69–71	175
6.73	177
6.75–76	85
6.76	177
6.86	85
6.87	179
6.70–71	175
6.79	176
6.99	178
7.147	78
7.172	175
7.87	179
270c–d	170

Epictetus

Discourses

1.6.23–29	78
1.9.4–6	28
1.13.4	28
2.19.24	168
2.30.26	78
3.12	175
3:13.2	175
3.22	166
3.22.23–26	173
3.22.45–61	174
3.22.51–52	134, 175
3.22.69	173
3.22.72–74	173
3.22.81	175
3.22.81–82	28, 173–74
3.22.95–96	173
3.24.64	175

Epictetus (continued)

Etymologicum magnum

| col. 498 | 171 |

Euripides

Phoenician Women

| line 1650 | 129 |

Herodotus

Historiae

| 5.7 | 164 |
| 7.111 | 164 |

Hesiod

Theogony

| 411–15 | 164 |

Hesychius of Alexandria

Lexicon

| 555, entry Kappa 1763 | 171 |

Homer

Iliad

| 9.312–13 | 82 |

Odyssey

| 19.521 | 83 |

John Stobaeus

Anthology

| 3.13.44 | 174 |

Florilegium

| 29.92 | 177 |

Julian

Against the Galileans

| 106ac | 56 |

Orations

6.183–89	173
6.197	165
6.198	176
6.201	175
7.211	179

Lucian

Apology

| 2 | 174 |

Demonax

7	174
11	172, 175
21	133, 166, 175
27	172
32	172

Dialogues of the Dead

1.331	178
1.332	179
2.425	178

Downward Journey

| 7 | 174, 178 |

The Fisherman

36	165
46	174
52	174

Peregrinus

| 17 | 171 |

Philosophies for Sale

| 8 | 174, 178 |
| 9 | 178–79 |

Index of Ancient Sources

10	165–66

Macarius Magnes

Apocritus

3.30	56, 96
3.31	56, 96
3.37	56, 96
3.38	56, 96

Marcus Aurelius

2.1	28
7.22	28
9.22–23	28

Maximus of Tyre

Orations

2	172

Meleager

Greek Anthology

7.419.7–8	85

Menander

Theophoroumenē

Act 2, Scene 1	153

Petronius

Satires

141	176

Philostratus

Life of Apollonius

1.19	129

Zeus Refutatus

15	169

Plato

Apologia

32b	172

Gorgias

521d	172

Menexenus

238e–239a	26

Meno

	70, 100
100a	172

Protagoras

352ff.	70, 100

Plutarch

De defectu oraculorum

9.414E	153

De Pythiae oraculis

407c	153

How to Tell a Flatterer from a Friend

59C–60B	173
61D–62C	173
73D–74DE	173

Moralia

557D	164

On the Fortune of Alexander

329B–D	27

Progress in Virtue

80B–C	173

Plotinus

Enneades

II.9.18	26

Porphyry

scholion on *Odysseus* 1.1	82

Pseudo-Diogenes

Epistles

12	134, 175
14	134, 175
16	177
27–29	173
28	173, 176
28.3	175
29	173
31	134, 175
44	171

Pseudo-Heraclitus

Epistles

4.2.5	78
4.10–13	172
4.17	172
4.20–26	172
5.14	172
7.2	175
9.15–19	172

Pseudo-Lucian

Epistles

1	179
5	167

Pseudo-Socrates

Epistles

6.1	167
9.3	167
24	173

Quintus Curtius

History of Alexander

10.3.11–14	27

Seneca

Epistulae morales

18.5–13	175
41.1	78
108.15–16	175
108.23	175

On Superstition

frr. 34–37	159

Strabo

Geographica

25.759.29	178

Xenophon

Anabasis

VII.2.25	26

EARLY CHRISTIAN WRITINGS

Acts of Paul

3.1	72

Augustine

Against Two Letters of the Pelagians

Book III, chapter 22	115

City of God

6.9–10	159

Letter

40.4	58

40.6	58	*Hom. Gen.*	
Letter 54		2.3	57
(Book I of Replies to Questions of Januarius)		*Hom. Matt.*	
1.1	68	23	131
2.2	68	52	131
2.3	67	*Hom. Phil.*	
5.5–6	68	3.2	113, 115
On Lying		*Hom. Tit.*	
	58	3.1–2	57

Chrysostom
Laud. Paul.

Adv. Jud.		5.6	57, 97
1.11.1–2	115	5.7	57
2.3.5	116		
5.3.2	80		
5.3.3	80		

Clement of Alexandria
Protreptikos

Hom. 1 Cor.		6.71.1	78
8:7	57	7.75.3	78
12.1	57	*Stromateis*	
12.3–4	57	8.4	133
20	27	8.12.4–7	133, 166
21	71		
22.5	79		
22.6	57		
23	28, 44		
25	28, 44		

Didache

6.1–2	12
9.5	116

Hom. 2 Cor.			
2.2	57		
4.13	57		

Ignatius
To the Ephesians

Hom. Eph.		7.1–2	180
6.3	57	10	27

To the Magneians

Hom. Gal.			
2:11	57	8–10	12
3	57		

Jerome

Letter

104.17   58

Justin

Dialogue with Trypho

35   12

Martyrdom of Polycarp

1.2   27

Origen

Homiliae in Jeremiam

20.3   58

Comm. in 1 Cor.

3.43   79

Pseudo-Clementine

Homilies

2.19–20   131

Recognitions

7.32   131

Tertullian

Against Marcion

4.7.5   131

Apology

9.13–14   12

Flight in Persecution

6.3   131

To the Heathen

2.2   169

Made in the USA
Monee, IL
04 December 2020